Backpacking in the '90s

Tips, Techniques & Secrets

Backpacking in the '90s
Tips, Techniques & Secrets

Victoria Logue
Illustrations by Leigh Ellis

Menasha Ridge Press
Birmingham, Alabama

Third Edition, Second Printing

Library of Congress Cataloging-in-Publication Data
Logue, Victoria, 1961-
    Backpacking in the '90s: tips, techniques & secrets/Victoria Logue;
illustrations by Leigh Ellis-Neill.
        p. cm.
    Includes bibliographical references and index.
    ISBN 0-89732-163-4
    1. Backpacking—United States—Handbooks, manuals, etc.
    2. Backpacking—Equipment and supplies—Handbooks, manuals, etc.
    I. Title. II. Title: Backpacking in the nineties.
    GV199.6.L64 1993
    796.5'0973—dc20   92-43314
                                                                      CIP

Text and cover design by
Carolina Graphics Group

Cover illustration by Victoria and Frank Logue

Menasha Ridge Press
3169 Cahaba Heights Road
Birmingham, Alabama 35243

Dedicated to Griffin Logue, Jessie Neill,
Sierra and Bryce Gladfelter, Galen and Faye Nisbet,
Kate and Jack Schroeder, Brittany Sochard
and the rest of the next generation of backpackers.

Contents

Introduction

BREATHE DEEPLY.

Let the fresh, moist air fill your lungs. Inhale the scent of rain-frosted fir.

And listen.

The only sounds on this early morning hike are the quiet drip of the newly fallen rain and the pure, clear voice of the white-throated sparrow. The rocks gleam and the stunted firs are gnomes in the swirling mist. A few feet away a snowshoe hare nibbles at a tuft of grass—yet another apparition on this ghostly morning.

This is the epitome of backpacking: one hour in one morning during one day of a six-month hiking trip. Alone with nature and all you need to survive resting on your back. But, you don't have to be out for six months to have a morning such as this one. That early morning hike over New Hampshire's Mount Kinsman was not unique to our hike of the Appalachian Trail. We've experienced many such days since we began hiking—from hiking along a Georgia beach at sunrise to discovering hidden shrines and swimming holes in Kathmandu.

Although some enjoy backpacking for its physical aspect, most become involved because of the chance it provides to get close to nature. Once the pack breaks you in, you'll forget the pain (if you suffer any) and begin to enjoy the trail. You will start to experience, on many different levels, the trail's environment. It won't be long before you realize that you've learned things without being told—the habits of wildlife, where water can be found, the patterns of weather.

You'll find as much pleasure in a walk on a misty morning as on a clear, bright day. The same stretch of trail will offer something different each time you hike it. The season, the weather, and your mood all contribute to your perceptions as you hike. My husband, Frank, and I vividly recollect a section of trail that made us feel as if we were walking across a vast plain hidden in fog. We were the only humans left on earth. It was a wonderful, almost mystical feeling. Later, we questioned other hikers about this section of trail and no one had

had anywhere near the same experience. It turned out that the trail was on a ridge rather than on the endless plain we'd imagined that foggy morning.

More and more people are turning to nature to escape the stress of city life and jobs. They seek the solace of the earth to help them with changes in their life, whether it be as dramatic as death or divorce, or as simple as seeking an added dimension to their lifestyle. Others prefer the outdoors to enclosed gyms for their exercise.

Fortunately, as people search for a new communication with their earth, programs are underway to provide them with somewhere to discover their planet. Both greenways and the National Trails System are growing each year as the federal, state and local governments, volunteers, and corporations work to provide Americans with a chance to "get back to nature."

People have been carrying loads on their backs for years—from hunters to soldiers to expeditions—backpacking has been a method for getting one's gear and one's self to the required destination. It wasn't until the turn of the century that backpacking began gaining interest as a recreational sport. The Appalachian Mountain Club was formed in 1876 to build trails in the White Mountains of New Hampshire; the Sierra Club in 1892 to both protect and experience the Sierras. Many trails and trail clubs were formed prior to World War I.

The pace slowed during World Wars I and II; but following both of those wars, surplus stores parlayed excess gear into thousands of dollars by selling packs, tents and other equipment to prospective backpackers. It was between the two wars that many trails, including the Appalachian, were conceived and constructed.

Groups such as the Recreational Equipment Inc. co-op (REI) on the west coast and the Appalachian Trail Conference on the east coast also evolved between the wars. Following

World War II, the number of backpacking expeditions began to increase; and as gear continued to improve throughout the '50s and '60s, the number of backpackers began to grow.

The hippie movement in the late '60s and early '70s saw an increase in backpacking as people sought to commune with nature. The next ten years saw a decrease in the number of backpackers as people became more interested in the material world. But when the environmental movement regained its momentum in the mid-'80s, it also caused a resurgence in the number of backpackers. Now as we approach the turn of the century, backpacking is experiencing another burst of growth.

Equipment continues to improve at a phenomenal rate—stoves, boots, packs, tents and sleeping bags are improved daily. The magnitude of information relating to backpacking is endless. Entire books have been written on single aspects of backpacking, including desert hiking, hiking with children and so on. So, I am writing this book because it is the book we wished we had when we took our first major backpacking trip. It includes all the information you need.

In *Backpacking in the '90s*, we try to focus on the basics of backpacking—what you really need to know to head off into the woods without too much discomfort. Unfortunately, we cannot guarantee an entirely comfortable backpacking trip. We're not sure there is such a thing. When you leave your climate-controlled home for the great outdoors, you open yourself up to any number of potential discomforts; be it vicious bugs, endless rain, steep inclines, icy streams, excessive heat or physical pain, it's doubtful you'll have a trouble-free trip. Keeping in mind that you'll probably be uncomfortable at some point, even on an overnight trip, there are ways to increase the pleasure of the hike.

Backpacking in the '90s: Tips, Techniques and Secrets presents you with everything you need to know to plan a basic backpacking trip, including tips on how to make your trip as pleasurable as possible. This includes choosing the right equipment. The type of tent you carry or stove you use is as much a matter of preference as pragmatism, and we provide information about the equipment so that you can make the choice that's best for you. You will find information on the latest equipment—stoves, tents, sleeping bags, boots, clothing and packs—the good and the bad. From where to find water and how to treat it to what to eat and how to prepare it, we touch on the information important to a good hike. We have also included a section on the miscellaneous items you need when backpacking such as toiletries, first aid kits, lighting, rope.

We cover injuries you might face, especially on longer hikes, and how to treat those problems. Animals you might run into are introduced, although it's unlikely anything other than bugs will present any threat. Camping in extremes (very hot or cold temperatures) will also be briefly discussed because several long distance trails consist of both desert and snow and ice hiking. Tips on hiking with children and with dogs are included for those who wish to share the sport with the ones they love. A chapter dealing with first hikes offers special tips for making your first outing a little bit easier. Another chapter is devoted to long distance hiking and to letting you decide beforehand whether or not you're suited to that type of backpacking trip. If you decide long distance is for you, we offer some suggestions on how to make that trip flow a bit more smoothly. And, because it is the '90s and the "Earth Decade", we offer some tips on hiking "green."

My husband and I are not what you'd call heavy duty backpackers. Although backpacking is a big part of our life, it is not all important. Basically, we're just people who like to head out into the woods every once in a while. Once there, our everyday problems and worries just seem to slip away. We

---

>>Hiking Tip<<

Beginning backpackers often choose an area they have heard about many times as the site for their first backpacking trip. If you do so, you will probably be choosing a heavily used area and may not find the wilderness experience you're looking for. Instead of picking a well known destination, such as Yosemite or the Great Smoky Mountains for your first hikes, seek out a lesser known trail. Outdoor retailers in your area should have a number of maps and guidebooks to choose from.

---

enjoy the crunch of leaves under our feet, the weight of the pack on our back and the whisper of the wind through the trees. We treasure the freedom that comes from having everything we need to survive resting on our backs.

Frank and I have had the opportunity to hike several thousand miles, most of which occurred during a trip of a lifetime when we hiked the Appalachian Trail from Georgia to Maine. Since that trip, we have continued to backpack but on a much smaller scale. We realize that most people don't have the time and opportunity to hike thousands of miles at once, and we had the average hiker in mind when we wrote this book. You don't have to hike long distance to enjoy the pleasures of backpacking. You can find as much joy in nature on an overnight trip as on a six-month trip, perhaps more.

It would be nice to say that our knowledge of backpacking is all encompassing; but in writing this book, we have relied on the knowledge of friends and family as well as our own experience. We may swear by our stove, but a friend may insist that his stove is better. We let you in on these varying opinions. We don't believe that you have to do it our way to do it right.

On the other hand, there are some wrong ways to hike and

camp. For example, trying to set up camp on a 40-degree day in rain-soaked clothes could potentially lead to death. While it may not matter in that situation if you choose an MSR Whisperlite or Coleman Peak One stove to make yourself something hot to drink, it does matter that you change into dry clothes immediately upon making camp.

Before I close, special thanks go to Randy Logue for his invaluable assistance on the section about water, and to Mike and Nicole Jones for their time and advice in guiding this book from an idea to ink on paper.

· 1 ·
Where To Hike

A SHORT HIKE on sidewalks will take me from my father's house in Alexandria, Virginia, to a hiking-biking path that runs from Mount Vernon to Washington, D.C. From there, the Chesapeake and Potomac Canal Towpath leads west toward Harpers Ferry, West Virginia and the Appalachian Mountains. Having hiked to Harpers Ferry, I would have the choice of turning north on the Appalachian Trail where I could hike all the way to the Canadian border via the Long Trail where it splits with the Appalachian Trail in Vermont. Should I decide to head south on the Appalachian Trail, I would eventually find myself in Georgia, and, in the future, I could continue along the Pinhoti Trail through Alabama to Florida where it will join the Florida Trail. But, even more astounding is the soon-to-be-completed American Discovery Trail. At its juncture with the Appalachian and C&O Canal Trails in Harpers Ferry, I could turn west on the American Discovery Trail and hike all the way to California.

Thousands of miles of trail are already accessible to me less than a mile away from my father's suburban home. From the long trails system to the natural corridors called greenways that are appearing across the United States, Americans are seeking the outdoors. And in many cases, the outdoors is right at their doorstep.

Greenways

Linking the urban world to the outdoors, greenways can be as complex as a hiking-biking-riding route or as simple as a protected, yet untamed, stretch of stream or river.

More than five hundred projects are underway in the U.S. Thousands of volunteers are linking parks, natural features and historic sites into linear paths criss-crossing the country. Long trails such as the Pacific Crest, Continental Divide and Appalachian Trails are being joined by greenways in the country's major cities—Brooklyn/Queens, Washington D.C., San Francisco and Minneapolis.

Historical and scenic sites, urban riverways, environmental corridors, recreational trailways, and regional and local trail systems are among the efforts to provide Americans (more than 80 percent of whom live in cities) with the opportunity to take advantage of the outdoors.

But greenways are not meant for humans alone. The protection of these scenic regions is beneficial to the migration and needs of many animals. The rapidly disappearing Florida panther could be rescued from the brink of extinction by the addition of only 15,000 acres of greenway to a 58,000-acre wildlife management area near Loxahatchee, Florida. This is true for many of the indigenous species whose survival is based on the need for large, undisturbed territories or ranges.

Greenways are "the paths to the future" as they link people to the outdoors. They meet an ever growing need, a need to leave the hectic city (if only for a moment) and to experience earth beneath your feet and fresh air in your lungs—to feel life and to feel alive.

❦ *Hiking Secret* ❦

Looking for solitude on America's public lands? Alaska is the place to go. That state's Kenai and Arctic National Wildlife Refuges alone offer more than 20 million acres of wilderness.

For something a little closer to home, try these lesser visited areas: Great Basin National Park, Nevada; Isle Royale National Park, Michigan; Bob Marshall Wilderness, Montana; Guadalupe Mountains National Park, Texas; and if you stay away from the large tourist draws, Adirondack State Park, New York.

Rails-to-Trails

An especially promising new trails system follows abandoned railway beds. Rail-to-Trail conversions are springing up everywhere. Transforming these abandoned tracks into trails is especially popular in urban areas where large tracts of land are expensive or unavailable. The level grade and narrow corridor of railroad beds are often perfect for hiking-biking paths.

Each year, more than three-thousand miles of railroad tracks go out of service as trucking becomes the most popular way to haul freight around the country. The Rails-to-Trails Conservancy was formed to promote the transformation of these potential trails to greenways. Of the approximately 150,000 miles of abandoned lines, more than 3,100 miles in 35 states have become trails.

Citizens are being joined in their effort by private corporations and companies. The American Gas Foundation is considering running greenways over pipeline rights-of-way and other companies are doing their part to fix up areas in cities, particularly in decaying neighborhoods.

National Trails System

Each year millions of people take advantage of this country's national trails system. From the thousands who hike a short section of the Pacific Crest Trail in California's Yosemite Valley to the intrepid few who attempt to hike the Continental Divide Trail's 2,600 miles, the system offers a wide variety of experiences. On the east coast alone, approximately four million spend a day or more along the Appalachian Trail's 2,146 mile length. Stretching from Georgia to Maine, the Appalachian Trail is one of sixteen trails belonging to the National Trails System; its four million users account for only a fraction of the number of people these trails see each year. Built and maintained by volunteers, these trails were designated by Congress to "copy the great Appalachian Trail in all parts of America," President Lyndon B. Johnson declared in 1968.

Completed in 1937, the Appalachian Trail was designated the country's first National Scenic Trail in 1968. That same year Pacific Crest Trail was established as part of the National Trails System. Ten years later, five more trails were added, including the first National Historic Trail—the Oregon Trail. Historic Trails follow roads and rivers as well as footpaths.

Once established by Congress, the law directs the Department of the Interior to fix the route of the trail and publish it with maps and descriptions. Then states along the trail have two years to acquire any land along the trail's corridor that is privately owned. Once the two-year period ends, the park service takes whatever action is necessary to preserve and protect the trail. If all else fails, the park service is allowed to use the law of eminent domain (condemnation of land) to purchase the trail corridor. Acquiring land for a national trail corridor is dependent on annual funding by Congress, funding that does not always come through.

Appalachian National Scenic Trail
The Appalachian Trail is the only member of the National
Trails System that has been completed. Its 2,146 miles cross
northward through Georgia, North Carolina, Tennessee,
Virginia, West Virginia, Maryland, Pennsylvania, New Jer-
sey, New York, Connecticut, Massachusetts, Vermont, New
Hampshire and Maine.

Less than seventy-eight miles of the trail's corridor remain on unprotected land. The most popular sections of the
trail pass through Great Smoky Mountains National Park,
Shenandoah National Park and the White Mountains of New
Hampshire.

Continental Divide National Scenic Trail
Established in 1978, the Continental Divide Trail begins at
the white obelisk marking the divide at the U.S./Mexican
border. Traversing New Mexico, Colorado, Wyoming, Idaho
and Montana, the trail ends at the Canadian border. According to the Continental Divide Trail Society, more than 2,100
miles of this 2,600-mile trail have been completed. The
Continental Divide Trail passes through the Rocky Mountains and both Glacier and Yellowstone National Parks.

Florida National Scenic Trail
Established in 1983, more than 1,000 miles of this 1,300-mile
trail have been completed. Traversing the length of Florida
and passing through the Everglades and Cape Canaveral
National Seashore, the trail links the western end of the
Florida panhandle to Lake Okeechobee and continues on to
Big Cypress National Preserve. Because some segments of
the trail are on private land, only members of the Florida
Trail Association can hike the entire length of the trail.

Ice Age National Scenic Trail
More than 450 miles of this 1,000-mile trail have been
completed in Wisconsin. The Ice Age Trail was established in
1980 and follows the ridge of hills defining the southern
advance of glaciers that occurred thousands of years ago. This
chain of moraines criss-crosses Wisconsin from the Door
Peninsula to the Saint Croix River.

North Country National Scenic Trail
Established in 1980, 1,200 miles of this 3,200-mile trail have
been completed. The trail will pass through New York,
Pennsylvania, Ohio, Michigan, Wisconsin, Minnesota, and
North Dakota—from the Adirondacks of New York to the
Missouri River in North Dakota.

Natchez Trace National Scenic Trail
This southern trail, established in 1983, travels from Natchez,
Mississippi, through Alabama and on to Nashville, Tennes-

see. It lies within the boundaries of the Natchez Trace Parkway whose 450-mile length commemorates the historic Natchez Trace, an ancient road that began as a series of animal paths and Native American trails and was later traveled by settlers. Because of the historic significance of this trail, it may soon be changed to a National Historic Trail.

Pacific Crest National Scenic Trail
To date, all but eight miles of the Pacific Crest's 2,638 miles have been permanently located. Beginning at the border of Mexico in Southern California, the trail traverses the length of the state before crossing into Oregon and Washington, and ending at the Canadian border. The trail passes through many National Park and Forest Service units including Yosemite, Lassen, Shasta, the Cascades, Mount Ranier, and Crater Lake.

Potomac Heritage National Scenic Trail
Passing through Virginia, District of Columbia, Maryland and Pennsylvania, approximately half of this 704-mile trail has been completed. None of this trail, however, has been officially designated or marked as the Potomac Heritage Trail. The existing parts of this trail, which was established in 1983, pass through Harpers Ferry, the C&O Canal Towpath and the George Washington Memorial Parkway along the Mount Vernon Trail.

Iditarod National Historic Trail
This unusual Alaskan trail is to stretch 2,350 miles (1,150 of which are completed). Currently, these 1,150 miles are used each winter for the trail's noted dog sled race, the Iditarod, that is run between Seward and Nome. The last of the five national trails established in 1978, the Iditarod is unusable during Alaska's summer months because the ground becomes too boggy. The Iditarod was made famous by prospectors and

their dog teams during the late 19th and early 20th centuries.

Juan Bautista De Anza National Historic Trail

A party of thirty families, twelve soldiers, and one thousand cattle, horses and mules spent three months crossing the deserts of the Southwest before reaching the missions of the California coast. These Spanish colonists set out from Mexico under orders from King Carlos to found a garrison and mission overlooking San Francisco's Golden Gate. The journey up the coast to the Golden Gate took another six months. The 1,200-mile route the group followed under their leader De Anza was established as a National Historic Trail in 1990.

Lewis and Clark National Historic Trail

Meriwether Lewis and William Clark were commissioned by President Thomas Jefferson to explore the newly-acquired Louisiana Territory and the "Oregon Country" beyond. They set out from what is today Wood River, Illinois, and, following the Missouri River upstream, they eventually reached the Pacific Ocean at the mouth of the Columbia River.

Established in 1978, this trail system is an optimistic 3,700 miles. Work has not yet begun, though eventually it will trek through Missouri, Kansas, Nebraska, Iowa, South Dakota, North Dakota, Montana, Idaho, Oregon and Washington.

Mormon Pioneer National Historic Trail

When the Mormons emigrated from Nauvoo, Illinois, in 1846 they became one of the primary forces of settlement in the west. Crossing into Iowa, they spent the winter in Council Bluffs, Iowa, and Omaha, Nebraska. The next year, Brigham Young led an advance party along the Platte River to Fort Bridger, Wyoming, and then turned southwest to the Great Salt Lake basin in Utah.

>>Hiking Tip<<

One alternative to setting up a two-car shuttle is to split the hiking party into two groups. Group A can be dropped off while Group B drives to the other end of the hike and parks the car. When the two groups cross paths, Group A receives the keys from Group B and then returns to the original drop-off point to pick up Group B. (Also, two cars can be used, switching keys mid-route.)

Only 47 miles of this planned 1,300-mile trail have been completed, although the 1,624-mile auto route that closely follows the trail's route is well marked. Established in 1978, the Mormon Pioneer Trail will pass, east to west, through Illinois, Iowa, Nebraska, Wyoming and Utah.

Nez Perce National Historic Trail
This commemorative trail traces the route the Nez Perce Indians followed while attempting to escape the U.S. Army. Leaving their homes along Idaho's Snake and Salmon Rivers, the Indians fled eastward toward the Rockies crossing Lolo Pass and making their way along ancient buffalo trails to reach the Great Plains. Unfortunately, just short of reaching the Canadian border in Montana, the Nez Perce were overtaken and subsequently surrendered.

Work has not yet begun on this 1,170-mile trail that traverses, west to east, Idaho, Wyoming and Montana. Established in 1986, the Nez Perce passes through Yellowstone National Park.

Oregon National Historic Trail
Although established in 1978, no part of this 2,170-mile trail has been completed. Plans for this east-west trail have it

stretching from the Missouri River in Independence, Missouri, through Kansas, Nebraska, Wyoming and Idaho and ending at the Willamette River at Oregon City, Oregon. During a twenty-year span from 1841 until 1861, approximately 300,000 people traveled this route by foot and covered wagon. Today, the trail corridor includes some 300 miles of discernible trail ruts and 125 historic sites.

Overmountain Victory National Historic Trail
During the American Revolution, patriots in the Cumberland Valley of Virginia trekked for two weeks across the Appalachian Mountains of Virginia, Tennessee and North Carolina to the Piedmont Region of North and South Carolina. There they defeated British troops at the Battle of Kings Mountain. This defeat contributed to the surrender of the British at Yorktown. Each fall, history buffs re-enact this event.

The shortest of the national trails, the Overmountain will be 272 miles once completed. Currently, twenty miles of the trail exist off-road. There is also a 310-mile commemorative auto route. Established in 1980, the trail passes through Virginia, Tennessee, North Carolina and South Carolina and crosses the Blue Ridge Parkway and Cowpens National Battlefield.

Santa Fe National Historic Trail
Using ancient Native American trade and travel routes, U.S. and Mexican traders developed the Santa Fe trail in the early 19th century. Of the 1,203 miles of primary route and cutoffs between Old Franklin, Missouri, and Santa Fe, New Mexico, more than 200 miles of ruts and other traces of the trail remain visible. In 1990, the Richard King Mellon Foundation acquired and presented to the Federal Government the 5,500-acre Forked Lightning Ranch (New Mexico) where important trail-related sites, structures and ruts can be

found. Approximately thirty miles of this east to west trail, established in 1986, are already federally protected. The trail will cross through Missouri, Kansas, Colorado, Oklahoma and New Mexico.

Trail of Tears National Historic Trail
Although a route for this trail has been planned, east-to-west through Georgia, North Carolina, Tennessee, Kentucky, Illinois, Missouri, Arkansas and Oklahoma, its length has not yet been determined. The Trail of Tears was established in 1987 and a comprehensive management plan is still underway. The planned route will follow some of the trails taken by the Cherokee Indians when they were forced to move to Oklahoma in the 1830s. The Indians were removed from North Carolina and Georgia by the U.S. Army following the discovery of gold in those states. The officially-recognized trail follows two routes: a 1,226-mile water route along the Tennessee, Ohio, Mississippi, and Arkansas Rivers; and an 826-mile overland route that is marked along the nearest highways. Few, if any, traces remain of the original trail.

The American Discovery Trail
Although not yet a National Scenic Trail, the American Discovery Trail will be the nation's first coast-to-coast hiking corridor. Sponsored by *Backpacker* Magazine and the American Hiking Society, the ADT will link existing scenic trails and backcountry byways. Winding through the nation's varied landscapes, towns, and ways of life, the trail will begin in

the Bay Area of San Francisco and end in Delaware. In the summer of 1991, legislation was introduced in Congress to begin the process of declaring the ADT as a National Scenic Trail.

Other trails being considered for National Trails System status are the California Trail and the Pony Express Trail, which would be named National Historic Trails.

Trails on Federal Lands

Backcountry trails in national parks and national forests are the best known resources on public lands. The National Forest service boasts more than 120,000 miles of trails and the National Park Service has 12,000 miles. These trails offer access to some of the nation's best known parks—the Great Smokies, Yellowstone and Yosemite—as well as many lesser appreciated areas such as the Idaho Panhandle National Forest or South Carolina's Sumter National Forest.

There are also thousands of miles of hiking trails (primarily in western states) on land managed by the Bureau of Land Management and throughout the country on National Wildlife refuges.

The most popular National Parks may require permits obtained in advance. Call as you begin making your plans to avoid disappointment later. Reservations and permits are usually not required for other federal lands.

State Parks and Forests

Another resource for hikers is state forests and parks. They offer a variety of trails and there is often one close to home. To find parks and forests in your area, check the state government in your local phone book. Call the offices of the state parks and forests in your state's capital to find out more about the trails in these areas.

· 2 ·
Water

THE SUN BLAZED brilliantly against the white sand as we stood in the shade of the ranger office and filled our gallon jugs with water from the fountain. We had been forewarned that water in Cumberland Island's backcountry required treatment and had decided to carry all we'd need for our two-day trip rather than boil or use iodine.

As we trudged down Grand Avenue with gallon jugs swinging heavily against our backs, I began to regret my decision to experience "real" backpacking. I longed for the half-mile walk to Seacamp and its raccoon boxes, cold-water showers and pleasantly shaded campsites. About half-way to our destination, we were startled by a loud and sloshy crash. We whirled around to find one of the gallon jugs sitting forlornly in the middle of the road's sandy bed. Its sides were split and water formed the pattern of a starfish around it. Well, we weren't about to go back! With only a gallon of water and an "attack of the killer seed ticks," we cut short our trip by one day.

Several years and backpacking miles later, we returned to the backcountry of Cumberland. This time, we carried only enough water to get us to our first campsite—a couple of liters. We also carried a filter to treat the water we pumped from the "iffy" well. We had a wonderful time. But experience need not be your teacher. It is possible to learn from the experience (i.e., the mistakes) of others.

Depending on where you hike, the quantity and quality of water will vary. Whether there's too much or too little, hikers can always get by if they use a little common sense. The longer you're out, the more likely you are to be uncomfortable with your water situation at some point. We have cursed both carrying too much and too little.

How much water you'll need, even how much you carry, is always a matter of personal preference. Though it may be uncomfortable at times, you will not die of thirst while hiking if you keep a few things in mind. Remember, first of all, that like the earth, the human body is seventy-five percent water. If you lose one and a half liters of water (through respiration, perspiration, etc.), you lose twenty-five percent of your body's efficiency. And, if you're expending energy in 110-degree, dry, desert heat, you could easily double the amount of water lost and lose another twenty-five percent of your body's efficiency.

Fortunately, this is a worst-case scenario; death from dehydration is unusual, except in the desert. It is always wise to be conservative when it comes to keeping yourself hydrated. Drinking at least four liters a day will replace the minimum you expend. Water is essential for life.

Where to Find Water

For many trails, there are guidebooks that tell you where to find water. But don't depend on guidebooks. Springs can run dry and are often intermittent. The same goes for small streams. Local trail clubs and the National Forest and Park Services often post signs along the trail to let hikers know where the nearest water supply can be found.

While hiking, you will get your water everywhere—from a pump to a spring to a beaver pond. Along the dry desert stretch of the Pacific Crest Trail, many hikers pull their water (albeit illegally) from the Los Angeles Aqueduct. Hikers who have tried this have some very entertaining stories to tell. We know of a couple of hikers who lost several bottles while fishing for water in the aqueduct before finally getting a "bite."

Water sources vary from stagnant pools dribbling from their source half a mile or more away from the trail (and downhill to boot!) to clear, ice-cold springs gushing forth alongside the trail.

Although there are exceptions, the higher you are, the harder it will be to find water. Conversely, the lower you are, the more water there is, and the more likely it is that you'll have to treat that water.

How Much Should You Carry

Like everything else, how much water you carry is up to you. We carry between two and three liters most of the time. That is usually adequate on most trails. I can think of only a couple of times when we were forced to eat cold meals for supper or go drinkless. Granted, there have been a few times when we spent more than half an hour waiting to fill our canteens as water dripped from an improvised funnel, but that type of situation is rare. Be prepared. Before planning a hike of any distance, find out the water situation in the area you plan to hike. You may have to carry more than is usually necessary.

On a hot day, even a beaver pond can look good and it takes a lot of restraint not to dip your Sierra cup into the inviting liquid. I remember times I wanted water so badly that the sound of the last remaining drops of water sloshing inside my canteen almost drove me mad. But I saved that tiny bit of water just in case.

One to two liters is standard when it comes to the amount of water carried by hikers. As a couple, we find we use approximately two liters of water at each meal: for oatmeal and hot chocolate or coffee at breakfast, for powdered drink mix at lunch, and for the meal and drink at supper time. We use the most water at supper because it is always our biggest meal and the hardest to clean up. Keep this in mind when planning your trip, especially when you intend to hike through water-scarce areas. Not only must you drink water to keep your body functioning properly and to avoid dehydration, but you must also use water to clean up after meals.

Also, and this is very important, take a serious look at how much liquid you take in on a normal non-hiking day. Do you drink a lot, even when you're not exerting yourself? You may need to carry more than the standard two liters of water. For example, on a cool day, I can easily get by with a cup or two of drink at breakfast and a half-liter at lunch and dinner. On hot days, I go through a liter or more at each meal. But I am an exception. Some people will want to sip on water constantly while hiking.

If you're a heavy drinker, so to speak, never pass up a good water source. Keep your canteens full of water. On hot days, Frank and I often slake our thirst at a cold spring before filling our canteens. When the temperature is high, it is best to drink cold, but not icy, water. Cold water is absorbed by the body more quickly than warm or hot water, and thus speeds up your rehydration.

Your body does not always warn you that it needs water. As a matter of fact, your body's thirst indicators are usually overridden when you start to dehydrate. Whether you feel like it or not, do not pass up the opportunity to drink water. The worst that can happen to you is that you'll have to head into the bushes a few more times.

One of the first warning signs of dehydration is the color

of your urine. If it is dark gold in color, you're heading into trouble. Drink now, not later. Coffee, tea, alcohol and soft drinks (unless they're caffeine free) are a no-no because they are diuretics and will increase your fluid loss. Obviously, if you have nothing else, you'll have to drink them; but the best way to avoid this situation is not to carry these drinks at all. If you carry instant coffee rather than a thermos-full, you can have your cake and eat it too. Drinking three full cups of liquid at each meal will help reduce the need to drink in between meals. On really hot, sweaty days, drinking an electrolyte solution such as Gatorade may help restock your body with more than just water though many physiologists advise against using drinks like Gatorade because it causes water to leave tissue and flood the digestive system—leaving muscle tissue to fend for itself.

Four activities contribute to your body's loss of water:
1) Respiration: 1-2 liters per day average
   6 liters per day in extreme cold/high altitude
2) Perspiration: 1-2 liters per day average
   1-2 liters per hour when exerting oneself in hot, dry weather
3) Urination: 1-2 liters per day average
   1-2+ with overhydration; -1-2 with dehydration
4) Defecation: .1 liter per day average
   As much as 25 liters a day with diarrhea

In most situations, without any water at all, a human can live for three to four days. Let's take a worst-case scenario—you're lost in the desert. Your best option is to find a shady spot and wait to be found. Why? Because if you have four liters of water, you could live as long as four days; ten liters, five days; and twenty liters, a week. But, get up and start walking (at night—during the day you wouldn't stand a chance) and you decrease your life span from a week to four days with twenty liters of water.

What to Carry It In

When they think of camping and backpacking, most people picture the canvas-covered metal or plastic containers slung around the neck of the hiker. Fortunately, that type of canteen is as outdated as heavy canvas tents and backpacks.

When we first started backpacking, we chose aluminum canteens to carry our water. We soon regretted that decision because the canteen's mouth was small, and hard to fill and mix drink in. The canteens were also cumbersome and difficult to get at because they were a bit too big to fit in the side pocket on our packs. We stuffed them in anyway, and consequently, had to help each other work them back out.

We eventually ended up with the Nalgene bottle (about $4). Its wide mouth is easy to fill (and to mix drink in); it is also easy to drink out of and hold. We each carry a one-liter Nalgene bottle, but they are available in a variety of sizes. I have a holder for mine that attaches to my hipbelt. Talk about easy access. Two bottles are easy to carry—one within easy reach and another packed away for later use. The screw-on tops are also recommended. (There are some that have a plug and screw-on top, but these seem prone to leaking.) The Nalgene type of bottle is used by most hikers. Some even wear special holsters, similar to the one I bought for my hipbelt, that hold their bottles in an easy-to-reach position: no more stopping to get a drink!

Also good for this purpose are the new drink bottles used by athletes—the ones you squeeze to squirt the liquid into your mouth through a spout. There are even some bottles on the market that have a tube running from the spout so that you don't even have to remove your bottle to drink. A little more flimsy, but still a viable alternative, especially in a

desperate situation, are empty plastic soda bottles. The one-liter size is used the most. They tend to leak a bit around the cap, but are great when a heat wave hits and you need to carry extra water for a limited time. The same goes for plastic milk jugs with screw-on caps.

There are two new water containers on the market that can be fitted with a filter to treat your water. An adaptor for this filter must be purchased from the manufacturer.

The first of these products is the Coldbuster Thermos by Upstream Products. It is designed as a fanny pack and carries 2.5 liters of water. This insulated, collapsible thermos can be fitted for both the Katadyn and First Need filters. At approximately $40, it is a bit expensive for most hikers but would prove invaluable when hiking in especially cold or hot areas because of its insulation.

The second is a waterbag by MSR that uses their MSR Waterworks filter. The Dromedary Beverage Bag comes in two models—plain and deluxe. Deluxe models have cords and grommets for attaching to your pack or suspending in camp. In two- and four-liter sizes, the bags range in price from $13 to $20.

Something extra (but worth it) to carry is a collapsible water bag. They're wonderful at camp because they hold more than enough water for dinner, cleanup, and sometimes even a sponge bath. Water bags, however, are unwieldy to carry filled in your pack as your only water holder. Water bags also tend to stay damp and leak a bit. We carry ours in a plastic bag to prevent it from getting the others things in our pack wet. A cheaper alternative to purchasing a water bag (which runs about $6) through an outdoors store is to recycle the bladder found in the five-liter "boxes" of wine. They're strong, lightweight, and fold up easily when empty. They are susceptible to punctures, though, so use them with care.

Most distributors of water bags also sell shower attachments that connect to the spout. We bought one but have never used it. The weather always seems to be either too cold or hot enough to swim. My stepfather, on the other hand, uses his religiously.

Giardia

"During the past fifteen years giardiasis has been recognized as one of the most frequently-occurring waterborne diseases in the United States," said Dr. Dennis D. Juranek of the Centers for Disease Control in Atlanta. According to Juranek, Giardia isn't just a contaminant of beaver ponds or of burbling brooks that flow through cow pastures (and you'll get your water from both). Anywhere there are animals, including humans, there's a chance of Giardia. Believe it or not, fifty to sixty percent of all giardiasis comes from tap water.

One reason Giardia causes intestinal problems may be that the parasite interferes with chemicals the body needs to digest certain foods, including dairy products. For as long as the parasite remains in its host, the intolerance to certain foods remains.

"The disease is characterized by diarrhea that usually lasts one week or more," Juranek said, "and may be accompanied by one or more of the following: abdominal cramping, bloating, flatulence with foul smelling gas, vomiting, fatigue, and weight loss." If left untreated, the infection may disappear in a month or two. But, in some cases, the microbe hangs on causing recurring attacks for many years.

Some people become infected but experience no symptoms at all (though they can still spread the disease), and the parasite vanishes in a couple of months. While most Giardia infections persist only for one to two months, he said, some people undergo a more chronic phase. Others can have several of the symptoms but no diarrhea or have only sporadic episodes of diarrhea every three or four days. Still others may not have any symptoms at all.

"The problem may not be whether you're infected with the parasite or not," Juranek said, "but how harmoniously you both can live together, or how you can get rid of the parasite (either spontaneously or by treatment) when the harmony does not exist or is lost."

Juranek said that there are three drugs available in the United States to treat giardiasis: quinacrine or Atabrine, metronidazole or Flagyl, and furazolidone or Furoxone. All three are prescription drugs; they are listed in the order of their effectiveness, although Flagyl is the most often prescribed. You may want to ask your doctor about a prescription if you are worried about picking up Giardia, especially if you intend to be out hiking for a week or more. But we know of only one hiker who carries a prescription with him, and he has never needed it.

"Fortunately," Juranek said, "the Giardia parasites do not invade other parts of the body or cause permanent damage." So, though rarely dangerous to adults, giardiasis can prove life-threatening to both the very young and the very old because of the severe dehydration it can cause should the victim be afflicted with vomiting and diarrhea.

Treating Water

Don't succumb to the urge to drink water before you've purified it. It is easier to carry an extra pound or two of water than suffer the discomforts of Giardia and other stomach ailments that dehydrate you and cause you to lose your strength. Diarrhea and cramps are harder to handle while hiking because of the physical strain you're already placing on your body.

We know of only a few hikers who have picked up Giardia while hiking. If you are careful, the chances of contracting this parasitic disease while backpacking are few. But Giarida cases are increasing at an alarming rate—an estimated figure (because so many cases go unreported and/or misdiagnosed) is more than 120,000 nationwide.

"Water treatment steps range from doing nothing at all, to boiling water, to high-priced purifiers," said Bob Dowling, a long distance hiker and victim of Giardia. "For the most part, I felt confident about the water sources I chose. Then I caught Giardia from an area I considered the most pristine--the wilderness stretch (of the Appalachian Trail) in Maine. This set me rethinking my practices on drinking water. A common question you hear is 'How is the water?' the response usually being 'Fine'. How do they know? Did they test for giardiasis or other contaminants? Hell no! How can you be

>>Hiking Tip<<
Remove large particles from debris-filled water by filtering it through a bandana first. This will save wear-and-tear on an expensive replacement filter.

sure? The answer is: you can't be sure. A hiker must treat all water as suspect. What to do? Use some common sense to decrease the chance of contaminated water."

Suspect water should always be treated, and, according to Juranek, portable devices with microstrainer filters are the only way to filter out Giardia. To be safest, Juranek says, the filters should have a pore size of one micron or less.

"Theoretically, a filter having an absolute pore size of less than six micrometers (microns) might be able to prevent Giardia cysts of eight to ten micrometers in diameter from passing into your drinking water, but for effective removal of bacterial and viral organisms, as well as Giardia, the less than one micrometer pore size is advisable."

General Ecology's most practical filter for backpackers is the First Need Deluxe, which has a pore size of 0.4 microns and weighs fifteen ounces. The charcoal-based filter purifies a liter of water in two minutes and costs about $70. It can be backwashed to extend the filter life. The filters must be replaced after about 400 liters and will cost around $30. The 1995 model fits on nalgene-style bottles. While hiking in Nepal, we successfully used the First Need to turn the filthy brown liquid to clean, pure water and experienced no problems in two months of steady use. The smaller Microlite tends to clog easily, and needs a new $10 cartridge every 120 liters.

The Katadyn filter, although expensive (about $250), is made for heavy duty use. A ceramic filter of 0.2 microns, it has been said to be effective even against nuclear debris, although I don't recommend trying that at home. It is easier to

· **Water Filters** ·

Filter	Pore Size	Weight	Impurities Filtered	Cost
GE First Need Deluxe	0.4	15 oz.	B,P,C	$ 70
GE Microlite	0.5	7 oz.	B,P,C,V	$ 30
Katadyn Mini	0.2	8 oz.	B,P,C	$150
Katadyn	0.2	23 oz.	B,P,C	$250
MSR Waterworks	0.1	18 oz.	B,P,C	$125
OB Trecker Travel Well	N/A	6 oz.	B,P,C,V	$ 65
PUR Explorer	1.0	20 oz.	B,P,C,V	$130
PUR Scout	1.0	12 oz.	B,P,C,V	$ 65
SweetWater Guardian	0.2	11 oz.	B,P,C	$ 50

Pore size is given in microns (absolute). B-Bacteria, P-Protozoa, C-Chemicals (including pesticides and fertilizer), V-Viruses

GE-General Ecology, OB-Outbound

pump and clean than the First Need and filters about one liter per minute. Replacement filters for the Katadyn cost about $90. Although we have no personal experience with the Katadyn, some of our river rat pals swear by theirs.

The MSR Waterworks has gained popularity in recent years because of its ease-of-use. Costing about $125, it can be screwed onto a standard wide-mouthed bottle such as Nalgene. The MSR filters to 0.1 microns, and a set of its three replacement filters and screen cost about $75.

Most filters screen out bacteria, protazoa and organic chemicals. Some filters also remove viruses with a chemical filter, such as the iodine elements in the PUR Explorer and Scout or the Outbound Trekker Travel Well. Viruses, including hepatitis, are the most serious threat to travelers in third world countries; they pose less of threat in the United States.

The problems with filters are their bulkiness, weight, and cost. There are two other, lighter ways to get rid of Giardia, both with their own drawbacks.

Giardia can be killed by bringing your water to a boil. According to Dr. Dennis Addiss, also of the Centers for Disease Control in Atlanta, water need not be boiled to kill Giardia, only brought to boiling point. Giardia is actually killed at a lower temperature; bringing your water to a boil is just insurance that you have killed the parasite. But, by boiling your water for a minute or more, you will also kill other viruses, bacteria, parasites, etc.

Obviously, the drawbacks to heating water are the time and fuel it takes to boil it as well as the time it takes to cool down. If you're boiling the water for a meal anyway, you can be assured the Giardia will be killed. You do not have to account for altitude when you're boiling water to kill Giardia.

Iodine and Halazone also can kill Giardia. One tablet in one liter of relatively clear, not too cold water for half an hour will effectively kill Giardia, says Addiss. The major drawback to this method is the taste. Iodine leaves a not-too-pleasant taste in your water, and, once again, you have to play the waiting game.

One way to combat the bad taste, according to Addiss, is to leave your water container uncovered for a while; this helps to dissipate the iodine.

Some hikers use two or three drops of chlorine (usually in

❦ *Hiking Secret* ❦

Add an iodine tablet to a liter of water, and, once it is dissolved, heat that water to boiling. Then, divide it into two or three containers and top those containers off with unpurified water. The heated iodine water more effectively kills contaminants and doesn't taste as bad once it is diluted.

the form of bleach) to treat their water. According to Addiss and Juranek, this is not a very good idea.

"There are too many variables that influence the efficiency of chlorine as a disinfectant," says Juranek. Among those variables are water pH, water temperature, organic content of the water, chlorine contact time, and the concentration of chlorine.

"There's just no way to be sure that you've accounted for all the variables," says Addiss.

Treating your water is important but keep in mind that bacteria can also grow in your water bottle, especially if you use it to carry flavored drinks. Make sure you keep your water bottle clean. Pay particular attention to the threads on bottles with screw-on caps.

When to Treat Your Water
The truth is, most hikers take chances and don't treat their water, especially when the source is a spring or at a high altitude. Pristine areas (such as springs high in the Rockies) are as likely a source of Giardia as your kitchen faucet. Because you can get Giardia from your tap water, day care centers, swimming pools, food, pets and sexual contact as well as from streams, ponds and springs, how can you possibly know if the water is safe? You can't. But the following chart will give you some idea of how safe your water might be.

Best to Worst Sources of Water	Confidence
Faucet or hose	high
Piped spring	high
Unprotected spring (Look for animal tracks around the spring.)	moderate

Streams   low
    (Consider source of stream: Does
    it run by civilization or cow pastures
    or does it stay in protected wilderness?
    Also, how cold is it, how near is its
    source, and how fast is it running?
    May need to be treated.)

Ponds or Lakes   none
    (Assume the worst; treat water.
    Take the time to be safe even if
    you feel lazy or tired.)

All hikers we've talked to agree with this analysis, and though many rarely treat their water, almost all agree in retrospect that it's better to be safe than sorry. As long distance backpacker Nancy Hill put it, "Do as I say not as I do."

It all comes down to a judgement call: when the source is questionable, you're the one taking the risk. Many hikers agree that they are less likely to treat their water when they are tired, depressed, etc.

When hiking through snow or on cold days . . .

- Never drink icy water in the winter or even on cool days. The cold water can cause your body temperature to drop. To avoid this, warm snow or water in your mouth before swallowing.

- Protect your water when temperatures drop below freezing by burying it deep in your pack. At night, stash it inside your tent or at the end of your sleeping bag. You can also turn your water bottles upside down so that ice won't block the spout.

- Keep your bottles full of water by topping off with snow after each drink.

- Use water to melt snow. An inch of water in your cook pot will melt snow more quickly. Add the crustiest, iciest or wettest snow to your pot—it'll produce more water.

- It probably goes without saying to avoid yellow snow, but also steer clear of pink or "watermelon" snow. This snow gets its name from its color, taste and scent produced by microorganisms that can cause diarrhea.

- Burying your water in the snow will help insulate it. A lidded pot buried a foot or so under snow will not freeze. Remember to mark the spot carefully.

- Keep in mind that melting snow will take more fuel and more time. With a cold wind blowing, it can take an hour and a stove full of fuel to melt and boil a quart of water.

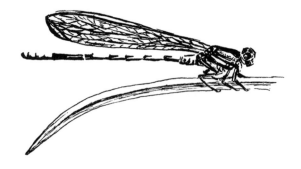

·3·
Food and Cooking

BACKPACKERS ARE NOTED for their tremendous appetites. Anyone who has done any long distance hiking or met long distance hikers has a tale to tell about how much a backpacker can eat.

From gallons of ice cream to All-You-Can-Eat (AYCE) buffets, hikers consume copious amounts of food whenever they hit a town near the trail. While hiking the Appalachian Trail, Phil Hall was so impressed with Shoney's AYCE breakfast bar in Virginia that he hitched a ride back there when he reached New Hampshire.

Long distance hikers often leave a town dreaming about the next and what epicurean delights it might have to offer. Because you really do want to keep your pack light, you must often hike with a less than satisfying amount of food in tow. This is because the heavier the pack, the more you exert yourself, and the more you exert yourself, the more calories you burn. Because of the often small portions, dehydrated foods—specialty, store-bought and homemade—though increasingly appealing, are often less than satisfying following a tough day of hiking.

Dehydrated/Freeze-dried Foods

Until someone invents something amazingly lightweight, filling, tasty, inexpensive and convenient, hikers will have to make do with what's available. Thanks, no doubt, to the ever increasing number of women in the workforce, supermarkets are filled with easy-to-fix, just-add-water dinners. A couple of years ago, we would have recommended that hikers stick to the low cost supermarket brand dinners such as Kraft, Lipton and others, but specialty dehydrated foods designed for backpackers have come a long way. Though still expensive, they offer variety to the macaroni-and-cheeses and ramen-noodle-dinners many hikers subsist on.

We decided to test a few different brands and meals and were pleasantly surprised by what came out of our cook pot. For breakfast, we tried an omelette with potatoes and sauteed onions. The two-serving egg dish was not a bad buy. A bit of a pain to clean up, it definitely adds variety to the staples of oatmeal and toaster pastries. Pancake mixes are also available in foil pouches.

For lunch, you have your choice of the many main courses the manufacturers of backpacker foods prepare as well as the standards—soups and sandwiches. If you want to cook your lunch, as opposed to eating a cold meal, dinner-type meals and soups offer you a variety of choices. Think about lunch at home or work—soups, sandwiches, salads and occasionally main courses. The same relates to backpacking except for salads, which are generally impractical.

For supper, we tried a dinner described as "grains, brown rice, turkey, vegetables and wild rice in a tangy sour cream sauce." The no-cook entree (not actually true—when you hike, even boiling water is cooking) was actually quite palatable. The dinner says it serves two although a hungry hiker, especially a hungry male hiker, would probably have to eat the entire dinner just to get half-way full. We had freeze-dried ice cream for dessert. The two-serving portion of neopolitan ice cream was good but expensive—one serving for a hungry hiker. We were intrigued by the thought of dried ice cream but we'd definitely recommend sticking to the cobblers, pies and more filling desserts.

Among the companies that supply backpackers with dehydrated and freeze-dried foods are Adventure Foods, Alpine Aire, Harvest Foodworks, Mountain House, Natural High, Nature's Pantry, Richmoor, Trail Wise and Wee Pack.

A new type of trail food, boxed in tiny "milk" cartons, is manufactured by Taste Adventure. These vegetarian, dehydrated meals prepare quickly and are inexpensive. We tried both the black bean chili and lentil soup, which were tasty and provided large portions for two people.

Although we would still not recommend relying solely on these specially dehydrated and freeze-dried foods, we do believe they are a wonderful way to add variety to the diet. Keep in mind, though, that main dishes tend to cost two to three times as much as store-bought macaroni, pasta salads and rice dishes.

Supermarket Fare

Add the ever-growing market of backpacking foods to the supermarket fare listed below and the backpacker in the '90s is already further down the trail than his compatriots of a decade earlier.

Grocery stores offer a wide variety of fare to choose from. You're limited only by what the store has in stock. By searching for meal ideas at oriental and health food stores as well, you open yourself up to more variety. On our long distance hike, we chose to purchase food along the way rather than send any ahead. This meant there were times when we ate macaroni and cheese three times in one week and other times when we had a different meal to choose from every night.

Breakfasts

Breakfasts are easier to choose than lunches since there are so many breakfast products on the market. Most are vitamin-fortified, a gimmick to make mothers feel that they are providing a healthy breakfast for their child even when the product is stuffed full of sugar. The extra carbohydrates are an added boon for hikers!

❏ **Suggested Breakfasts**
Cold cereal with powdered milk
Oatmeal (Fruit-and-Cream and Swirlers and plain variety)
Toaster pastries (such as Pop Tarts)
Eggs (will keep for several days)
Canned bacon
Bread with peanut butter
Bagels with cream cheese (cheese also keeps for several days)
Snickers or other candy bars
Granola bars
Gorp in powdered milk
Pancakes (bring the dry mix, add powdered milk and water)
Granola in powdered milk
Instant hash browns
Instant grits
Cream of Wheat
Bacon bars
English muffins
Breakfast bars (such as Nutrigrain Breakfast Bars)
Raisin bread

❦ Hiking Secret ❦

Boiling eggs for five seconds will increase their pack life. Eggs will keep several weeks, even in summer, if first treated in this manner. Another secret to increase the life of eggs is to coat them in petroleum jelly.

Lunches

Lunches are always a problem for us, both at home and on the trail. Unless it is really cold, we never feel like taking the time to cook a lunch; but on the trail, there are only so many things you can do to improvise a cold lunch. We recommend that you do what suits you best. Some people hike better after a big, hot meal, but most do best with a simple repast. The temperatures during your hike may also determine your midday meal. When it is cold, we often choose to keep moving, eating snack foods while we hike, rather than stopping to prepare a meal.

❏ **Suggested Lunches**

Sardines

Cheese

Nuts

Pemmican (complex protein bars)

Cookies

Crackers (a number of varieties can be purchased already spread with cheese or peanut butter)

Beef jerky

Peanut butter and jelly sandwiches

Dried soups

Candy bars

Pepperoni

Graham or other type cracker and peanut butter

Sausage (hard types like salami, summer sausage, etc.)

Apples, oranges, and other fresh fruit

Lipton Noodles and Sauce

English muffins and peanut butter

Crackers and tuna

Corned beef or Spam

Hard boiled eggs

Dried fruit (including rolls, bars, etc.—raisins are a good choice)

Cheese sandwiches (pita is a great hiking bread—stuff it with salami and cheese for a calorie-packed sandwich)
Granola bars
Snack foods (Little Debbie brand is especially popular)
Gorp (a mixture of dried fruit, nuts, M&Ms, sunflower seeds, etc.)
Vienna sausages
Fruit cake

Supper
Supper should be your most time-consuming meal of the day. It is time to relax, settle down for the night and enjoy the great outdoors. You no longer have to worry about whether or not you'll reach your goal for the day. Your camp is set. Dinner is your only concern. Despite the fact that many backpackers eat macaroni and cheese night after night, there are many alternatives when choosing dinner on the trail.

❑ Suggested Suppers
Lentils
Instant rice dishes (instant gravies and cheese sauces can be added)
Macaroni and cheese (a real favorite; meat or dried soup often added)
Lipton brand noodle dinners
Instant mashed potatoes
Stove Top or other stuffings
Chef Boyardee spaghetti
Instant soup
Ramen noodles
Pasta salads
Couscous (a middle eastern wheat dish similar to grits)
Pilafs (such as lentil, wheat and rice)
Instant potato dinners (au gratin, etc.)

Tuna and other canned meats (used with any dinners)
Pepperoni, dried beef and sausages
Sardines and fish steaks (hotdogs also show up occasionally)
Specialty dehydrated meals

Beverages
As I mentioned in the chapter on water, drinking is a very important part of hiking. Becoming dehydrated will seriously impair your body's ability to perform normal functions. The best thing to drink is water, but when the water tastes like iodine you'll probably want to disguise its taste with a powdered drink mix such as Kool-Aid. Because we prefer the flavor, we have developed the practice of constantly carrying a full liter of a Kool Aid-type drink mix and a spare liter (or two, depending on the heat) of water.

The next best thing to water is an electrolyte solution such as Gatorade or Gookinaid ERG. These help replace the electrolytes, as well as the water, that you lose when you perspire, respire, etc. Some physiologists debate this claim and believe that electrolyte solutions do more harm than good.

There are very few of us willing to give up our morning cup of coffee when we hit the trail. If you do drink coffee or cocoa (unless decaffeinated), keep in mind that they are diuretics and you will need to drink more water to compensate.

❏ **Suggested Beverages**
Water
Powdered fruit drinks (such as Kool-Aid—unsweetened or your preferred sweetener added)
Powdered iced tea (often mixed with fruit drinks)
Powdered fruit teas
Jello mix (used as a tasty, hot drink that also supplies extra calories)
Instant coffee
Non-dairy creamer (for tea or coffee)
Powdered spiced cider
Powdered egg nog
Gatorade (powdered)
Gookinaid E.R.G.
Hot tea
Cocoa/Hot Chocolate

Desserts
Desserts are a nice way to finish your evening meal. They supply you with a few extra calories and help fill that last empty spot in your belly. They also make dinner special. Although pudding is a favorite, there are a number of easy-to-make desserts on the market.

❑ **Suggested Desserts**
Instant puddings
Instant cheesecakes
Cookies
Instant mousse
Jello or other flavored gelatins
Powdered milk (mostly used to add to other foods)
Snack cakes
Easy-bake cakes
Specialty dehydrated desserts

Spices and Condiments

Not everyone uses spices, and no one carries all of those indicated below; but those who bring spices tend to use a variety. For their weight, spices and condiments can add a lot to a meal.

A good way to carry spices is to put them in film containers. This keeps them both dry and compact. Shaker tops are available through most outdoors stores for about $2 for two lids.

❑ **Suggested Spices**
Garlic
Salt
Pepper
Italian seasoning
Seasoned butter
Tabasco
Red pepper
Curry powder
Chili powder
Oregano
Cumin
Onion powder

Squeeze margarine (lasts approximately one week in hot weather and almost indefinitely in cold weather)

Trail Snacks

I've never been a snacker, but I find it important when hiking. Because you don't want to stuff yourself at meals—for comfort's sake as well as the fact that a too-full stomach can make you drowsy—it is a good idea to snack on high energy food during breaks and while hiking. One of the most popular trail snacks is Gorp, a mixture of nuts, dried fruit and M&Ms. Actually, Gorp can consist of anything you like, but the following is a list of some popular ingredients. Mix and match your favorites: peanuts, almonds, pecans, walnuts, filberts, cashews (if you can afford them), M&M's (plain, almond or peanut), Reese's Pieces, shredded coconut, chopped dates, raisins, banana chips, dried pineapple, figs, prunes, sunflower seeds, and cereals like Cheerios.

Other trail snacks include: hard candy, Skittles candy, semi-sweet chocolate, mixed nuts, fruit bars and rolls. There are many packaged snack bars on the market these days. Use your imagination. As long as it is within easy reach and will keep in the outdoors for more than a day, it will make a good snack. Remember too that "snacks" can round out dinners and often make up your entire lunch.

Self-dehydrated Foods

Many hikers depend on food they dehydrate themselves. Dehydrators can be purchased through most outdoors stores. All manner of food can be dehydrated—fruit, meats and vegetables.

Although it takes time and effort, dehydrating your own food can be an inexpensive alternative. My mother swears by her dehydrated tuna, and Bill and Laurie Foot by their beef. Cindy Ross and Todd Gladfelter, who have hiked more than twelve thousand miles between them, dry most of the food they use for their trips.

Dehydrators cost between $50 and $100, and are for use before you hike since they are both too heavy and bulky (not to mention electric) to carry with you.

Fresh Food

Fresh foods are available to hikers although you can't rely solely on fresh foods for your backpacking diet. Those hiking short distances have more freedom in the different types of foods they can carry because they have more room in their packs to carry the heavier, bulkier foods. If you're going for an overnighter, you can carry steaks, hamburgers, fish or chicken to cook over your grill. Although long-distance hikers have the option to carry fresh meat, vegetables or fruit, they have to eat this motherlode their first night back on the trail after a shopping stop or risk rotten and decaying food. The weight is also a problem and the sooner you eat the heavier food, the more immediate the relief to your back.

We usually stick to hotdogs (turkey or chicken) on longer hikes because they are the only meat that won't drip blood all over our packs. Hotdogs roasted over a fire with some cheese make a delicious meal alternative and you don't have to worry about ketchup, mustard, etc. We also occasionally carry apples, oranges, pears, carrots and other fruits and vegetables that are not easily bruised.

With a little planning, weekenders can still enjoy fresh foods. For example, if you intend to have hamburgers your second night out, freeze the meat before you go. By the end of the second day, it should be thawed. Make sure you keep it in a zipper-lock bag or you could end up with a messy backpack. One of the greatest advantages of short hikes is that your diet is limited only by the amount of time you want to spend cooking.

Nutrition

Nutrition on the trail is a "Catch-22." While it is easy enough to carry sufficient food to account for calories burned during a day or weekend hike, it is difficult and often impossible to do so for extended trips.

The more food you carry, the heavier your pack. The heavier your pack, the more calories you burn. The more calories you burn, the more you need. It's a vicious circle for long-distance hikers as well as those who are already on the thin side. While you're sure to lose weight on an extended hike, there is no need to sacrifice your health.

Since you'll be burning close to five thousand calories per eight-hour day on a backpacking trip, it is important that the food you carry has high nutritional value and a high carbohydrate count. The complex carbohydrates should make up about fifty percent of the backpacker's daily caloric intake. Fortunately, this is an easy requirement to fill. Bread, pastas, cookies, dried fruit, candy and honey are all high in carbohydrates.

Twenty percent of your day's calories should consist of fats, which the body converts into stored energy. You need a higher percentage of fats in the winter, and you can get your fats from margarine, cheese, peanut butter, nuts and salami. High altitude hikers and climbers need to increase their carbo intake, and lower their fat consumption during climbs because the body will confiscate oxygen to process fats into stored up lipoproteins. Most climbers can't spare the oxygen for this process, and have more energy on a high carbohydrate diet.

Protein is also important to the backpacker; but if you eat too much, it will be converted to glycogen and stored as fat. You can get your proteins from peanut butter, oat and wheat cereals with powdered milk, sausage, cheese, beef jerky or other dried or fresh meats. A better solution is to get your protein from plants—raw or cooked beans, soybeans, nuts and olives—that also supply important vitamins, minerals, carbohydrates and fiber.

Whether or not you should take vitamins on an extended trip is debatable. During our six-month trek, we took vitamins when we remembered (which wasn't often) and both of us caught a severe cold. Two years later I began taking vitamins religiously (when carrying my daughter, Griffin) and I have suffered only one brief cold in two years. Whether or not it is the vitamins or the lack of exposure, I couldn't tell you. Once again, it is a matter of preference; but I would recommend taking some sort of vitamin supplement on an extended trip, particularly vitamins C and B. It is hard to maintain a balanced diet under such strenuous conditions, so a multi-vitamin is your best bet during a long-distance hike.

Food sources high in calcium are particularly important to long-distance hikers. Powdered milk, milk products such as cheese and sardines in oil are good sources of calcium. Dried fruit, though not particularly high in calcium content, can add greatly to the total calcium and vitamin A intake when eaten on a regular basis.

Experts recommend that you vary your backpacking diet as much as possible. While it may not bother you to eat cold cereal for breakfast, gorp for lunch and macaroni and cheese every night for dinner, your body may soon tire of it. I learned the hard way with macaroni and cheese. We ate so much of it that by the end of our trip I literally had to gag the stuff down and often couldn't finish my serving. The most important aspect of a varied diet is the guarantee that you will be getting all the nutrients your body needs to function efficiently.

I know of backpackers who subsist on the same thing for every meal, seven days a week. I also know of backpackers who thought they were in peak condition until they had to undergo open-heart surgery. Your body can only do so much

>>Hiking Tip<<

A Frisbee can be cleaned off and used as a plate. Having the toy do double duty as a dish will help you justify those extra ounces. If you have energy after setting up camp for the night, you'll never want for a game to play in good weather.

---

on its own. It depends on you to do what's right for it. As The Fonz said, "You live in your body most of your life."

Things to consider
There are several other things to consider when shopping for backpacking trips. The weight of the food, ease of preparation, taste and cost are of varying importance to different people.

Remember that your pack can only hold so much. While you may want steak every night, the weight alone precludes your carrying it. The lighter the food the better and, fortunately for backpackers, there are a lot of options on the market.

Ease of preparation also is important. After a long day of hiking, it is unlikely that you will want to spend hours preparing your meal. Read package labeling before purchasing a food product. How long will it take to prepare the meal? How long do you want to wait? On days when we reached our destination early, we didn't mind waiting twenty minutes for our lentils and rice to simmer. Other days, we could hardly wait for the macaroni to finish cooking and often ate it a bit more al dente than we usually liked. Buying food with various preparation times (an emphasis on the short side) will give you some options when you stumble into camp for the night.

Taste is something else to think about when purchasing food. If you can't stomach peanut butter at home, you sure as heck won't like it in the outdoors, especially if you're forced to eat it. Macaroni and cheese was not the only thing I got sick of while backpacking. During our six-month trip, it seemed we always ate our sardines on cold, rainy days. It wasn't long before I associated being miserable with those smelly little fish.

Although I can eat both macaroni and sardines again, they are no longer a staple when it comes to backpacking meals. If you are unsure whether a certain backpacking food will be unsavory to you, try it before you hike. There is nothing worse than end-of-the-day hunger when you're facing an unpalatable meal. A lot of your time hiking will be spent anticipating your next meal.

Backpacking food (as with anything) can cost as much or as little as you like. From the expensive, extra-lightweight, specially packaged foods to the inexpensive home-made alternative, the backpacker has many choices. You know how much you have to spend. Once again, the key is diversity. Don't buy a week's worth of blueberry pancakes and lasagna; round it out with eggs and toaster pastries, macaroni and cheese, pasta salad and lentils.

Packing your food
Packaging is only a problem if you are unable to repackage the food yourself. Don't buy rigid, heavyweight containers if they must go straight into your pack. Unless you have room for food at the top of your pack where it won't get smashed, make sure the packaging is sturdy enough to survive the weight you intend to subject it to.

Proper packing is essential. Hikers joke that the "yellow-and-blue-makes-green" Gladlock brand plastic bags are one of the great backpacking inventions of our time. This might be a little exaggerated, but not much. In the interest of space, weight, and waterproofing, you will want to repackage your food into plastic bags or some other waterproof container. Other options include reusable, plastic, squeezable food tubes. A clip at the bottom is used to squeeze the food upward toward the spout. I have only seen these used for peanut butter and jelly; but because both peanut butter and jelly now come in plastic containers, it is just as easy to use them in their containers. Also, it isn't a simple process to transfer these sticky foods from one container to another.

Rigid plastic egg cartons are also available for less than $3 from most outdoors stores. They come in both the dozen and half-dozen size and are a wonderful way to carry eggs if you eat a lot of them while hiking. These containers will hold small and medium size eggs only.

To pack food for backpacking, sort your boxes and other packages into meals. Open the boxes and pour the contents into plastic bags of appropriate sizes. You do not need to do this with meals that come in foil or other waterproof pouches. On short trips, you can cut down on weight and space by adding the powdered milk, salt, pepper, etc. to the bag at home and leaving the condiments behind. If you need the directions, cut out the portion of the box the recipe is written on and put it in the bag with the meal.

Some food products do better in plastic bags with twist ties. If you are carrying powdered milk, for example, it is best to double bag it and shut it with a twist tie because the grains of milk tend to get caught in the "zipper" and keep it from closing properly.

Food for a week or more
If you are hiking for more than a week, will you be able to buy food along the way? Would it be better to send something ahead to a post office? The majority of long distance hikers suggest using both methods. Buying some food ahead of time and some as you hike allows you to be adaptable along the trail and leaves some leeway as to where and when you stop.

It also allows for much less preparation before the hike and is easier on the support crew at home.

The option to purchase food along the way eliminates the need to time your arrival in town to coincide with the hours of a post office. (It's nice not to have to depend on the U.S. Postal Service for food.) It also allows you to satisfy any cravings you may have!

For more information on buying food for long distance hikes, see Chapter 15.

The Outback Oven

This clever device turns a backpacking stove into an oven to bake bread, cakes and even pizza. The backpacker's model— Outback Oven Ultralight—comes with a reflector collar, diffusor plate, thermometer and convection dome. The eight-ounce kit effectively spreads out the heat output by your stove with the diffusor plate and uses the reflector collar and convection dome (an aluminized fiberglass fabric cover for your cook kit) to lock the heat in. The oven cooks on simmer, so fuel use is low even though many recipes will take 45 minutes to cook. The Ultralight costs $30.

The Outback Oven Plus Ten adds a 10-inch teflon pan and lid to the above. At 24 ounces, the weight is hard to justify for extended hikes, but we use ours for short trips. It costs $45.

Traveling Light, the makers of the Outback Oven, sell baking mixes made to use in their stove. Like other pre-packaged trail foods, you just add water and cook (or bake in this case). The oven and food may sound like just something else to carry, and it is, but pulling a fresh-baked pesto pizza out of your backpacking stove when you are 15 miles from the nearest road is nothing short of miraculous.

Cleaning up after meals

Cleaning pots, dishes, and utensils is an absolute necessity. Many hikers have found out the hard way that giving cleaning the short shrift can result in severe gastrointestinal problems not dissimilar to giardiasis. Cleaning should be done away from the campsite or shelter, as well as far from the water source.

There are several reasons to clean your pots as soon as you have finished eating, not the least among them being the growth of bacteria. Dirty pots also beg for the appearance of pests such as raccoons, skunks, mice, and even bears (not to mention the hardships caused by dried-on macaroni and cheese that is harder than Super Glue to clean up).

The best solution is to carry a little biodegradable soap and a pot scrubber. Bill and Laurie Foot offer these suggestions: "Use two pots for hot meals. You should never need to cook food in your large pot. It is for heating water and rinsing dishes only. Add your hot water to the entree in the smaller pot, and after you've eaten, add more water and some soap to the smaller pot to use as a washpan. The remainder of the hot water in the large pot becomes your rinse water."

Living Off the Land

Unless you know your edible wild plants backwards and forwards, I would suggest sticking to store-bought and home-made foods when backpacking. Many edible plants can be easily confused with poisonous plants.

While attending a lecture on mushrooms, we were dismayed to find that a mushroom we had feasted on in Maine was potentially fatal. This mushroom has the color and taste of lobster and is parasitic, growing off both a safe and a very dangerous mushroom. Obviously, we were lucky and we've decided we'll never take a chance like that again.

There are some obvious edibles though. Blueberries grow profusely in the wild and are great in pancakes, on cereal, in oatmeal and so on. Blackberries, gooseberries, currants, raspberries and wild strawberries can also be found trailside.

Mulberries, unless fully ripe, can be dangerous. Another safe wild plant is the ramp or wild leek. It's strong onion odor distinguishes it—use as you would an onion.

For more information on edible plants, I would suggest reading *The Basic Essentials of Edible Wild Plants and Useful Herbs* by Jim Meunick (ICS Books, 1988).

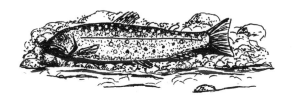

·4·
Stoves and Fuel

OUR FIRST EXPERIENCE with a pack stove was a disaster. It was hot, the ticks were vicious, and we had forgotten to bring the directions for our new stove—the Camping Gaz Bleuet. We had absolutely no idea how to load the butane cartridge that fueled the lightweight stove. Our first attempt ended with us watching, wretchedly, as the gas fumes exploded through the puncture before we had the cartridge properly mounted. We wasted an entire can of fuel in five minutes! Our second effort was a success and we haven't had problems with the little stove since. As a matter of fact, we had to hide our grins on our next trip as we fired up our stove and got the coffee water boiling while a friend struggled to light his Coleman.

But, when we decided to take an extended backpacking trip of six months, we no longer felt safe using the Camping Gaz because of the unavailability of its fuel cartridges. Neither did we feel safe about sending them ahead of us. So we opted for the MSR Whisperlite.

Using a campstove while backpacking is almost mandatory now because there are so many areas where fires are prohibited. In areas where fires are permitted, the woods around shelters and campsites have often been picked clean of downed wood by other hikers. Fortunately, stoves are now light-weight and efficient, as well as inexpensive.

White Gas/Kerosene Stoves

Stoves that use white gas are preferred for backpacking because they are the most versatile. They are more likely to reach a boil in cold weather and their fuel is more widely available.

All fuels have their advantages and disadvantages. White gas evaporates quickly, has a high heat output and is widely available in the United States. However, priming is occasionally required, the spilled fuel is very flammable and self-pressurized stoves using white gas must be insulated from snow or cold. Although kerosene will not ignite readily, it also does not evaporate quickly. Kerosene stoves can sit directly on the snow, and they have a high heat output. Kerosene is also available world-wide. A disadvantage is that all kerosene stoves require priming.

No matter what the stove type, a 16- to 22-ounce container of Coleman fuel generally lasts seven to twelve days. In the winter, because fuel consumption is slightly higher, you can count on no more than a week's worth of fuel from any 22-ounce container. In the summer, one container may last as long as two weeks.

Hikers rarely experience any difficulty purchasing fuel for their gas stoves. Unleaded fuel is usually an available substitute. A number of hikers use unleaded fuel exclusively (particularly with the MSR Whisperlite) without any problems, though this is not recommended by the manufacturer.

MSR fuel bottles can be purchased in three sizes: 11-ounce, 22-ounce and 33-ounce, though the latter are probably not necessary for most hikes. Sigg offers fuel bottles ranging from 8 ounces to 48 ounces. Both brands are made of non- corrosive aluminum and are relatively inexpensive (under $10). Fuel faucets are available for both the MSR and Sigg bottles. The screw-on cap allows you to turn the top to pour and turn again to seal without a leak. Nalgene bottles, which do not fit the MSR stoves, can also be purchased—pint size and quart size.

The following stoves are among the favorites because of the availability of fuel and their versatility in hot and cold weather:

MSR Whisperlite Internationale 600
The Mountain Safety Research (MSR) Whisperlite is something of a standard in backpacking stoves. The stove earned its name by barely whispering in comparison to the then dominant stove, the SVEA 123 (now the Optimus 123). Though you can still buy the original Whisperlite, this updated model is less than $10 more in most stores and boasts two features worth the extra hard-earned cash.

The main complaint many hikers had about the original Whisperlite is that it clogged frequently. It was easily cleaned, but hikers demanded something simpler and MSR responded. This model is equipped with a cleaning tip for the fuel jet built into the stove. Each time you pack your stove up after use, turn it upside down and right it again several times. This will drop the weighted cleaning tip through the jet and clean the stove. Our field tests show that this feature lives up to the manufacturer's claims.

The second new feature is that the stove is now approved by the manufacturer for burning unleaded auto gas. It also comes with a replacement jet for use with kerosene, which is a popular fuel in Europe. Though auto gas is less expensive and easier to find than white gas, you should think twice before using it in your Whisperlite or other backpacking stoves. Auto gas has additives that can not only clog the fuel jet, but will foul the fuel supply line over time. It is also more volatile than white gas.

For easy lighting of your Whisperlite, open the thumb valve a little while looking and listening for the fuel to fill the priming cup. Then turn the valve off immediately. Light the priming cup and let it burn out completely. Finally, light the burner area while turning the valve back on.

One other complaint about the Whisperlite is that it won't simmer. This is unjustified. While it doesn't have a simmer setting, like Peak One's Apex II, it will easily simmer. Pump the stove up fewer times to pressurize and the stove will turn down to a simmer later. For example, a full fuel bottle (always leave two inches of air at the top) needs about 20 strokes to be fully pressurized. By pumping the bottle just 10-15 times, you will have sufficient pressure to boil and will be able to turn the stove down to a simmer later. You will occasionally have to pump the bottle a few times to simmer for a long period of time (such as when baking).

The International 600 also has a larger fuel tube than the original Whisperlite. It is designed to cut back on the clogging problems experienced after long-term storage. The fuel tube can be cleaned in the field.

This multi-fuel Whisperlite boils a liter of water in about 4 minutes and is easy to set up and take down. With the changes in design, this stove reclaims the Whisperlite crown as one of the best buys on the market. The Internationale also weighs 12 ounces, but unlike the Whisperlite, can support an 11-ounce fuel bottle. It costs about $60.

The original Whisperlite is still a fine stove. It boils a liter of water in about four minutes, weighs in at 17 ounces and costs $50. Take the cleaning tip along and it is a very reliable stove.

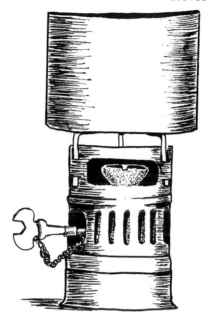

Optimus 123 Climber

The Optimus 123 Climber (formerly the Svea 123) is also a
favorite but appears to be losing its popularity. One of the first
alpine ascent stoves, the 123 is very similar in performance
to the Whisperlite, and once you've heard the Svea's distinctive roar, you will understand how the Whisperlite got its
name.

"The Svea is wonderfully reliable and has a high heat
output," commented hiker Bill Foot. "Buying the optional
special cap with pump makes lighting it very easy. We carried
the repair kit and didn't need it, nor did we ever have a clogged
jet."

Another backpacker, Peter Keenan, suggested carrying
an extra key or chaining your key to the stove. If it gets lost,
it will be tough to improvise, according to Peter, who was
forced to improvise with a pair of needle-nosed pliers. The
stove gets very hot once it has been fired, so remove the key
as soon as possible unless you want to burn your fingers later.

The 123 weighs about 18 ounces, has a 6-ounce fuel capacity and boils water in approximately seven minutes. It is sold with one small pot (5" x 4 1/2") and handle, and may become unstable if larger cooking pots are used.

Optimus Hunter 8R

This white gas stove features a built-in cleaning system, an easy-fill tank that pops out in front when its case is opened and infinite flame control from simmer to full-on burn. And, although it appears complicated with its extensive parts diagram, the Hunter is one of the more reliable stoves.

Easily set up, it is difficult to prime, and like the 123, it can get very hot—even causing blowouts from the pressure relief valve. Priming paste can be used with your Optimus to prevent carbon build-up.

The Hunter weighs 22 ounces and has a maximum fuel capacity of 4 ounces. It boils water in approximately eight minutes. The optional fuel pump, which weighs 2 ounces, is recommended and should be mandatory.

Peak 1 Multi-fuel

The Peak 1 Multi-fuel stove runs on both kerosene, white gas and even jet fuel, although you must install a vaporizer to use white gas. Conversions to kerosene-burning or white gas-burning are simple, though. The Peak 1 is a pump stove, and though popular, it weighs a bit more than other stoves—18.7 ounces with a fuel capacity of 11.8 ounces. This high-output stove is good at simmering and will boil water faster than most (five to eight minutes in summer and winter—with the latter taking a bit longer). But it can be finicky. Repairs in the field are difficult. One hiker we spoke with joked that he had to soak the Peak 1 in gas before it would ignite in cold weather.

On the other hand, Namie Bacile, who has hiked more than three thousand miles using his Peak 1 stove, says his stove has never clogged or needed to be primed once. "I've never had to borrow a stove to cook my dinner, but I have loaned mine to a few Whisperlite owners so they could cook theirs," Bacile said.

The Peak 1 Feather 400 and 442

This redesigned version of the Peak 1 offers the same power as the older model and, although its name implies that it weighs less, it actually weighs more. The Feather 400 weighs 22 ounces and has an 11.8 ounce fuel capacity.

It makes up for the added weight with speed, boiling a quart of water in just over four minutes during the winter and in about five minutes during the summer—quite unusual for any pack stove. It is also easier to light than the older model and only requires a bit of priming in really cold temperatures. Its drawbacks, other than its weight, are stability and packing. The Feather 400 can be unstable with larger pots and can roll quite a distance if tipped over on a slope. Unless packed carefully, the on/off switch can be bumped to "on" causing quite a mess. This can be avoided if the stove is packed into its stuff sack, which is a good place to put it because it won't fit in most cook sets.

Similar to the Feather 400 in design, the 442 was built specifically to burn unleaded fuel, although it will burn Coleman fuel as well. It also boils water in about four minutes and also weighs 22 ounces; but the Feather 442 is more expensive than the Feather 400.

The Peak 1 Apex I and Apex II Stove Systems

With its patented fuel-feed system, the Apex uses a pump that mixes the fuel with air so that by the time the fuel reaches the stove it's fully atomized. Therefore, there is no need for a pre-heating priming cup. Our tests show that this stove does indeed light easily without priming. The stove and fuel bottle together weigh just 19 ounces.

The 32-ounce fuel bottle, which is part of the system, is filled two-thirds full to allow room to pressurize. The Apex stoves are self-cleaning. The Apex also comes with lightweight, built-in wind guards. Perhaps the handiest feature are the two flame controls that make it easier to hold the Apex stoves at a true simmer indefinitely. The stove is very stable on its adjustable legs.

The Apex I burns white gas exclusively and costs $50. The Apex II is a multi-fuel version of the original Apex. It burns unleaded auto gas and can burn kerosene by using the replacement jet included.

Butane Stoves

Butane stoves are often less popular with backpackers because very few of them will achieve a boil in cold temperatures and fuel often must be sent ahead on extended trips. On the other hand, they are wonderful, easy-to-use stoves for short, warm-weather trips. Hikers using the butane cartridge stoves said about one-and-a-half of the full-size butane cartridges lasted them a week.

Depending on the type of trip you're planning, butane's disadvantages may outweigh its advantages. While it is true that there is no fuel to spill, no priming required and immediate maximum heat output, butane costs more than white gas and kerosene. The fuel has a lower heat output and straight butane must be kept above freezing to be used effectively. To compensate for the cold temperature problems, many manufacturers (including Camping Gaz) are now selling a mixed butane/propane fuel, which burns better at and below freezing than straight butane. Butane cartridges are not always interchangeable, with many stove manufacturer selling their own fuel. Most fuel cartridges can be purchased for less than $5.

Camping Gaz Turbo Bleuet 270 and Tristar 270
This Bleuet stove burns a mix of 20 percent propane and 80 percent butane to give good heat output, even in cold weather. Depending on how much fuel you have left in the cartridge, the Bleuet will boil water in four minutes or more. As the pressure decreases in the tank, the boiling time increases.

On extended trips, the stove's butane cartridges must be sent ahead, because very few stores sell the CV270 or CV470 cartridge this stove uses. The CV270 holds 270 grams of fuel with the CV470 holding 470 grams. The cartridges are more expensive than other forms of fuel at about $4 for the CV470.

Lighting the Bleuet is also easy—as simple as lighting the gas burner on a stove with a match. Because the fuel can't spill, no priming is required and maximum heat output is obtained immediately. The Bleuet is a dependable little (and lightweight) stove. At $30, this is one of the most inexpensive stoves available and weighs 9.5 ounces without the cartridge.

Camping Gaz also powers its Tristar 270 stove with the new cartridges. It has a detached burner and built-in windscreen. The Tristar weighs seven ounces and costs $40.

An added bonus with the Turbo and Tristar 270s is that the new CV cartridges, unlike earlier Camping Gaz cartridges, are resealable. You can take the stove off the cartridge and replace it with Camping Gaz's Bivouac 270 lantern to provide 100 watts of light after your meal. The lantern costs $30 and weighs seven ounces without the fuel cartridge.

Olicamp Scorpion II
Heavy for its size, the Scorpion II is thirty percent faster than the original. A larger windscreen traps heat and reflects it back to cut cooking time and fuel usage. This works well only in warm weather, and even then it takes about ten minutes to boil a quart of water. In freezing temperatures, the Scorpion cannot reach a full boil. Like Camping Gaz, Olicamp is

working on a mixed fuel cartridge (blended propane and butane) that will increase its versatility in cold weather.

The Scorpion uses screw-on butane cartridges, that are also hard to find on extended trips. The Scorpion II weighs 15 ounces without fuel, and like the Bleuet, it is inexpensive.

MSR Rapidfire

This butane stove is very similar in appearance to the other MSRs but runs with screw-on canisters of isobutane fuel. Simple to use, lightweight (12 ounces), easy-to-light and clean-burning, the Rapidfire boils water in approximately five to ten minutes depending on the condition of the fuel cartridge, which is self-sealing. Like most butane-burning stoves, the Rapidfire's fuel cartridges respond well to hand-warming in colder weather. Although the stove itself is stable, the tube that connects it to the cartridge often pulls the cartridge over causing minor flareups on the stove. Like the other MSRs, the repair kit and windscreen should be considered standard equipment. As with any butane stove, cartridges must be sent ahead on extended trips.

Other Stoves

The following stoves, The MSR XGK II and the Zip Ztove, do not really fit into the other two classes of pack stoves.

MSR XGK II

This updated version of the MSR XGK stove (another popular backcountry stove) is advertised to burn nine types of fuel and can probably handle more. Like Mountain Safety Research's other stoves, the XGK II can be repaired easily in the field. Given proper care and maintenance, it can last for years. The 17-ounce, high-output stove was designed for use on mountaineering expeditions and it has been compared to a blast furnace. Although it boils water in a mere five to ten minutes, a complicated on/off ritual must be used for simmering.

For general purpose hiking, it would probably be overkill. It costs nearly twice as much as the Whisperlite, and in spite of its abilities, is not as popular with backpackers as its cousin.

ZZ Corp. Zip Ztove

Zip Ztoves are inexpensive and lightweight. Zip Ztoves use small twigs, bark, pinecones, and charcoal for fuel and run a fan off a small battery that superheats the fire. This stove operates better in cold weather and at higher altitudes than do gasoline and propane stoves.

The Zip Ztove's biggest advantage is that you don't have to carry fuel for it. Long-distance hiker Phil Hall said finding fuel for his Zip Ztove was not difficult, and he did not have any problems lighting his stove in the rain.

One of the drawbacks is that heating food can take a long time although ZZ Corp. boasts a four-minute boil time not including time spent searching for fuel. Other disadvantages include the possibility of a dead battery or a burned-out motor rendering the stove useless. It also requires you to constantly feed it with fuel. Trouble with the Zip Ztove is rare, according to the company that manufactures it, and people we know who use the stove said they've had no problems in thousands of miles of hiking.

Pyromid Pack-Lite Plus

This fuel-independent stove can burn charcoal briquets, wood, sterno, or be outfitted with a propane burner. It weighs 40 ounces with its own mess kit and costs $80.

Other backpack stove manufacturers include Bibler Tents, Denali International, Inc., Epigas/Climb High, Markill/Apex, Mountainsmith and Taymar. Most backpacking stoves can be purchased for less than $100.

· Stoves ·

Stove	Fuel	Average Boil time	Weight Empty	Cost
Whisperlite Internationale 600	K/WG/U	4 minutes	14oz.	$60
Optimus SVEA 123	WG	6	16oz.	$75
Hunter	WG	5	18oz.	$90
Peak 1 Apex I	K/WG	4	19oz.	$50
Peak 1 Apex II	K/WG/U	4	19oz.	$60
Peak 1 Multi-fuel	K/WG	5	19oz.	$60
Peak 1 Feather 442	U/WG	4	22oz.	$50
Bleuet CV270	B-P	3	8oz.	$30
Scorpion III	B-P	5	10oz.	$35
Rapidfire	B	5	13oz.	$40
XGK II	Multi	4	18oz.	$85
Zip Ztove Sierra	Wood	4	15oz.	$45

WG-White Gas, K-Kerosene, U-Unleaded, B-Butane, B-P-Butane/Propane blend, Multi-XGK II uses nine types of fuel.

Operating and Maintaining Your Stove

- Practice taking your stove apart before you hike.
- Carry a repair kit from your manufacturer.
- Use a heat deflector and a wind screen to reduce fuel consumption.
- If you can't prime your stove directly, carry an eyedropper. You can extract the fuel from your fuel bottle with the dropper—much safer than pouring fuel from the bottle into the priming well. This works especially well with the Optimus stoves and produces much less flaring.
- Don't fill white gas stoves more than three-fourths full. The extra air space will help you generate pressure.

- After each trip, empty the fuel from your stove. What you can't pour out, burn. Fuel left in stoves leaves residues that will clog your fuel jets and filters.

- Burning a cap of Gumout Carburetor Cleaner along with a half tank or half-a-pint of gas will help dissolve residues. Do this once a year to keep your stove clean.

- Just as they build up in your stove, residues also build up in your fuel source (Coleman fuel can) if you don't use it up within a year. If your fuel is getting old, get rid of it. Don't put it in your stove.

- Keep your stove in a dust-free environment (such as a fabric sack) when it is not in use.

- A foam beverage insulator can be slipped onto butane cartridges to keep them warm.

Stove Safety
The following tips will help ensure safe and efficient use of your fuel:

- Never try to heat your fuel canisters with a candle flame or lighter: the results could be disastrous. Instead, try warming the cartridge in your hands or keep one in your sleeping bag at night for easier lighting in the morning.

- Unless the fuel cartridge is self-sealing, do not remove it while your stove is inside your tent. The escaping fumes can be dangerous.

- Since most stoves get very hot once lit, never set the stove directly on the floor of your tent. Instead, place it on a non-burnable pad such as a ceramic tile or a flat rock. Also, make sure your stove is firmly set before lighting to avoid a tipover.

- Never light a white gas/kerosene or other liquid-burning stove inside your tent. Flare-ups are very common and tent/sleeping bag materials are susceptible to flames as are your hair, eyebrows, beard, etc.

- If you must cook in your tent, make sure it is well ventilated or try cooking under the vestibule to avoid becoming ill (if not worse) from the fumes generated by the stove.

- To maintain pressure in gasoline stoves, do not overfill. By leaving an inch of air space in the tank, the pressure will hold longer and be more even.

- By pre-filtering any low-grade fuel you might be using, you can avoid clogs and repairs later. Most manufacturers offer filters for their stoves and Coleman sells an all-purpose, 1.5-ounce aluminum filtering funnel for only $4. This will filter fuel before it is stored in your fuel bottle.

- Most importantly, don't forget to pack out your fuel cartridges!

Windscreens
Windscreens are an indispensable addition to your stove setup. Most are offered as options like the repair kits; but both should be a part of your stove purchase.

Windscreens/heat reflectors help your stove work more efficiently. The MSR stoves come with windscreens but replacements can be purchased. The Gaz Bleuet has an optional windscreen, and Coleman sells one for its Peak 1. General purpose windscreens can be purchased as well, although the MSR windscreen can also be used for the Optimus 123 or as a booster for the Scorpion. Windscreens are an inexpensive addition to your stove setup.

>>Hiking Tip<<

Blackening the bottoms of your shiny silver cook pots will reduce your cooking time and save on fuel consumption.

Cooking Pots and Utensils

The cooking pot may seem innocent enough, but it is one of the hiker's most important tools. It is a multi-use vessel used to boil water for drinks and meals, to gather water from a nearby source, to eat out of instead of a bowl, and even to hold your stove while hiking.

Although hikers use both the one-quart and the two-quart pot, the two-quart is probably the most useful. We met many hikers who found that the one-quart pot tended to overflow during cooking. The food that boiled over the side was much harder to clean. Improperly cleaned pots can lead to an uncomfortable hike: they increase your chance of food poisoning and serve as an irresistible lure to hungry animal neighbors in the night.

Most couples we know carry nesting pots. We use one pot to cook our dinner in and the other to mix drink (or to warm the drink when it's cold outside).

Many stoves offer special cooking pots to go with their setup. MSR offers both the Alpine Cookset and the XPD Cooking System. The Alpine includes a 1.5-liter pan, a 2-liter pan, a fry pan that doubles as a lid and an aluminum pot lifter. Both the Whisperlite and Rapidfire can be stored in the cookset. The set weighs 20 ounces and is relatively expensive. The XPD includes a heat exchanger with the Alpine Cookset. The 7-ounce exchanger, constructed of aluminum and stainless steel, claims to make your cookset twenty-five percent more efficient (boiling water at least a minute faster) thereby cutting back on the price of fuel. It rolls up for storage in your Alpine Cookset and costs half as much as the cookset.

Coleman/Peak 1 offers a container/cookset. The stove nests inside the 10-ounce aluminum (square) container, which can also be used for 1-quart and 1/2-quart saucepans. It will house both the Peak 1 and the Feather 400. Also available from Coleman are the Peak 1 Short Stack Kit, the Peak 1 Outfitters Kit, the Peak 1 Solo Kit and the Peak 1 Trekkers Kit. These kits offer a variety of options in style as well as in price.

Mess kits are also available from Primus, Open Country and other manufacturers ranging in price from $11 to $55 and serving from one to six people.

An important option to consider when purchasing a cook set is a potlifter. If your set does not come with one, they can be purchased separately and cost less than $3. They are necessary to remove your very hot pot from an even hotter stove. Not only will a potlifter keep you from burning your fingers, it can also help you avoid spilled meals.

When it comes to carrying implements, hikers opinions are split. We carried spoons, bowls and the Swiss-made, Opinel-brand, disposable pocket knives. Single hikers tend to prefer a fork, spoon, and a pocket knife; and they use their cooking pot as a bowl. Couples usually carry bowls, and almost no one uses plates.

Cups are a matter of preference. We have carried the Sierra-style cup that features indentations showing measurements, but we don't really like them. Now we use the more standard, plastic thermal cups.

A three-inch lock-blade pocket knife or a Swiss Army knife will prove adequate for most hikes, though hikers usually say they aren't used often.

Extras, such as grills and coffee pots, are rarely used on longer hikes though may be worth their weight and bulkiness on short trips if you drink a lot of coffee or intend to grill the fish you catch or steaks you brought. For extended trips, most hikers stick to instant coffee and eat their steaks when in town to resupply.

On Going Stoveless

Other, not-quite-so-popular options are to eat only cold foods or to build fires. We've met only a few hikers that depend on cold meals during their backpacking trips. It is not an impossible option, although most hikers can't live without their morning coffee, and hot liquid is vital in cold, wet weather. Hikers who opt to go stoveless subsist for the most part on sandwiches--both cheese and peanut butter—along with toaster pastries, tuna,and cereal.

We have never met any hikers who depend only on fires to cook their food. While a Zip Ztove might be easy to start in the rain, we often have trouble lighting campfires in wet weather. Cooking over campfires creates other problems (including stability): hikers can lose their meals to the flames when an unbalanced pot tips over into the fire!

Campfires are wonderful for the warmth they produce, and their smoke is indispensable during mosquito season. Although fires are fine for cooking in an emergency, stoves are the best cooking option when hiking. Remember to check local U.S. Forest Service, National Park Service, or state park regulations concerning fires before you go on a hike if you decide to cook by fire.

Although we recommend using stoves to cook your food, it is still in your best interest to be able to build a fire if necessary. A time may come when you just can't get your stove to work and you desperately need a fire for warmth, drink, food, etc.

Most outdoors stores offer a number of gadgets that will help you start a fire in inclement weather. Frank and I always carry windproof and waterproof matches along with our trusty butane lighter—the simplest of solutions. Also available are fire starter kits containing waterproof matches, tinder and fire starter sheets; fire sticks that will light even when wet; fire ribbon, a fuel paste; and magnesium fire starter that uses magnesium shavings as a flame source. Another alternative is to carry a few votive candles. Once lit and set in the tinder, they last a lot longer than matches.

If you are one of those people who wish to carry everything for every situation, you could also carry a cake pan to build a fire in and a small grill for your pot in case you have to build a fire to cook. Unfortunately, if you carry everything you might possibly need, your pack will end up weighing more than you do.

If building a fire is absolutely necessary, balance your pot by using large, flat rocks for support. A trough between the rocks contains either the fire or the coals from an adjacent fire.

Another option is to cook your meal over the fire by hanging your pot from a stick suspended between two y-shaped sticks wedged in the ground. The disadvantages to this method are numerous. There are many places where you will either not be allowed to cut down limbs to form your suspension system or you will not be able to find limbs to cut at all. From experience, it is very difficult to get the two y-shaped limbs embedded in the ground. You must also keep the weight of your pot in mind. Your supper could end up all over the ground if the horizontal limb is not strong enough to bear the pot's weight. The crossbar must also be wet or green enough to keep from catching on fire.

Building a low-impact fire, one that leaves little testimony of its presence, is an important consideration in the '90s. There is nothing uglier in the wilderness than the scars left by fire rings. If you must build a fire, try to build one in an established fire ring. If there is not a ring available, try building a fire in a pan or keep the fire small and remove its

>>Hiking Tip<<
Instead of starting a fire try using a hot water bottle to keep you warm on chilly nights. Heat the water up on your stove, fill the bottle, and cuddle up against it in your sleeping bag. It's a good alternative to sparks and smoke.

traces as much as possible. Obviously, if it is an emergency, you will be more concerned with getting a fire lit than the impact it will have on the environment. So, once again, don't build a fire unless 1)it is an emergency and/or 2)there is an established hearth or fire ring.

Fire Safety
If you must build a fire, there are a number of precautions you should take:

- Never build a fire on pine needles, leaves, etc. The fire can smolder for days (even if you think you've extinguished it) before bursting into flames and torching an entire forest.
- Make sure the area you build your fire in is well-cleared so if sparks fly, wood pops or ashes take sail, there is nothing for them to light on as they fall to earth. (Clearing the ground is yet another reason for not building a fire unless absolutely necessary.)
- Always build your fire in a clearing with no over-hanging branches. The rising sparks will ignite the leaves and small branches in dry weather.
- Should you decide to build a fire, a ring of rocks or fire ring is an absolute necessity because it will contain the fire and keep it from spreading. Don't use damp or wet stones when building a fire ring. Some stones will explode when dried and heated by the fire's warmth.
- Never leave your fire unattended, even for a second. Unless you have someone to watch the fire for you as you

search for downed wood, collect all the wood you will need before you light your fire.

- If it is a windy day and the area is under a fire hazard (that is, it is dry and fire could spread easily), don't even think about lighting a fire.
- Don't use wood that causes a lot of sparks—the sparks can start forest fires not to mention put holes in your tent or sleeping bag. Soft woods like pine burn quicker but cause more sparks; use hard woods to keep the sparks to a minimum.
- Never chop down a tree for a fire—always used downed wood.
- Never build a fire against a large rock because the black scar left by the fire will last for centuries.
- Finally, make sure your fire is completely out. Stir the ashes to make sure no coals remain and then drown it with water and cover it with dirt.

If you're a smoker, don't be surprised if you find you are not allowed to smoke in certain areas while hiking. Some forests are routinely under a fire hazard during much of the year, usually summer and fall. Once, we were sent on a detour around a forest because it was on fire and the ensuing roadwalk was miserable—hot asphalt, exhaust fumes and 100-degree heat. All because someone didn't properly extinguish his cigarette!

· 5 ·
Tents

WE WATCHED THAT DAY as mackerel scales drifted into mares tails and by the time we reached the shelter just outside of Rangeley, Maine, massive storm clouds were building over the Saddlebacks.

Fortunately, there was still room in the lean-to and we quickly rolled out our sleeping bags and hung our packs from the ceiling. By dusk, the shelter was full and although there's a saying among backpackers that when it's wet there's always room for one more in a shelter, it would have been quite a squeeze to fit someone else. When Ed Carlson, who calls himself Easy Ed, walked up he surveyed the lean-to then began looking around for a campsite. Although we offered to pack him in, he maintained that he'd rather sleep in his tent, and was soon setting up his Sierra Designs Clip Flashlight a couple of hundred feet from the shelter. It poured all night long, lightning flashing, thunder booming angrily in response.

The next morning Ed appeared smiling as always.

"Did you sleep well?" someone asked.

"Great," he replied.

"You didn't get wet?" we wondered in amazement.

"Oh sure, I got wet," Ed said, "but I slept like a baby."

That's a hard attitude to maintain when you've been sleeping for days in a soggy tent but a necessary one for most trails. Almost any hiker you speak to can tell you of a time they were glad they had their tent. They could also tell you of a time they cursed it. Tents have their advantages over tarps and over sleeping under the stars though all are feasible. It all depends on how much discomfort you're willing to withstand.

Strictly speaking, a large piece of plastic and some rope is all it takes. When asked what type of tent he prefers, the backpacker will give you a range of answers. From tarps to roomy dome tents (costing from $10 up for a tarp or tent, to tents costing more than $500), hikers will tell you that their tarp or tent has proven adequate.

For most hikers, a tent will be the most practical alternative for staying dry on a rainy night. Tents keep out the rain and bugs, they are warm on cold nights because your body temperature warms the tent (sometimes by as much as ten degrees), and the tent itself dulls the force of the wind. When it's cold, wet and buggy, tents are invaluable.

Important Features of Tents

Shape
Backpacking tents are designed in a variety of shapes, each with its own benefits and drawbacks.

A-frame: This classic shape is also known as the pup tent. Roomy and easy to set-up, A-frames tend to be stable except in the wind. They are usually inexpensive but they are rarely self-supporting and many models have a support pole in the middle of the entrance.

Dome: The dome is probably the most popular backpacking tent because it was designed to solve the limitations of the A-frame. Free-standing, roomy, stable and taut in the wind, the dome also offers plenty of head and elbow room and maximum space for its weight. Consequently, its price runs a bit higher than the A-frame. Domes tend to be a bit heavier as well, and some dome tents do not fit easily into a pack.

A note from experience—dome tents are stable in the wind only if there is something inside them weighing them down. They make great kites if left empty on a windy day, especially if the door is open.

Tunnel: The tunnel tent is gaining in popularity because of the relation of floor space to the overall size (and weight) of the tent. Much lighter and more compact than other tents because of the "covered wagon," two-hoop design, tunnels are rarely free-standing and must be pitched in the right position to provide optimum stability in wind. Sleeping in an unstaked tunnel tent is similar to bedding down in a bivy sack—it keeps you out of the elements.

Ultralight or bivy: As noted above, it is the barest minimum of tent in the tunnel design. The lightest and most compact of tents, the ultralight or bivy is not for the claustrophobic.

Weight

When you are making your tent wish list, remember that you will have to carry the tent. When questioned, most hikers say that the weight of a tent is its most important feature, leading a few to purchase a tarp and sleep screen.

Carrying more tent than the trip calls for can be almost as much of a mistake as not having an adequate tent. As a rule of thumb, try not to carry more than four pounds of tent per person (three pounds is better). If two people are splitting the load, you will be able to carry a roomier tent. Having one person carry the poles and fly while the other carries the rest is one way to split it up. Another would be for one person to carry all the tent and the other person to carry the cooking gear and more food.

Weight is the major reason for carrying a tarp. For example, the Moss Parawing weighs a scant one pound, four ounces with stakes. Backpacker Doug Davis carries a two and a half pound, 10-foot by 12-foot plastic tarp. "The tarp has proved to be lightweight, spacious, and waterproof, which is everything I could ask for," he noted.

Room

The second most important thing to look for in a tent is roominess. Are you tall? Is there enough room to stretch out to your full length? What about headroom? Do you have enough room to sit up comfortably if you so desire? Decide how much room is important to you before purchasing a tent. Also, will you be cooking inside your tent? On cold mornings, it isn't unusual to see steam rising from beneath the vestibules of tents as hikers heat water for coffee and oatmeal. If you think this is a possibility (something we never planned on but ended up doing countless times), make sure the vestibule has enough space beneath it so that it won't ignite. Whenever possible, we place a flat rock beneath our stove for further insurance.

If a tent claims it holds one to two people, it means exactly. Two people will be a tight fit without gear, one person will fit with gear. Keep that in mind when considering how much you want your tent to hold.

Ventilation

Ventilation is another important tent feature. On hot, buggy nights there is nothing worse than being stifled in a poorly ventilated tent. Many tents these days offer plenty of no-see-um netting for cross ventilation as well as protection from bugs. If you are planning only cold-weather camping, this

>>Hiking Tip<<

Never shake out your shock-corded poles to snap them together. The violent action causes nicks to form at the joints that will tear your tent-pole sleeves.

feature won't be necessary. On the other hand, if you intend to hike in every season, a good fly will compensate in cold weather for the extra ventilation needed in hot weather.

Tent Materials

Most backpacking tents are made of a strong but lightweight nylon taffeta or ripstop nylon, which weighs approximately two ounces per square yard. The floor and flys are usually coated with urethane or another moisture-repellent substance to prevent moisture from passing through. Although the body of the tent is often left uncovered to increase the transfer of respiration and perspiration through the tent's walls, it is not unusual to wake up in a damp tent. We have found that moisture often gathers beneath our sleeping pads. A groundcloth under a well seam-sealed tent should ensure that the water on the floor came from you and not the rain water puddling outside.

Tent Poles

In the past few years, tent poles have evolved from unyielding aluminum to shock-corded poles. Segments of the pole are threaded over elastic (shock) cord that allows the user to merely snap the poles into shape rather than piece them together. When dismantling the tent, the segments are pulled apart and folded compactly.

There is still some controversy as to whether fiberglass is superior to aluminum when it comes to designing tent poles. Fiberglass is less expensive and more flexible than aluminum. It does not require pre-bending or any special attach-ments. It also provides a better packing size when folded. Its major drawback is that it is affected by weather and can break. Unlike aluminum, which can be splinted when it breaks (although it is more likely to bend), fiberglass breaks into clean splinters and must be replaced. Durability is one of aluminum's main advantages along with the fact that it is easily replaced.

Workmanship
Although any tent may be adequate for your needs, you may want to consider how long you would like your tent to last. Good workmanship means a long-lasting relationship with your tent. A well-made tent should have lap-felled seams around the floor seam. Lap-felled seams (like the seams on the sides of your Levis) provide extra strength because they are actually four layers of interlocking fabric joined by a double row of stitching. On uncoated nylon tents, check for taped seams. Because nylon tends to unravel, taping or hiding the end of the fabric behind the seam with another piece of fabric will stop or stall this process. Finally, make sure that all stress points are reinforced either with extra stitching or bar tacking. Tug at the material to make sure the load is equally distributed across the reinforcement. Unequal distribution can cause premature wear on your tent.

Waterproofing
Hikers agree that waterproofing is an important feature to consider. There is nothing more miserable than sleeping in a wet tent. The better the material (i.e., Gore-tex), the more likely you are to sleep dry. But there are some days that it rains so hard that no matter how good your tent, you're going to get wet. It may rain for days on end or you may not have the time to spare to dry your tent. As long as your sleeping bag

is dry, you can sleep warmly, if not entirely comfortably, in a damp tent.

To keep your tent as dry as possible, it is important to seal its seams. Although parts of the tent are coated, the needle holes in the seams will allow water to enter your tent. Buy some sealer (available at most outdoors stores) and follow the directions. Then seal them again. Depending on how much you use your tent, the sealer can last up to two years. If you use your tent a lot, seal the seams more often. On an extended backpacking trip (five months or more), it may be necessary to reseal your seams at least once, if not several times.

Set-up

You will also want to consider how easily a tent can be set up and taken down—important when it comes to pitching a tent in the rain or wind. Practice setting up your tent before you begin a long hike. The time saved by knowing your tent could mean the difference between soggy and dry clothes.

Color

While color is a matter of personal preference, there are reasons why you may choose one over the other. Bright, neon-like colors are good only in search-and-rescue conditions because the blinding material will stand out against the snow or the green and brown of the woods or the sand in the desert. For the same reason, bright colors might be annoying to other backpackers, causing a visual disturbance in the wilderness.

If your tent is pale green or blue, the bright sunlight filtered through your tent will form a soft light inside. On rainy or overcast days, the light inside your tent could be slightly depressing. These colors are also a bit more inconspicuous in the backcountry.

Orange and yellow fabric are great in foul weather because they produce a brighter light inside your tent. Grey, light grey, white, and tan are popular colors now and are also pleasing to the eye inside and outside the tent. Blue and gold are also used in many tents.

Tents to Consider

There are several styles of tents: shelters, family camping tents, backpacking tents and four season or snow campers. Because this is a book on the basics of backpacking, we will ignore the others and concentrate on tents designed specifically for backpackers. Lightweight, compact and easily assembled, backpacking tents are usually two-layered, about 20-square-feet and three pounds per person.

There are numerous tents to choose from, but here are some of your best bets.

Sierra Designs Clip Flashlight

A list of suggested tents should start with the popular Sierra Designs Clip Flashlight. This tunnel-design tent weighs in at about 3.75 pounds. Its "Swift Clip" suspension system allows for quick and easy set up and comfortably sleeps two people. The Flashlight comes with a fly and 5-square-foot attached vestibule.

Sierra Designs Meteor Light

This free-standing dome tent holds two people, offers 40-square-feet of room with nearly vertical walls, and includes a 6-square-foot vestibule. Like the Flashlights, the Meteor uses shock-cord poles that are "clipped" to the tent. The Meteor Light weighs five pounds, fourteen ounces.

Sierra Designs Half Moon 3

This rectangular dome tent is also free-standing. It offers 44-square-feet of room and comes with an 11-square-foot attached vestibule. A three-person tent, the Half Moon weighs five pounds, nine ounces.

· Tents ·

Tent	Sleeps	Sq.ft.	Seasons	Weight	Price
Diamond Free Spirit	2	35	3	6lbs.12oz.	$160
Diamond Lite House	1	30	3	4lbs.14oz.	$215
Eureka! Skylite	2	35	3	4lbs.14oz.	$185
Eureka! Gossamer	1	21	3	2lbs.14oz.	$110
Eureka! Timberlite	2	31	3	4lbs.11oz.	$175
Kelty Domolite 2	2	37	3	8lbs.6oz.	$155
Kelty Ultralight	2	34	3	4lbs.2oz.	$160
Kelty Windfoil II	2	41	4	8lbs.2oz.	$525
Moss Outland	1	25	3	5lbs.12oz.	$300
North Face Lunar Fire	2	36	3	5lbs.8oz.	$320
North Face Lunar Light	2	28	3	4lbs.4oz.	$240
North Face VE-25	3	48	4	9lbs.14oz.	$600
Quest Preying Mantis	2	34	3	5lbs.8oz.	$315
REI Half Dome	2	33	3	5lbs.5oz.	$100
SD Clip Flashlight	2	32	3	3lbs.14oz.	$170
SD Half Moon 3	3	44	3	5lbs.9oz.	$260
SD Meteor Light	2	40	3	5lbs.14oz.	$250
Walrus Swift	1	30	3	3lbs.4oz.	$150
Walrus Tri Star	3	50	3	9lbs.4oz.	$325

SD-Sierra Designs

Sierra Designs offers a number of tenting options along with the Flashlight series and Half Moon, including the Airstream, Clip 3, Comet, Clear Light, Mondo Condo, Lookout, Nightwatch, Stretch Dome, Stretch Prelude, Sphinx, Super Flash and Divine Light.

The North Face Lunar Fire/Lunar Lite
The North Face Lunar Fire and its smaller brother, the Lunar Lite, are new versions of two extremely popular backpacking tents—the Bullfrog and Tadpole (they were

known as the Star Fire and Star Lite in 1994). They are roomy and lightweight, and offer excellent ventilation. Both are two-person, free-standing, tunnel-shaped tents. The Lunar Lite weighs just over four pounds, and the Lunar Fire, which offers an extra 8-square-feet of room, weighs five and a half pounds. The Star Fire and Star Lite are now offered as extreme tents for three and a half seasons of use.

The Leafhopper, Starship, Westwind, Aerohead and VE 25 are also available from The North Face.

Eureka! Timberlite

The Eureka! Timberlite is a good A-frame tent for most uses. It is another popular tent among backpackers. This four pound, eleven ounce two-person model is relatively inexpensive and comes in a three-person size as well.

Eureka! offers a range of tents, including the Geom EX3, Sentinel, Cirrus, Gossamer, Eureka! Dome, TL Deluxe, Alpine Meadows, Aurora, Prism, Tetragon, Stony Brook, Timberlite, Rising Sun, Autumn Wind, Expedition Equinox, Equinox, Wind River, Traverse, Outfitter Timberline, Outfitter Equinox and Expedition Denali.

Kelty Domolite

This three-season tent comes in two- and four-person sizes. The walls are much steeper than in most dome tents to give you more usable space inside. There are netted panels in the roof of the tent to let in breezes or allow stargazing at night. The two-person size Domolite weighs six pounds, eleven ounces and offers 38 square feet of floor space.

Kelty also offers the GeoDome, Canyon Ridge and Quattro Mountaineer.

REI Half Dome

A classic tent for basic backpacking, the modified half-dome design sleeps two and is easy to set up. The Half Dome weighs five pounds, eight ounces and is another inexpensive back-packing tent. REI also offers the Traildome, Mountain Hut, and Geodome.

Walrus Swift and Arch Rival
This ultra-light, one- to two-person tent features the tunnel design, no-see-um netting canopies and 31-square-feet of space. It weighs only three pounds. The Arch Rival is a slightly larger version of the Swift, sleeps two, and weighs four pounds, three ounces. Other Walrus tents include Apogee, Eclipse, Moonrock, Three Star, Two Star and Rocket.

Other tent manufacturers include: Adventure 16, Bibler Tents; Black Diamond Equipment, Ltd.; Diamond Brand Canvas Products Co., Inc. (too heavy for most backpackers); Eastern Mountain Sports; Famous Trails; Gregory Mountain Sports/Noall Tents; Invicta/Uvex Sports, Inc.; Kelty Pack, Inc.; LaFuma USA; L.L. Bean, Inc.; Liberty Mountain Sports; Moss Inc.; Mountainsmith, Inc. (two tents—one sleeps four, the other eight); Outbound; Quest; Remington Outdoor Products; vauDe USA; Wild Country USA; and Wild Things (only produces a one-man bivy sack).

Ground Cloths
One time we didn't take a ground cloth because we didn't think we'd need it and found out our first night on the trail that we were wrong. A plastic ground cloth, cut to fit under the bottom of your tent, may not completely protect the tent from the damp (or wet), but it helps. Ground cloths come in handy especially when setting your tent up on ground that has been wet for days.

If the ground cloth is larger than your tent, you are likely to wake up in the middle of a rainy night sitting in the puddle that has formed beneath your tent. By cutting it to within an inch of your tent's width and length, you'll wake up much drier. Another possibility (rather than setting your tent on top of the ground cloth) is putting the ground cloth inside the tent, said Peter Keenan. The bottom of your tent gets wet, but the equipment and people inside stay drier.

Digging a trench around your tent can help keep the rain from running under it, but this is hard on the environment; we recommend that you do not follow this outdated practice. We never met a hiker who had the time or the inclination for such a job. After a day of hiking, who wants to spend the time in the rain and mud digging a trench?

Taking Care of Your Tent

Never store your tent when it is damp. Make sure it is thoroughly dry if you are going to put it up for more than a day. Otherwise, next time you pull it out of its stuff sack, you're bound to find it spotted with mold and mildew. It is important to make sure that even the seams are dry and that all the dirt has been cleaned from the stakes, poles and bottom of the tent.

When packing your tent, stuff it rather than rolling or folding it. If the fabric is stressed at the same points every time, it will eventually crack and peel. Never store your tent in your car or its trunk. Cars can become hot as a furnace, and those high temperatures can damage the coating on the tent's material.

To clean your tent, use a damp sponge and mild soap. Set it up before wiping it down and then let it air dry. If your tent is smeared with pitch or grease, use a bit of kerosene to remove it. Never machine wash your tent.

Never leave your tent set up in the sun for long periods of time. If you are camping in one spot for several days, cover your tent with its fly during the day to protect it from the sun's ultraviolet rays, which can damage the nylon material. A rainfly is less susceptible to the sun's damage and can be replaced at less expense than the tent.

>>Hiking Tip<<

Taking off your boots before entering your tent will increase the life of your tent by cutting down on the wear and tear caused by Vibram soles.

Keep your tent poles clean to avoid corrosion of the metal. A silicone lubricant applied occasionally will help protect your poles and will keep them in good working order. Apply the silicone to your tent's zippers to keep them working smoothly when it's freezing outside. Also, avoid damaging your tent by carrying your poles and pegs in a separate stuff sack.

Repair kits for your tent are very helpful and are available from most outdoors stores. There are several kits available, but the best, in my opinion, is made by Outdoor Research. This inexpensive kit contains adhesive-backed ripstop and adhesive-backed taffeta fabric to repair holes in tent and fly fabric; mosquito netting, needle and thread to repair holes in no-see-um fabric; an aluminum splint and duct tape to repair broken tent poles; and braided Dacron utility cord in case you need to jerry-rig a guyline, tent-peg loop, etc. A small tent repair kit should take care of most of the mishaps that can occur to a tent on a backpacking trip (unless you set the tent ablaze with your cooking stove or campfire).

Tarps and Sleep Screens
One of the problems with a tarp is that it doesn't keep the bugs out. When the mosquitoes or black flies start to swarm, you won't want to be sleeping under the stars or under a tarp. Some hikers who rely on tarps for shelter from the rain also pack sleep screens to keep the bugs at bay. Escaping from bugs is no joke, and most hikers agree that a tent or sleep screen is indispensable when the mosquitoes, deerflies and blackflies arrive to torture innocent hikers. When hiking out

west (because of snow, grizzly bear, etc.), you're probably better off in a tent. On the other hand, should you be hiking a beach trail in the summer, a sleep screen and tarp to protect you from bugs and rain would likely be more than adequate. If you decide on a tarp, you have a number of options. Tarps are both inexpensive and lightweight, although some can end up weighing and (in the case of the Moss Parawing) costing as much as a tent.

One option tarpers have is to purchase a polyethylene sheet (one brand is Visqueen) that is a translucent white and comes in both 9- by 12-feet and 12- by 12-feet sizes. Unfortunately, these tarps do not come with grommets for you to attach your ropes and you will need to find some sort of clamp—be it a stone wrapped in the material and secured with a rope or the popular Visklamp that uses a rubber ball and a device to secure the ball and rope.

A number of tarps are available with metal grommets, including ripstop woven polyethylene and coated nylon. While the reinforced polyethylene is cheaper, it will decay faster in the sun than the nylon. The best tarp size is the 10- by 12-feet.

Once you have chosen your tarp, you will need the following to set it up: approximately fifty feet of one-quarter inch braided nylon rope for the tarp's ridgeline; a hundred feet of one-eighth inch braided nylon rope for guylines; six to eight tent pegs to secure the tarp should there be a lack of other objects (trees, roots, rocks, bushes); and of course, cloth tape or a tent repair kit.

Setting up a tarp
There are many ways to set up a tarp, but the most common is the shed roof. This is the easiest method of rigging a tarp and requires only two trees reasonably close to each other. The high side of the tarp is suspended six to eight feet off the ground (facing away from the wind) with one corner attached

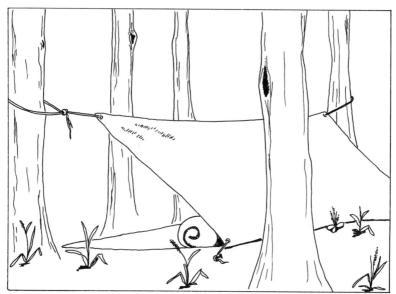

Shed Roof Tarp

by rope to each tree. The low side faces into the wind with two to four tent stakes pegged flush to the ground.

The A-frame is another common tarp set-up. The tarp is set up between two trees at least ten feet apart. Your fifty feet of rope is used as a ridgeline for the tarp and attaches to each tree six to eight feet off the ground. Make sure the ridgeline is pulled tight so that the tarp does not sag in the middle. Depending on the weather, guylines are then tied to grommets or clamps on both sides of the tarp and then nailed to the ground with tent pegs in bad weather or settled several inches off the ground in good weather for more room and ventilation.

Should the area you are hiking afford no trees or boulders large enough to rig your tarp, another possibility is rigging the A-frame with four makeshift poles—sound branches, driftwood or whatever-is-handy—at least a few feet long. One end of the ridgeline is pegged into the ground. Making a teepee shape with the first set of poles, wrap the ridgeline

A-frame tarp

A variation on the A-frame tarp

rope twice vertically and horizontally around the top of the A-frame where the poles cross. With enough space left to lay your tarp over it, lash the other end of the ridgeline rope in the same way to the second set of poles. Make sure the ridgeline is tight then lash the end of the line to a peg and then stamp it into the ground. Throw your tarp over the ridgeline and lash the edges to the ground as needed.

Sleeping Under the Stars

If you have a wonderfully comfortable sleeping bag, sleeping out under the stars is a viable option as long as you have a tent or tarp as backup. If you are hiking in the mountains, weather can change in an instant and you will need a backup plan.

Advantages to sleeping outdoors (other than not having to set up a tent or tarp) are falling asleep under the stars and waking up to a sunrise. With your head outdoors, you can fall asleep and wake up to the wonders of nature.

As long as you're in a relatively safe area, the weather is good and your sleeping bag warm, there is no reason not to sleep under what Shakespeare called "this most excellent canopy . . . this brave o'er hanging firmament, this majestical roof fretted with golden fire."

But in some areas you may be putting your life in jeopardy. For example, in grizzly country you might find yourself nose-to-nose with a bear that is not too happy with a trespasser. As long as you use a little common sense, you should be able to reap the benefits of fresh-air camping.

Pillows

Some people cannot sleep without a pillow. Whenever I hike, I use my wool sweater as a pillow. I carry it anyway so there's not the added bulk of a camping pillow. I consider camp pillows needless weight even on short backpacking trips, but for those of you who wish to carry the extra half-pound, you

❦ *Hiking Secret* ❦

If you're searching for the warmest site to pitch your tent, try a spot fifteen feet higher than a stream, lake, or meadow. The slight change in elevation can result in a difference of fifteen degrees. The south and west sides of trees and rocks soak up sunshine during the day and radiate heat at night. Finally, cold air flows down a valley at night, close to the ground and into the mouths of sleeping bags! Face yours downwind, if possible; it will be a lot warmer.

have the choice of a small (10-12 by 16-20 inch) synthetic stuffed pillow or an inflatable pillow. Relatively inexpensive, backpacking pillows are a matter of preference. But remember, your body can only carry so much weight.

Pitching Tents in the Wind, Snow and Rain
Before going on any backpacking trip, you should know your tent (and all your other equipment for that matter) backwards and forwards. Set it up in your backyard (or if that is impossible, your living room) over and over again until you can do it in your sleep. This will be invaluable once you're in the backcountry and setting up your tent in a downpour or in a raging wind.

At the end of the day when you want nothing more than to crawl into your sleeping bag and drift off to sleep, you must first set up your tent. If there is a knock-you-off-your-feet wind blowing, first go over in your head the steps for setting up your tent. If you get panicky it will take twice as long.

Before unrolling your tent, get the poles, pegs, or whatever you need to set up, ready. As you slowly unroll your tent, stake it to the ground if it is not a freestanding tent. If it is freestanding, place heavy objects on the tent to keep it from blowing away.

Once pegged or weighted to the ground, insert poles windward side first. This sounds easier than it is, but with a little determination and imagination your tent will soon be up. If it is a freestanding tent, throw your pack inside to weigh the tent down until you get in. If it is a pegged tent, make sure none of the stakes threaten to pull loose.

If you plan a backpacking trip in the snow, make sure that you have pegs that will hold in both soft and hard snow. Most outdoors stores offer special anchors and pegs for snow camping. You may want to purchase a full-time replacement for the spindly pegs that come with your tent. Some of the heavy-duty options available are T-stakes, I-beams, half-moons and corkscrews. The salesman at your outdoors store will be able to tell you which stake best suits your purpose. Making sure your tent is securely pegged is important when setting up your tent on snow. Before you can set up your tent, you must first stamp down the snow, including an area for you to walk around while pitching your tent, a broad area for the entrance and troughs for the guylines, if you need them.

To keep your tent as dry as possible, make sure that you rid yourself of as much snow as possible before climbing in. A large garbage bag outside the entrance to your tent can work as a waterproof doormat.

If you intend to camp in extreme snow conditions, you will need either a snow shovel or something that can be used as a shovel such as a snowshoe. If your tent is buried in the snow, death is a possible result. If snow keeps falling for more than a day, take down your tent and rebuild your platform by shoveling snow onto the stamped down area and re-stamping. Finally, repitch your tent.

Pitching your tent in the rain is merely a matter of speed.

It all comes down to how quickly you wish to get out of the rain. The faster you set up your tent, the quicker you can get dry. Getting the rainproof fly on as quickly as possible is very important. When taking down your tent in the rain, you may be able to do most of the work beneath the fly, keeping the tent a bit more dry.

·6·
Sleeping Bags

ARISING WELL BEFORE DAWN on his first major backpacking trip, Frank hefted his pack onto his shoulders and continued his hike in the Sangre de Cristo Mountains of northeast New Mexico. His destination was Baldy Mountain at sunrise. Lying behind a rocky windbreak, Frank shivered in his sleeping bag as he waited for the appearance of the sun. Rated only to forty degrees Fahrenheit, Frank's synthetic bag could do little to protect him from the pre-dawn chill atop the 12,000-plus-foot peak. By the time the sun rose forty-five minutes later, he was too cold to enjoy the magnificent view. Only photos taken that morning with numb fingers provide proof of what should have been a wonderful memory. Frank recalls only how cold and miserable he felt. Fortunately a year later, he was able to return with a warmer 20-degree bag and enjoy the experience.

Because about a third of your day is spent sleeping and because most people usually have an uneasy night's sleep in a strange place, choosing a sleeping bag that you'll be comfortable in is very important. It's probably wise not to go for an extreme unless you plan to buy several bags. Sleeping in a 0-degree bag (see Comfort Ratings below) on a muggy summer night in Pennsylvania can be as much torture as a 45-degree bag when you're snowed-in in the Sierras.

Important Features of Sleeping Bags

We won't even begin to recommend a bag because they (as with any piece of equipment you will purchase for backpacking) really are a matter of preference and there are so many options available. Those represented in the graph on the following page are merely an example of different combinations and possibilities.

Choosing a bag really isn't as daunting as it may seem. The first consideration is how much you wish to spend (sleeping bags can be bought for under $100 and in excess of $500 and everywhere in between); then decide on temperature rating, fill, and weight. From there, you can narrow down your options by taking into consideration bag shape and shell material. The trick is to find a balance point between comfort and practicality. Care, cleaning, and the bag's construction should also be kept in mind.

Comfort Ratings

A comfort or temperature rating is assigned to most sleeping bags by the manufacturer or retailer. The rating, basically, is the lowest temperature at which the bag remains comfortable.

Unfortunately, most comfort ratings are overly optimistic and vary widely between manufacturers. They assume you are an average hiker under normal conditions. The problem lies in trying to define who is "average", what conditions are "normal", and what is considered "comfortable". What it really means is that you are neither fat nor thin and you are not overly fatigued. It is also assumed that you are using a sleeping pad and are not sleeping out in the open. What it does not account for is whether or not you are using a bag liner or

· Sleeping Bags ·

Sleeping Bag	Temp.	Filling	Weight	Price
Caribou Approach	25°	Primaloft	3lbs.5oz.	$145
Caribou Cold Snap	-5°	Primaloft	4lbs.3oz.	$230
FF Swallow	20°	700-fill down	1lbs.15oz.	$250
FF Widgeon	-10°	700-fill down	3lbs.6oz.	$420
Kelty Soft Touch	20°	Polarguard HV	3lbs.4oz.	$150
LL Bean Goose Down	20°	550-fill down	1lbs.5oz.	$170
Marmot Pinnacle	15°	650-fill down	2lbs.15oz.	$285
Moonstone Optima	15°	Lite Loft	2lbs.13oz.	$210
NF Cat's Meow	15°	Polarguard HV	3lbs.3oz.	$160
NF Superlight	0°	550-fill down	3lbs.2oz.	$270
NF Dark Star	-40°	Polarguard HV	5lbs.12oz.	$295
Outbound Hot Tube	15°	Polarguard HV	4lbs.	$130
P-1 Tier 2	15°	Quallofil	4lbs.12oz.	$150
P-1 Tier 3	-5°	Quallofil	4lbs.14oz.	$175
REI Nod Pod	15°	Lite Loft	2lbs.9oz.	$145
REI Nomad	35°	Hollofil II	4lbs15oz.	$ 65
REI Fat Cat	0°	550-fill down	4lbs.5oz.	$240
SD Calamity Jane	20°	Lite Loft	2lbs.15oz.	$150
SD Northern Lite	0°	Lite Loft	4lbs.	$195
Slumberjack Conquest	20°	Lite Loft	2lbs.14oz.	$170
Slumberjack Discovery	15°	Microloft	2lbs.12oz.	$160
Therm-a-Nest Tapered	20°	Polarguard HV	4lbs	$120

FF-Feathered Friends, NF-North Face, P-1-Peak 1, SD-Sierra Designs

overbag, what type of sleeping pad you are using, and what you might be wearing. You'll be a lot cooler sleeping in the nude and a lot warmer wearing long johns. Keeping all that in mind, comfort ratings are helpful when compared to each other: a 10-degree bag will keep you warmer than a 20-degree bag.

Before deciding on a comfort rating, try to determine the range of temperatures in which you will most often be hiking. If you intend to do a lot of cold-weather camping, you'll probably want a bag rated between zero and twenty degrees. What if your hiking will take you through both cold and hot weather? You may want to buy a 20-degree bag and a bag liner, which can raise your bag's temperature by as much as fifteen degrees. Of course, if money is no object, you may prefer to buy several bags with ratings ranging from zero to forty-five degrees or so.

A 20-degree bag is adequate for three-season camping unless you live in Alaska. But if you get cold easily, a 20-degree bag may be a bit chilly when the temperature dips below freezing. It is better to buy a warmer bag (or at least, a bag liner or overbag) than to face a 20-mile day after a cold and sleepless night. If it's too warm to slip into your bag, you can always sleep on top of it!

On hypothermic days, a sleeping bag may save your life. Some people choose to cut down their backpack weight by carrying a blanket (and in one case we know of, a table cloth) instead of a sleeping bag. Whether hiking on the west coast, east coast or anywhere in between, it is unwise to forfeit your sleeping bag for the sake of weight. Any meteorologist will admit that weather is unpredictable, seemingly changing at whim from hot and muggy to cold and stormy within twenty-four hours. During our backpacking career, we have had both our coldest and hottest days in Pennsylvania in June. We definitely recommend that you purchase a sleeping bag, even if you only intend to make overnight trips. It could be the difference between life and death.

Fillings

There are only six fillings to consider when purchasing a bag for backpacking. They are the lightest and warmest to be found on the market currently: Quallofil, Hollofil, Polarguard HV,

Lite Loft, Microloft, Primaloft and down. One thing that will influence your decision when choosing a fill is what happens to that fill when it gets wet. Once again, your choice will be a question of preference.

Quallofil: The fibers of this polyester filling are hollow, each with four microscopic tubes that allow for good insulating ability and more surface area. Quallofil, which is as soft as down, is non-allergenic, and retains most of its loft when wet. (Loft is the thickness of the filling.) So, when Quallofil gets wet it doesn't become thin and hard or lose its warmth.

Hollofil: Also polyester, Hollofil fibers are about two inches long and must be sewn to another backing to prevent clumping; this leads to cold spots in a sleeping bag. Similar to Quallofil, Hollofil has a single hole in the fiber; but it allows for more "air" per ounce and thus provides more insulation. The added insulation is gained at a price because the backing materials used for the filling mean added weight. Like other polyester fills, Hollofil loses only about a tenth of its warmth

---

>>Hiking Tip<<

Keep yourself warm in your sleeping bag by wearing a hat, drinking plenty of fluids, and warming yourself up before climbing in. A hat retains heat lost from the head, dehydration inhibits your body's ability to warm itself, and a quick stroll or a few jumping jacks will provide your sleeping bag with some heat to retain.

---

when wet. The new Hollofil II has silicone added to make the fibers easier to compress and the bag, therefore, easier to fit into a stuff sack.

Polarguard HV: Polarguard HV is a continuous filament. The fibers, which are long and interwoven, don't become matted, which eliminates the need for a backing to prevent cold spots. Polarguard HV also retains its loft—thus its warmth, when wet. The new Polarguard HV is 20 percent warmer than the old Polarguard for the same weight.

Lite Loft: Thinsulate Lite Loft by 3M is the warmest synthetic insulation available for its weight. Its microfine polyester/olefin fibers make it lightweight, even when wet, and easily compressible.

Microloft: This is the latest from Du Pont. Microloft boasts the smallest of the micro fibers. These tiny fibers enable Microloft to trap more heat and remain soft and supple.

Primaloft: It mimics the structure of goose down with tiny fibers interspersed with stiffer fibers. Unlike down, Primaloft is water repellent and retains its warmth when wet.

Down: Down has long been lauded and is still number one when it comes to providing maximum warmth and comfort for minimum weight and bulk. Down sleeping bags breathe better than polyester fiber bags and are less stifling in warmer temperatures than their synthetic counterparts. But when a down bag gets wet, it loses almost all of its warmth and gains much more in weight than synthetic bags. Down bags also mat and clump worse than synthetic bags. Down bags are notoriously bad for hay-fever-sufferers. If you're allergic to feather pillows, you'll be allergic to down bags.

Both goose down and duck down are used as fillings with the difference discernible only under a microscope. But, goose down is generally considered structurally superior. The fill power or loft of down is measured in cubic inches and simply represents the number of cubic inches one ounce of down will expand to in a twenty-four hour period. For example, 600 cubic inches is considered to be a superior loft, 500-550 is very good, and so on. That infamous tag (Do not remove...) called the bedding or law tag will inform you of the bag's loft. By the way, the consumer is allowed to remove the law tag once the product has been purchased.

According to tests conducted by Recreational Equipment Incorporated (REI), "a synthetic bag will lose about ten percent of its warmth while gaining about sixty percent in weight" when the sleeping bag gets wet. Conversely, they said a water-soaked, down-filled bag "will lose over 90 percent of its warmth, gain 128 percent in weight and take more than a day to dry."

What this all means is that your ability to keep a down bag dry is a major factor when deciding to purchase a bag. All six fillings have strong proponents. When purchasing a bag, decide how much trouble you want to go through to keep your bag dry. Stuffing your sleeping bag into a plastic garbage bag before putting it in a stuff sack will keep it dryer. And if you will be fording a stream or are expecting hard rains, put the stuff sack into another bag for extra protection.

A few companies—Feathered Friends, Gold-Eck of Austria and Wiggy's Inc.—make their own synthetic fibers to fill their bags. These fibers are all similar in merit to the six listed above.

Down bags are clearly a favorite with hikers but they may lose ground to the new synthetics—Lite Loft and Primaloft—that are designed in the image of down without its failings.

Weight
The lighter your bag the better. Unfortunately, the lighter the bag, the more it's going to cost. Try not to buy a bag that weighs more than five pounds. A bag in the two to four pound range is probably your best bet for cost-efficiency and warmth.

Weight is related to the comfort rating and the filling. Usually, the lower the comfort rating, the more the bag weighs. Fillings other than the six mentioned above weigh a lot more than you'll be willing to carry, even on overnight trips.

Keep in mind that it is likely that the bag you buy will eventually get wet, and that will increase its weight somewhat.

Shape
Sleeping bags come in three basic shapes—mummy, rectangular and semi-rectangular. Most backpackers choose the mummy-shaped bag because it offers the most warmth and space for the least weight. Most bags offer what is called a draft tube behind the zipper to prevent air from leaking into the bag. If you intend to use your bag in windy or even cool weather be sure that the bag you choose has a draft tube.

Mummy: The name describes the shape. Formed to the contours of your body, the mummy has the least amount of air to warm and takes less material to make (and, therefore, to stuff) This saves on weight as well. The mummy's "head" is designed to draw down over and around your own on cold nights, limiting your body's heat loss. Most mummy bags also feature a "boxed" foot section which keeps the insulation in place over your feet so that they stay warmer. But like everything, the mummy has its drawbacks. There is absolutely no room to turn around in it. You either toss and turn the entire bag or sleep in one position through the night. Also, the short zippers hamper ventilation.

Rectangular: This is the roomiest and the heaviest of sleeping bags. Three sides of the bag are zippered allowing you to ventilate to the point of making the bag a blanket. Room and ventilation become the bag's drawbacks on cold nights because there is more air to heat up and no hood to prevent heat from escaping through your head.

Semi-rectangular: The taper of a mummy bag without the hood, this design saves some on weight, provides good ventilation because it, too, is zippered on three sides, and has a bit less air to heat up. Like the rectangular bag, there is no hood for cold nights.

When purchasing a sleeping bag, make sure it fits. A bag that is too narrow or too short will affect the quality of your sleep. Because a mummy bag follows the contours of your body, make sure that it is not too tight in the shoulders and around your head. If you are planning extended backpacking and/or cold weather trips, you may want to buy a bag with extra room at the feet. The extra room will accommodate water bottles, boots, socks or any other things you may want to keep from freezing.

Shells
Another important consideration when buying a bag is the shell or outer covering. Although there are numerous materials to choose from, you will want to consider only shells

made from ripstop nylon, nylon taffeta and waterproof/breathable fabrics.

Ripstop nylon: This material features heavier threads interwoven in the fabric every quarter inch or so to prevent rips from running down the bag. It also forms a web of reinforcement to reduce stress. Strong for its weight, ripstop nylon is also wind resistant. On the other hand, it does not repel water and therefore gets wet easily—although it dries quickly.

Nylon taffeta: This flat-weave fabric is softer than ripstop but isn't as strong or as resistant to wind. It, too, gets wet easily. Nylon taffeta is often used as an inner lining.

Waterproof/breathable fabrics: These are being used more and more as shells because they ventilate better than other fabrics and repel water. Brand names such as Gore-Tex and VersaTech are the more popular waterproof/water resistant products. Microfiber fabrics, which feature a super tight weave that repels water, are also gaining in popularity. No bag is truly waterproof, but these fabrics will keep fillings dry in a tent and are often wind-resistant enough to improve a bag's temperature rating by ten degrees.

The following is a list of some of the many sleeping bag manufacturers: Bibler Tents; Boulder Designs; Caribou Mountaineering, Inc.; Down to Earth/Liberty Mountain Sports; Eastern Mountain Sports; Envirogear, Ltd.; Feathered Friends; Gold-Eck of Austria; Integral Designs; Invicta/Uvex Sports, Inc.; Kelty Pack, Inc.; L.L. Bean, Inc.; LaFuma USA, Inc.; Marmot Mountain International; Montbell America; Moonstone Mountaineering, Inc.; Mountain Equipment/Climb High; MZH Inc./Cloud 9/American Trails/Expedition Trails; The North Face; Outbound; Peak One/Coleman Outdoor

Products; REI/Recreational Equipment Inc.; Remington Outdoor Products; Ridgeway by Kelty; Sierra Designs; Slumberjack; Tough Traveller; vauDe USA; Western Mountaineering; Wiggy's Inc.; Wild Things, Inc.; Jack Wolfskin.

Caring For Your Bag

Synthetic sleeping bags can be washed by hand or in a commercial washer with warm or cold water. They should be cleaned with a mild soap such as Ivory, and, if not air dried, they should be dried at a low setting in your dryer. When air drying any bag, make sure it is well supported. Never hang it by one end because the weight of the wet filling may tear out the inner construction and ruin the bag. Supporting the bag on a slanted board is a good option.

Down sleeping bags should be hand washed. If washed in a machine, your bag could lose its loft because the detergent breaks down the natural oils of the goose down. Down bags should not be dried in a household dryer; rather, they should be drip dried for several days. The bag can then be placed in a commercial dryer on low heat to fluff it. Throwing in a clean pair of tennis shoes will break up matted down.

Sleeping bags should not be stored in the tiny stuff sacks that they are normally carried in on a hike. A big, loose bag is the best container for keeping your bag in good condition when you're not on the trail. Stuffing your bag into a small sack every day while hiking is all right because you're taking your bag out almost every night. But if you store it that way at home, the filling becomes packed together and it is hard to restore its loft. Never roll your bag up neatly because this compresses the insulation. Stuffing the bag into its sack assures you of a different pattern of compression each day, which is better on the loft.

Another way to increase the life of your bag is to wash up

each night before crawling into it. The dirt and oil on your clothes and body will find its way into your bag's fill and inhibit its ability to insulate. If you can't wash up, change into clean clothes.

Mated Bags

For couples interested in hiking, some sleeping bags may be zipped together. Many sleeping bag manufacturers offer bags with right and left zippers.

If you intend to buy mateable bags, you may want to consider one lightweight (approximately 40-degree) and one heavier (about 20-degree) bag. That way, if it's warm, you can use the cooler bag on top—and vice versa.

Bag Liners

Purchasing a bag liner is a good way to warm up your bag without adding much cost or weight. There are three types of bag liners—overbags, vapor barriers, and plain inner liners. Overbags: The overbags slide on over your sleeping bag and have a filling that increases the warmth of your bag by as much as twenty degrees. They cost approximately $50 to $100 and weigh about two to three pounds—kind of bulky for extensive backpacking but not too bad for short, cold-weather trips.

Vapor barriers: These liners are inserted inside your sleeping bag and can raise its temperature by as much as fifteen degrees. Basically, with the vapor barrier, you're sticking yourself inside a plastic bag. They are constructed out of coated nylon or other materials and weigh only five to six ounces. Also, they cost much less than the overbags—approximately $20 to $30 a bag. The drawback to the vapor barrier is comfort; they are designed to make you sweat and use your own warmth to keep you warm. Vapor liners are recommended for temperatures well below freezing.

❦ *Hiking Secret* ❦

Use your sleeping bag as a cooler on hot days by inserting already cooled soft drinks or water into the middle of your bag. The liquid will stay cold for several hours.

Plain inner liners: You can also purchase simple bag liners made of flannel, cotton, breathable nylon, synthetics, and down costing anywhere from $5 to $100 and weighing three ounces to two pounds. The degree to which they warm your bag varies and should be clarified by the salesperson before you decide to purchase such a liner.

Sleeping Pads

Sleeping pads are a necessity. If you don't sleep on a pad, you lose all your heat to the ground. Although the padding is minimal, they are more comfortable than the hard earth.

The two sleeping pads favored by hikers are the Therm-a-Rest and the Ridgerest. The Therm-a-Rest is a self-inflating pad that can be purchased in three-quarters or full length. It is the overwhelming favorite among hikers, although it weighs and costs more than the Ridgerest. Most hikers find the three-quarters length pad sufficient for their comfort. The pads range in weight from just over a pound to close to 4.5 pounds. Prices range from $40 to $100. The Therm-a-Rest is an open-cell foam pad with a nylon cover and is available with a repair kit.

A "couples kit" also can be purchased for the Therm-a-Rest that allows two pads to be joined together. It is simply two nylon tarps that hold the pads so that they do not move around during the night.

The Ridgerest, although less popular among hikers we know, was awarded *Backpacker* magazine's product design award. It, too, can be purchased in three-quarters and full lengths. Both the three-quarters and the full-length pads weigh under a pound and cost less than $20. The "ridges" in the Ridgerest were designed to trap air to keep you warmer. It is a closed-cell foam pad.

Also available are three other pads: the Equalizer, a self-inflating mattress by Basic Designs, Inc.; the Insul-A-Mat, a self-inflating pad from Gymwell Corporation; and the Easy Nite comfort pad by Foam Design Consumer Products, Inc. The Equalizer is a bit heavy for most backpacking trips, weighing more than two pounds and costing more than $50. The Easy Nite weighs less than a pound and is less expensive.

Other options include the blue foam pads available at most camping stores and other foam pads. These pads weigh anywhere from eight ounces to one pound and can be purchased in the $10 to $15 range.

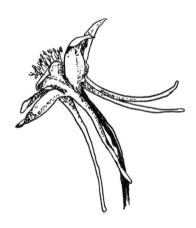

·7·
Boots

PLANNING FOR TWO MONTHS of trekking in Nepal was not easy. As a novice backpacker, I had absolutely no idea what type of boots I needed for the rough terrain. Although we weren't planning on snow or ice hiking, I wanted something heavy enough to support my sprain-prone ankles yet light enough that I didn't feel I was carrying around lead weights on my feet. I was too naive to realize that boots had to be tried on, fitted and broken in. I ordered a pair of Raichle Ecolites from a catalog and got lucky. Not a single blister suffered I, and the boots lasted me more than 2,000 miles. They carried me through two months of trekking in Nepal, and later through Georgia, north to Massachusetts on the Appalachian Trail.

The second time I pulled this stunt I wasn't so lucky. Even though the lightweight boots I purchased were reputed to be easy to break in, I still experienced some painful blisters. A bit of moleskin cleared them up in a few days, but some unlucky hikers get blisters so badly they have to go to the hospital for treatment.

Almost every hiker can tell you a boot story—from dissolving uppers and disappearing soles to swamp rot and ulcerous blisters. Boots can both protect and destroy your feet. And, since backpacking usually involves being on your feet all day, well-suited boots will be your most important gear acquisition.

Boot Weight

Your selection of boots will depend on where and when you want to hike, and how often. Lightweight boots are ideal for day hikes and backpacking on easy terrain. For example, most of the trails along the east coast can be hiked in lightweight boots. Rock scrambling and rougher terrain call for mediumweight boots, which are better suited to that kind of stress. Heavyweight boots are designed for those who intend to do intensive backpacking in mountainous terrain, including snow and ice hiking. Both the Pacific Crest and Continental Divide Trails, among others, involve this type of hiking.

While some people hike in running shoes (and I'll agree that there are some trails in this country where running shoes make a comfortable alternative to hiking boots), for all-purpose backpacking, I feel that lightweight boots, at the minimum, are a must. Because so many trails are made hazardous by rocks and roots, the ankle support that hiking boots offer is indispensable.

Lightweight Boots

Lightweight boots usually weigh less than 2.5 pounds per pair and are generally made of a combination of leather and a "breathable" fabric. Lightweights have been around for only a decade, but it would be impossible to hike any trail without running across someone wearing a pair. Beyond the fact that they don't weigh your feet down, lightweights rarely require a breaking-in period. If they do, you're probably wearing a mediumweight boot or you've purchased the wrong size or brand. This type of boot is more flexible than the mediumweight and heavyweight and it has shallower lug outsoles.

There are disadvantages to lightweights. Your feet will get wet quickly when it's raining or when you're walking through dew-soaked grass or leaves. On the other hand, they dry out more quickly than other boots. They offer less support than heavier boots, particularly in the ankles, and they don't last as long. Taking that into account, they usually cost a lot less than heavier boots.

For all their disadvantages, lightweight boots are still the best choice for day trips and light hiking. Be sure to look for a fully gussetted tongue when purchasing a pair of light-weights. This extra material sewn between the upper and tongue will help the boots shed both moisture and trail debris (dust, leaves, twigs, etc.).

Although Frank lost the soles of his lightweights, it is usually the seams that begin to fall apart. We know one hiker who burst the seams on four pairs of lightweights. That was an extreme, though. I currently own a pair of Hi-Tec Lady Nouveaus with more than nine hundred miles on them.

Mediumweight Boots

For most hiking conditions, mediumweight boots have re-placed the heavyweight boots of yesterday. Weighing be-tween 2.5 and 4 pounds, mediumweights are almost entirely, if not all, leather; although you will see some stronger fabric/leather combinations in this category. Higher uppers offer better ankle support and more protection in snow and on rocky terrain. Wider outsoles and heavy-duty midsoles, com-bined with a half-length to three-quarters-length steel shank to strengthen the sole, help to protect your feet from bruising stones. Unlike lightweights, it usually takes mediumweights longer to get wet, and conversely, longer to dry out.

Top priority for mediumweight boots is fit. You must try

them on before you buy them, or purchase them through a mail-order house with a liberal return policy.

Heavyweight Boots

Heavyweight boots usually weigh more than four pounds and cost more than $200 (as always, there are exceptions). They are designed for technically demanding hiking such as on ice with crampons or on snow and alpine rock.

Heavyweight boots are made of thicker, stiffer leather than mediumweights, and sometimes of molded plastic. They have close-trimmed soles and a half- to full-length steel shank in the sole. Some heavyweight boots offer a padded, insulated inner boot for protection against the extreme temperatures involved in mountaineering.

Boot Manufacturers

There are many manufacturers of hiking boots and prices can range from less than $50 (inexpensive) to more than $400 (expensive). The following is a list of some of the many boot manufacturers: Adidas USA, Inc.; Alico Sport; Alpina Sports USA; Asolo/Kenko International, Inc.; Coleman Footgear/ Wolverine Worldwide Inc.; Danner Shoe MFG. Co.; Dunham; Fabiano Shoe Co., Inc.; Five Ten; Georgia Boot Inc.; H.H. Brown Shoe Company; Hi-Tec Sports USA, Inc.; K-Swiss; La Sportiva USA; Limmer Boots (custom-made boots); Lowa USA; Merrell Footwear; New Balance Athletic Shoe, Inc.; Nike; One Sport/Brenco Enterprises, Inc.; Raichle Molitor USA, Inc.; Reebok International Limited; The Rockport Company; Rocky Boots; Salomon/North America; Saucony/Hyde Athletic Industries, Inc.; Tecnica USA; The Timberland Company; Trezeta/Climb High; Vasque; Vertical Footwear.

• Boots •

Boot	Type	Uppers	Weight	Price
Adidas Whistler II	L	SL	2lbs.1oz.	$ 90
Asolo AFX 520GTX	M	L/GT	2lbs.10oz.	$170
Asolo AFS Pinnacle	M	L	2lbs.12oz.	$190
Danner Mtn. Light II	M	L/GT	3lbs.10oz.	$185
Danner Sawtooth	M	L/GT	2lbs.15oz.	$160
Fabiano S.L. Trionic	M	L	3lbs.8oz.	$200
Five Tennie Extreme	L	L/N	2lbs.	$ 90
Hi-Tec McKinley	H	L	4lbs.	$200
Hi-Tec Kilmanjaro	L	SL	2lbs.3oz.	$ 80
Hi-Tec Sierra Lite	L	SL/N	1lbs.8oz.	$ 60
Peter Limmer Stock	H	L	5lbs.	$250
Merrell Leather	M	L	3lbs.8oz.	$240
Merrell Adirondack	L	SL/N	2lbs.8oz.	$ 80
New Balance MH815BG	L	L/N	1lbs.4oz.	$100
Nike Air Khyber WS	L	L/N	2lbs.12oz.	$105
One Sport Moraine	M	L	3lbs.12oz.	$190
Raichle Montagna	H	L	5lbs.5oz.	$225
Raichle Mountain Guide	M	L	3lbs.3oz.	$160
Reebok Pump Massif	M	L	3lbs.2oz.	$175
Salomon Adventure 7	M	SL/N	2lbs.10oz.	$150
Salomon Adv. 9 Mtn.	H	L/N	4lbs.8oz.	$245
Tecnica Patagonia Dry	M	L/S	3lbs.6oz.	$180
Timberland Eurohiker	L	SL/N	2lbs.5oz.	$ 75
Vasque Alpha GTX	L	L/GT	2lb.5oz.	$120
Vasque Skywalk II	M	SL/N/GT	2lbs.10oz.	$175

L-Lightweight (up to 2.5 pounds), M-Mediumweight (2.5 to 4 pounds), H-Heavyweight (boots over 4 pounds).
L-Full Grain Leather, SL-Split Leather, N-Nylon Cloth or Mesh, GT-Gore-Tex fabric liners, S-Sympatex.

Boot Construction

Uppers

There are four types of uppers—or the portion of the boot above the sole—including leather, fabric/leather, Gore-Tex and plastic. Because of its support, breathability, comfort, protectiveness and ability to be waterproofed, leather is most often used when constructing uppers. The highest quality boots feature an all-leather upper because there is less stitching for water to leak through and fewer seams to burst. Multiple-piece leather uppers are your next best option because they cost less than all-leathers and can be waterproofed.

Fabric/leather uppers reinforce canvas or nylon with pieces of leather to help the boots resist abrasion and to increase support. Only the leather pieces can be waterproofed because the fabrics will not take waterproofing treatments.

Some boots offer a Gore-Tex liner between the upper and the outer lining. Because the stitching in the upper does not penetrate the Gore-Tex, the boots provide more protection against wetness.

Uppers made of plastic are used only in heavyweight mountaineering boots. Although light, warm, strong and waterproof, plastic uppers are too rigid for most terrains. Uppers also include cuffs or scree collars that are stitched to the ankle top of most boots to provide some protection against the inevitable invasion of pebbles and twigs. Internal cuffs are better than external because they last longer.

The tongue of the boot should be gussetted for the best protection against moisture and debris. The gusset is a thin piece of leather or other material sewn between the boot upper and tongue. The best protection is found in a bellows tongue, which has a full-length gusset that covers the entire tongue opening. Overlapping tongues also provide a nearly water-tight closure. Well-padded tongues are more comfortable, offering some protection against tightly laced boots.

The protective piece of leather sewn over the back seam of most boots is called the backstay. Because it is next to impossible to replace, look for a backstay that is narrow. It will be less vulnerable to abrasion.

Toe and heel counters are also part of a well-made upper. These are stiffeners built into the toe and heel areas to provide some protection against rocks and roots.

Soles

The outsole, midsole and steel shank make up the sole of the boot. The outsole, often a Vibram brand these days, usually has either shallow or deep lugs to provide traction. Good traction is particularly important if you intend to do some rock scrambling or if you will be gaining and losing a lot of elevation while carrying a heavy pack. While shallow lugs are designed for easy to moderate terrain and are usually paired with lightweight boots, deeper lugs can be found on mediumweight and heavyweight boots and provide the traction needed for most backpacking trips.

Between the outsole and insole of the boot is the midsole. The thickness of the midsole varies with the boot but is designed to provide extra protection, extra support, and cushioning between your foot and the ground. Even lightweight boots feature a midsole, often of EVA or polyurethane, for added comfort.

Most boots have a steel (or plastic or nylon) shank that ensures that the sole of your boot flexes at the ball of your foot. Except for plastic boots, which have an inherently rigid sole, shanks range in length from a quarter- to full-length. The lightweight boots usually require only up to a half-length shank while the mediumweight to heavyweight boots need at least a half- to full-length shank for optimum rigidity.

Leather

There are several different methods used to cure the leather that makes up the hundreds of boots designed for hiking, backpacking and mountaineering. Tanning immediately comes to mind. This is curing leather by placing hides in a rotating drum containing a solution of chromium sulfate. It is called chrome tanning, and all leather undergoes this first process. Some leathers then undergo a vegetable process that involves tanning with plant derivatives. This step gives the leather extra body and solidity. Some leathers are put through a step called fatliquoring in which the leather is cured with either oils to make it softer, or waxes to make it firmer.

Hide straight off the cow is too thick for even the heaviest of boots. All leather is split into sheets of varying thickness. Full-grain leather, the outside layer of the hide, is the highest quality leather--resistant to abrasion, the most waterproof and the stiffest. All others layers are called "splits". Quality of splits varies but only the layer beneath the full-grain can be used in boots and it must be specially treated to make it resistent to water.

Most manufacturers use full-grain leather in their uppers. Because of the battering hiking boots receive, many

> **>>Hiking Tip<<**
> Spray the inside of your boots with a fungicide to prevent boot rot and bad odor.

manufacturers will turn the full-grain leather inside out before stitching it to the sole. This way, the water resistant side is facing inward and is less likely to receive nicks and scratches from rocks and roots that will allow water to seep into your boot. How can you tell which way the full-grain is facing? The outside of the boot will be smooth if the top layer is out, rough if the top layer is facing in. Boots designed for easy hiking often have the top layer facing out.

The Welt

The importance of the welt (or how the upper is fastened to the sole) never occurred to me until Frank lost the soles of his New Balance Cascades outside of Elk Park, North Carolina. Hiking sixty miles to the next town with his soles duct-taped to his uppers was pure torture, but what if a friendly hiker hadn't had the tape? A bare-footed jaunt to the next road carrying a forty pound pack was unthinkable . . . so, a plug for carrying duct tape (probably one of the better modern inventions along with WD-40—just ask MacGyver) and a strong suggestion to check out the welt on the boots you plan to hike in. It is usually accomplished with stitching and/or cement and affects both the strength and flexibility of the boot.

The Goodyear welt is accomplished with two rows of stitching. A horizontal stitch joins the upper to both the insole and a strip of leather. This strip of leather is then vertically stitched to the soles. This welt is very flexible and is often used in lightweight hiking boots. Both the outer and midsole can be replaced on boots using this welt.

The Norwegian welt also uses two rows of stitching—a

horizontal stitch to join the upper and lining to the insole and a vertical stitch to attach the upper to the midsole. While not as flexible as the Goodyear welt, the Norwegian welt is much stronger and is often used in mediumweight and heavyweight boots. Outer and midsoles can also be replaced on this boot.

Another type of welt is called the "inside fastened", the "Littleway" or the "McKay". This welt is achieved by rolling the upper between the insole and midsole and then stitching all three together from the inside. This is both a flexible and durable welt method and is often used on lightweight hiking boots. Like the other methods, both the outer and midsoles can be replaced.

Because they are not intended for heavy use, lightweight boots often have cement-welted soles. A narrow outsole is required, which can be a drawback. Advances in technology have produced strong adhesives, but boots with soles that are attached with an epoxy take a bit of extra care (i.e., common sense).

Don't dry them out too close to a heat source because the epoxy could melt and a few miles down the trail, the sole could separate from the upper.

Fit
Select your boot carefully. Backpacking is an activity that often involves spending the entire day on your feet as well as putting an extraordinary amount of weight on them. The strongest welt, toughest leather and super-traction soles will mean little if every step is agonizing because of improper fit. You may be proud of your small, shapely feet, but buying a boot because it enhances your appearance is foolish and may amount to a face lined with anguish by day's end.

Boot sizing is notorious for its inconsistency. You might normally wear a size 6 in tennis shoes but a 5 or a 7 in a boot. Make sure that the boots are not only long enough for you but

❦ *Hiking Secret* ❦

Try this technique for selecting the proper boot size. With the boot unlaced, slide your foot to the front of the boot. If you can just slide two fingers in between your heel and the boot the fit should be right. It will allow the little extra room you need without giving too much play.

wide enough as well. A number of boots come in several widths: find the one that's right for you.

The most important thing when purchasing a boot is whether or not it is comfortable. When trying on the boot, wear hiking socks. A boot might feel comfy over a thin cotton crew, but slip it on over a thick polypropylene and suddenly your foot feels like a sardine. Also, if you intend to wear insoles, which give you extra cushioning and arch support, bring them along when you are trying on boots because insoles also affect the way a boot fits.

How do you know if the fit is big enough but not too big? Is there a thumb's width between your toes and the tip of your boot? Can you wiggle your toes for good circulation? Take all the time you need to get a good fit.

While my first pair of boots didn't give me blisters, they were too short. On the downhill, my feet slid forward into the toe of the boot, resulting in painfully numb toes that throbbed all night long. Not even aspirin could dim that pain. Long distance hikers often lose toenails. A boot that is long enough will help alleviate that problem. On the other hand, make sure your heel doesn't slip. This could lead to blisters. The heel should be snug but it shouldn't pinch you.

Lace your boots up securely. Is there any part of the boot that is uncomfortable? Pressure should be even all over your foot, which contains more than 26 functional bones. Tell the salesperson what you feel. Is there unusual pressure at the instep? Let him or her know. They'll probably suggest a boot that will suit you better.

Finally, don't be surprised if you can't find a perfect fit. With more than 132 potential foot shapes, no manufacturer can fit everyone. Once you've found the next best thing to perfect, the boot can probably be altered with orthotics and broken in to fit.

Waterproofing

If your boots have any leather in their construction, they need waterproofing. Sno-Seal, and the newer Aquaseal, are two popular brands of sealant although there are a number of others. Devoutly follow directions for the waterproofer you purchase. It really does help to have dry feet!

Unfortunately, sealing your boots is not a one-time deal. It must be done periodically; and the more you use your boots, the more often you must seal them. For hikes of more than a week or two, you may want to carry sealant along with you. Or send some ahead if you plan to have mail drops.

Taking care of your boots will ensure a longer lifespan (for your boots, that is). After every backpacking trip, brush off dirt and debris before storing. If your boots are wet, try stuffing them with newspaper to soak up the inside moisture and let them dry in a cool, dry place. Don't try to dry them quickly by setting them near a heater, oven or open flame. It could mean the death of your boots. Once they are dry, reseal them with waterproofer. Seams and welts and the leather used in lightweight boots require a special sealant. All boot sealants can be purchased in outdoors stores.

Breaking in Your Boots

The single most important advice when it comes to boots is "break them in." Any experienced hiker will tell you (and it certainly cannot be stressed enough) that boots must be broken in if you intend to hike more than a mile or two in them.

Once you find a pair of boots that fit comfortably and you have sealed them properly, it's time to break them in. Start by walking around your neighborhood. Wear them to the store and on short errands. If you start to get a blister, put moleskin on it immediately—don't wait. If you catch a hot spot before it becomes a blister, you'll save yourself a lot of pain.

The next step is a day hike. Wear your boots for an entire day without a pack on your back. If this goes well, you're ready for the final step—backpacking. If not, continue to day-hike until the boots are comfortable. If you intend to use these boots only for day-hiking, you will want to try hiking with a day pack to see if they are still comfortable with weight on your back. If they are, your boots need no further breaking in.

Backpacking requires more breaking in. No matter how comfortable your boots are without a pack, that all could change once you add thirty or more pounds to your back. A lot of weight on your back changes the way weight is distributed over your feet and it could change the way your feet feel in your boots. One of the strangest feelings in backpacking is taking your pack off after a long day. Suddenly, it feels as if you're walking on air.

If you can backpack five to ten miles in your boots without creating any sore spots, your boots are ready for extensive backpacking.

Inserts

Some hikers find that they can make their boots more comfortable, and more supportive, by adding special insoles. Also, the insoles and arch supports that come with your boots begin to wear down after a while. Adding insoles that provide additional arch support can extend the life (and comfort) of your boots. They can also provide extra warmth and insulation. Insoles for boots can be purchased at most outfitters or department, discount, and drug stores.

Extra Shoes

Should you carry an extra pair of shoes with you when you hike? Well, that all depends on the distance you're hiking. For day trips, you probably don't need an extra pair of shoes, especially if you're wearing lightweight boots. Weekenders must decide if they want to carry the extra weight on such a short trip. It really is a matter of preference. Some people can't stand to be in boots once they've made camp.

If you are going to be out for more than a few days, you need to seriously consider additional footwear. We've seen all kinds carried—tennis shoes, espadrilles, flip flops, Nike Aqua Socks, sandals.

There are a number of reasons to carry additional footwear. Picture this typical scenario: You've been hiking all day in the rain; your boots are soaked, your socks are soaked. You arrive at your campsite, make camp, and prepare to bed down. Keep in mind that this entire time you've been sloshing around in wet boots. Because you're no longer hiking, your feet are getting cold. Then, when you're all cuddled up in your nice, warm sleeping bag . . . nature calls. Do you really want to put those freezing cold, damp boots on your feet just to make a quick run into the woods?

Another example. It's a wonderful, warm and sunny day and you have to ford a stream. There are very few times when you have the option to remove your boots and cross barefooted because of sharp and slick rocks. On the other hand, you don't really want to get your boots wet either. A second pair of shoes is a great alternative in this case.

Also, hiking boots are tough on campsites. Another pair of shoes (soft-soled) is an ecologically sound alternative. If you're hiking long distance, it is not unusual to wear a spare pair of shoes into town to purchase food, wash clothes, etc. And because many trails are not entirely routed in the woods, you may want to wear another pair of shoes on road walks. Asphalt wears down the tread on hiking boots.

These are all good reasons to bring along a second pair of shoes. But choose wisely: the last thing you need is an extra burden.

Laces and Lacing

While leather laces used to be popular, their tendency to stretch when wet has been their demise. Nylon has replaced them as the standard lace for hiking boots. The durable, soft-woven, unwaxed nylon laces also hold knots best.

Hiking boots usually feature three different methods of closure—grommets, D-rings and hooks. Lacing using only grommets is probably the sturdiest; grommets usually last well past the lifetime of the boot. The only problem with an all-grommet boot is that it can be difficult to lace, particularly when your hands are blocks of ice. Many boots have grommets in the lower half of the boot and hooks at the top.

My boots have D-rings on the lower half and hooks above. They are very easy to lace, even with numb fingers (it's the knot I have trouble with when I can't even feel the laces).

There are a few tips to keep in mind when lacing your boots. If the upper knot of your boot rubs against your shin, lace your boots to the top then back down a few notches and tie the knot midway down your boot to prevent a painful bruise. Another advantage of this method is that it keeps the knot from loosening under the pressure of your constantly bending ankle.

If your toes are feeling cramped, try loosening up the lower laces a bit, tie a knot, and continue lacing the boot tightly. Although this won't work on the downhill because the

---

❦ *Hiking Secret* ❦

If you are having trouble keeping your feet warm when the temperature drops below freezing, try a vapor barrier. A plastic bag, such as the resealable ones used for packing food, can trap moisture and thus prevent heat from escaping. Place your socked foot into the plastic bag and then slide the bag-wrapped foot into your boot. While not fashionable, it is cozy.

---

loose laces will cause your toes to slide painfully into the front of your boot. In this case, you might want to try the opposite approach.

Socks

It used to be that you needed to wear several pairs of socks with your hiking boots just to be comfortable. Fortunately, the way boots are made these days, all you really need is a pair of liner socks and a pair of hiking socks.

Liners are important. They wick away the perspiration and help keep your feet dry. Liners are made of silk, nylon, polypropylene, Thermax, or orlon. Keep your liners clean. At least rinse them out often so that they don't "clog up." Socks can be hung out to dry on the back of your pack. (You can use clothespins or safety pins to fasten drying clothes to the back of your pack.)

Choose your outer pair of socks wisely. Most experts suggest a blend of wool and nylon or wool and polypropylene. Cotton is never suggested because, unlike wool, it will not keep you warm when it's wet.

Some socks are made with added padding at the toe and heel as well as extra arch support. These socks are usually a nylon-orlon-polypropylene blend; liners are not necessary with them. Try several brands and find out what's right for you. I discovered that mostly wool socks retained too much foot odor for my taste. Frank had absolutely no complaints with his wool-polypropylene blend.

Footcare

Hardening your feet before setting out on a hiking trip is not an easily accomplished task. There is nothing like carrying a thirty to sixty pound pack to quickly break your feet in. But there are some things you can do to make the transition a little easier. Besides wearing your boots as often as possible before you set out on a backpacking trek, rubbing your feet each day with rubbing alcohol or tincture of benzoin for a week prior to your trip will help toughen them up.

While backpacking, continue to use the alcohol or benzoin each day on your feet. Airing your feet out during breaks will also help keep them tough as will sprinkling your socks with foot powder prior to putting them on. And most importantly, don't forget that as soon as you feel a hot spot on your foot cover it with moleskin!

· 8 ·
Clothing

WHILE BACKPACKING in the mountains of North Carolina and Tennessee, the last thing we expected in April was a snow storm. Fortunately, we were prepared. No matter what the expected weather, I always carry a wool sweater and long johns in my backpack. They've paid off countless times. We were nice and comfy in our wool and silk, and snuggled down in our sleeping bags, but a youth group who shared the old barn with us was almost hypothermic.

A heavy rain originally drove us into the rickety old barn. When the rain didn't let up by late afternoon, we decided to stay for the night. It wasn't long before the youth group began straggling in. Clad in jeans and t-shirts, the boys were already shivering when they entered the barn. Their leaders were wise enough to get them out of their wet clothes and into their sleeping bags. As dusk darkened the interior of the barn, the leaders finished hanging the last of the jeans and t-shirts. Soon everyone settled down, rocked to sleep by the barn that swayed back and forth in the gusting wind. As we slept, the snow storm blew in. We awoke to find ourselves dusted with snow, the barn decorated with frozen clothes. The perils of cotton!

For many situations, cotton is the perfect fabric—backpacking isn't one of them. Unlike wool, cotton does not retain heat when wet. Unlike synthetics, it takes forever to dry. Faced with jeans and t-shirts not even a snowman could wear, the youth group tried in vain to start a fire to thaw the clothes. Finally, tents went up in the frozen barn and clothes were pulled into the warmth. The group eventually donned their damp, but no longer frozen, clothes for the chilling five-mile hike through a foot of snow to the nearest road. Better equipped and wearing everything from long johns to rain gear, we continued our hike northward. The ability to layer clothes when backpacking can be a lifesaver.

The type of clothing you wear will virtually determine the comfort of your hike. Although the exertion of hiking warms your body, I've found myself hiking in long johns and a wool sweater on a barrier island off the coast of Florida in May. Clothing is undoubtedly a matter of personal preference, but there are some tips that could save you a lot of frustration. The most important tip is the famous Boy Scout creed—"be prepared".

You do not have to carry a backpack full of clothes to be prepared for all types of weather. Shorts, t-shirt, long johns, wool sweater and rain gear can all be layered to add warmth.

Hiking through the low desert on the Pacific Crest Trail in southern California is akin to a walk in hell. It is hard to stay cool even in shorts and a t-shirt. But when the sun drops below the horizon, it doesn't take long for things to cool off and you'll actually relish the warmth of your sleeping bag! You'll find yourself adding pants or long johns. There are even times when a wool sweater would be in order.

Europeans often express shock at the American penchant for clothes. The late French film director Francois Truffaut once remarked that he could not believe Mrs. Dean wore a different outfit every day of the Watergate trial. How could anyone feel sympathy, he said, for a man whose wife could afford so much clothing. We are notorious for our over abundance of luggage when traveling, and for buying inexpensive, poor quality clothing in order to fluff our wardrobe. When it comes to backpacking, at least, we should follow the European example. Buying a few, high quality garments will see you through many backpacking trips. Style doesn't matter on the trail, comfort and quality do. Fortunately, there are many reputable manufacturers of backpacking clothing and you can purchase quality along with style. One good pair of Patagonia Stand Up shorts will last as long as, if not longer, than five cheap pairs of shorts.

Layering
Take the time to select your clothes carefully and think about layering. Buy an ensemble that can be adjusted to fit the circumstances. Consider your clothing options if you awake to a warm but rainy morning—long johns or shorts, shirt, sweater or fleece jacket, rain gear. You may want to start out with the shorts, t-shirt, and rain gear; but as it continues to warm up despite the rain, you may drop the rain gear and opt for just getting wet. Come evening, you pull into camp and, no longer moving, you get a chill. Pull on your wool sweater and/ or your rain gear. On the other hand, if the morning had been rainy and cold, you could have layered your long johns under your shorts, rain gear and hat. Depending on the time of year, you may be comfortable in a pair of loose pants or tights instead of shorts.

Layering allows you numerous options and the clothes involved in layering are lighter, more durable, and allow you greater physical flexibility. The layering system works better than other methods (such as a separate outfit for each weather condition), especially when you get wet or sweat. It is important to layer with the right pieces—long johns, pants or shorts, a wool or pile garment and a waterproof shell. Layering cotton long johns under blue jeans may keep you warm at first, but as soon as the garments are wet with rain or sweat, you'll be miserable.

When you are layered correctly, you can open up easily in response to the warmth. If you are sweating, take off your hat first. Because you lose most of your heat through your head, removing your hat or hood will act as a kind of air conditioning. If you're still hot, unzip your rain jacket collar, and loosen the sleeves (buy rain gear that allows the sleeves to be cinched tight) to let the air circulate.

Remove and add layers as you get warm or cold. It may seem tiresome and time-consuming at the time, but you'll be much more comfortable for the bother.

Fabrics
Choosing the fabric of your clothes is as important a decision as choosing what clothes you will bring. But glancing through the pages of an outdoors catalog is a mind-boggling experience! Synthetics with names such as Supplex nylon, Polartek polyester, Thinsulate and PolarGuard polyesters, Taslan nylon, Lycra spandex, Cordura nylon, Tactel nylon, Orlon acrylic, Hydrofil nylon, Capilene polyester and Ultrex nylon make you feel like you need a degree in chemistry to purchase your clothes. Fortunately, it is not as overwhelming as it seems.

Cotton
Beginning with the basics, cotton is inefficient in the outdoors. It doesn't keep you warm when it's wet and it takes a long time to dry. For these reasons, clothes that might serve you well at home will not do as well on a backpacking trip.

The best example is blue jeans. Not only are they constricting, but when they get wet they double or triple in weight. They also take forever to dry. Other cotton clothing to avoid includes long johns, socks, sweaters, and 100 percent cotton t-shirts.

An alternative to 100 percent cotton clothing is cotton blends. For instance, Patagonia Baggies (shorts) are made of a nylon-cotton blend and are favored by many hikers because they are lightweight, roomy, and water-resistant. Many manufacturers make pants and shorts of nylon-cotton blends. T-shirts made of cotton and a synthetic are the most popular hiking shirts because they allow freedom of movement and dry more quickly than all-cotton t-shirts. For day hikes in pleasant weather and moderate altitudes, a cotton t-shirt is a good choice.

Wool

Wool is your best bet for winter wear, and when it is blended with polypropylene or other synthetics, it makes good socks. Wool keeps you warm when it's wet. A wool sweater can be a lifesaver on cold and/or wet days. Temperatures at high altitudes can drop below freezing even in the summer. I have never been on a backpacking trip that I haven't worn my sweater, even during the middle of summer. If you have the pack room on an overnight summer hike, a sweater may be worth the peace of mind. New synthetics—the "Polars" and Synchilla—are giving wool a run for the money.

Silk

Silk is one of the lightest fabrics and is often used in long underwear. Although silk is a strong, flexible fabric, it tends to be less sturdy than synthetics, giving way at the seams more quickly. It does give you warmth without the bulk, and provides an effective first layer. Silk must be hand-washed and line-dried.

Polypropylene

This petroleum-based synthetic is a lightweight fabric that keeps you warm when it's wet. Unlike wool, it drys out quickly. This is because it is non-absorbent. It will not retain moisture, wicking it away immediately. When used as your first layer of clothing, it keeps your skin dry by transferring moisture to your next layer. Polypropylene is primarily used in long johns and socks. One drawback to polypropylene is that it absorbs the scent of perspiration and must be washed in a special detergent to remove the odor. It is also renowned for its pilling, which can be annoying, especially to the fashion conscious. Polypropylene must be line-dried to prevent shrinkage.

Thermax and Capilene

Thermax is another synthetic used in garments designed to keep you warm. Like polypropylene, it draws moisture away from your body, and its hollow-core fibers trap air to provide insulation. Thermax can be machine-washed and tumbled dry, and it does not retain the odors of perspiration.

Capilene is a polyester fiber and is similar to Thermax in its attributes—it is odor resistant and can be machine-washed and dried. Both Capilene and Thermax are said to be softer than polypropylene and provide a lot of warmth for their weight.

Nylon

Because it's one of the easiest synthetics to manufacture, you will find many nylons on the market. Nylon is inexpensive, durable, abrasion-resistant, strong, and drys quickly. There are hundreds of types of nylon, from the rough-textured Taslan and the super-tough Cordura to the supple, softer nylons such as Supplex, Taslan and ripstop.

The best purchase we've made is our nylon jogging shorts.

Not only do they have a built-in liner (making underwear unnecessary), but they dry very quickly. The slick material also helps to keep our hip belts from rubbing us raw—a very common backpacking problem. I traded my cotton blend, boxer-style shorts for the slippery nylon expressly to heal a hipbelt wound, which had begun to bleed. The new shorts cleared up the problem instantly.

Polarplus, Polarlite, Patagonia Synchilla

These bunting or pile materials are good insulators. Comfortable jackets and pants in Polarplus, a double-faced pile of fine-denier Dacron polyester (denier is a unit of measure for textile fibers); Polarlite, a lighter and stretchier version of Polarplus; and Synchilla, Patagonia's well-known, double-faced synthetic pile, are bulky and heavy, but may be worth the extra bulk and weight on a cold night. For day hikes to higher altitudes, the insulation these materials provide offers good protection from wind and cold when taking a break. The materials are generally far too warm to actually hike in, but are said to be warmer per pound than wool and to dry more quickly than the natural fabric.

Although Polarlite is supposed to be lighter than Polarplus and Synchilla, it appears to weigh approximately the same, if not more, when used to fabricate similar garments. As with food, you may want to inspect a little more closely anything termed "lite."

Others

Lycra spandex is a very stretchy, strong synthetic used extensively in clothing—from cuffs and waistbands on jackets to bras, socks, running tights and shorts. Tights made of a blend of polypropylene and lycra are especially popular because they keep you warm and conform to your figure allowing you a lot of freedom of movement.

Fibers polymerized from acrylonitrile are called acrylics and are rarely used in their "pure" form in clothing except maybe in underwear. Acrylics such as Orlon are often found as a blend, especially in socks.

Rain Gear

"I used a rain jacket, rain pants, poncho, pack cover, and gaiters, and I still got soaked," lamented hiker Peter Keenan. Sometimes you're just going to get wet. It is easier to stay dry in the rain if you are standing still. Once you start hiking, you increase your chances of getting wet.

In warm weather, hikers often refuse to fight the battle, opting to get wet by hiking in the rain in just shorts and t-shirt. That's all well and good when it's steamy outside, but what about when its cold or even just a bit chilly?

Wet clothes can lower your body temperature to the danger point. Your greatest risk of hypothermia comes when you least expect it. It doesn't have to be freezing or even near it for you to become hypothermic. Hikers die of hypothermia every year when they ignore their wet clothes on cool days. Rain gear is probably one of the most essential items on your clothing checklist.

Ponchos
The least effective of all rain gear options, most backpacking ponchos are designed to cover both you and your pack. Ponchos do shield you from a lot of the rain under ideal conditions, but in the wind they are practically useless.

While a minority of hikers find ponchos meet their needs, most hikers who have tried ponchos dispose of them during their hike. Ponchos cost from $3 (for a vinyl poncho) to $30 (for a coated nylon backpacker's poncho).

Rain Suits
Rain suits (a jacket and pants) although usually designed in sets, can be purchased as separates. They afford the best protection against the cold and rain. In purchasing a rain suit, a major consideration is whether to get one in Gore-Tex or coated nylon.

Gore-Tex: This fabric, developed by W.L. Gore, has been adopted by a number of manufacturers of rainwear as well as many other clothing manufacturers. Gore-Tex is a hotly debated subject: hikers either swear by it or swear at it; it is everything it claims to be or too expensive for the little it does.

Clothing made with Gore-Tex promises to be both water repellant and breathable. The key to this is an extremely thin and very lightweight membrane patented by the W.L. Gore Company. Made up of two different substances, the Gore-Tex membrane keeps out the water while allowing moisture vapor to escape. The component that repels water is pure expanded polytetrafluoroethylene (ePTFE), which is similar to Teflon polymers and contains nine billion microscopic pores per square inch. Because the pores are smaller than a droplet of water but much larger than a molecule of water vapor, water (in its liquid form) cannot penetrate the membrane. On the other hand, vapor released from your body can escape through the membrane to the outside.

The second part of the membrane consists of an oleophobic or oil repellant substance that allows water vapor to pass through but keeps oil-based contaminants from penetrating the membrane. Oils, cosmetics, insect repellents and food substances would otherwise affect the breathability of the article of clothing. The oleophobic substance is also impenetrable to wind. This is said to make Gore-Tex both warm and water repellent, yet, according to the company, it keeps you comfortable by allowing water vapor to escape.

The Gore-Tex membrane is found between the outer layer and inner lining of the garment. Depending on the piece of outerwear you purchase, the membrane will either be laminated or bonded to the outer fabric or hang freely between the two layers.

The argument over whether or not Gore-Tex works centers around whether it is truly breathable and waterproof. Both Frank and I have hiked extensively in our Gore-Tex rain jackets. We have been cold and hot and dry and wet. Although the fabric seems to be sufficiently waterproof against light rain or brief showers, you still get wet in downpours and when backpacking all day in a steady rain. Excessive sweating and rain trickling into the jacket as it runs off your face and throat also cause the garment to get wet. The wetness caused by sweating should be eliminated by the fabric's "breathability." But in our experience, the fabric seems incapable of keeping up with the water vapor escaping the body while backpacking. Regardless, Gore-Tex is still the best fabric when it comes to rain gear—it keeps you as dry as nylon and it affords some breathability.

Gore-Tex rain suits can be purchased from $200 to $500 price; most cost approximately $300. You can also purchase suits in a variety of weights—some with extra rain protection, some with liners for added warmth. Among the designers of Gore-Tex rain wear are Columbia, L.L. Bean, Marmot, Montbell, Moonstone, Nike, The North Face, REI, Sierra Designs, Solstice and VauDe.

Nylon: As with Gore-Tex, coated nylon rain suits can be found in a variety of styles. Because coated nylon makes no effort to be breathable, it doesn't keep you as cool as Gore-Tex but it is also less expensive.

Coated nylon rain suits must have the seams sealed to be effective. Seam sealer can be purchased through outfitters and mail order houses. Following the directions carefully and resealing the seams occasionally will ensure proper water-proofing. Nylon rain suits range from about $50 to $150.

Hats
Hats are an indispensable part of your backpacking outfit. If your feet are cold, putting on a hat will warm them up because much of the body's heat is lost through your head. Warming your head will do more toward warming your feet than adding an extra pair of socks. Another pair of socks might actually make your feet colder by making your boots too tight and constricting the circulation in your feet.

A wool cap with a polypropylene liner will keep your head warm while wicking away perspiration. Thermax hats are also good for the same reason. If you will be doing a lot of cold weather backpacking, you may want to invest in a balaclava. This hat covers your head and neck and most of your face and is much lighter to carry than an extra shirt or sweater!

While not as warm, baseball-style caps are great for keeping the sun off your head and face. They are also great worn under your rain jacket hood to keep the hood from dripping rain on your nose and to help the hood move with your head. All types of baseball caps are available, including those that offer a neck flap for extra protection against the sun.

For those of you who go for the high–tech products, Sequel offers the Desert Rhat Hat. An adjustable chin strap keeps the hat on your head even in high winds, a large bill with a black underbrim provides sun protection for your eyes and face, a breathable lining of Tex-O-Lite metallic film shields the top of your head from the sun's intensity, a removable white cape reflects the sun, and a terrycloth headband absorbs the sweat—all for under $30.

Socks

There was a time when there was only one type of sock to wear with your hiking boots—it was wool or nothing. Now there are so many options, it's hard to decide. While wool socks are still very present in the sock market, they are giving way to synthetic blends designed especially for backpacking.

Wool, cotton/wool blends and cotton socks are not as good for backpacking compared to the wool/polypropylene or nylon blends and the Orlon acrylic/nylon blend of Thor-Lo socks. Wool socks retain foot odor while cotton socks do not retain their shape. The Thor-Los were designed specifically for sports and include designs for running, hiking, climbing and backpacking. The hiking socks average about $7 a pair.

Gloves

My hands get cold easily but I find that when hiking I rarely need gloves. Cold, wet days are the worst, especially once you make camp. I've used glove liners without the gloves fairly successfully—they are easier to manuever your fingers in because they don't have the bulk of leather gloves. But for those days when sticking your hands in your pockets just

>>Hiking Tip<<
You can dry socks and other garments while you hike by
clipping them with alligator clips to the back of your pack.

won't do (what if you take a tumble with your hands in your
pockets?), there are a number of glove/mitten options available. From Gore-Tex shell and wool mittens to gloves of wool,
wool-blends, Thinsulate, pile and other synthetics, you should
be able to find a pair of hand warmers that fits your needs.

Keep in mind that you can also purchase glove and mitten
liners (usually very lightweight and made of silk or synthetics
used in the manufacture of thermal underwear) for extra cold
days. If you're desperate, use plastic bags as vapor barrier-
style gloves.

Bandanas

In the backpacking world, you're not a true hiker unless you
have at least one bandana on your person. Bandanas are
wonderfully versatile. I use them as headbands, hats and
handkerchiefs. They can also be used to strain water before
filtering and to cool hot necks (dipping the bandana in water
and loosely tying about your throat). Similarly, they can be
used as a cloth for washing or as a towel for drying (your body
and your dishes). I always carry several with me when I am
backpacking.

Gaiters

Hiking gaiters are made of water-resistant materials. They
fasten below the knee and extend to cover the upper portion
of your boots. Their purpose is to keep water and snow out of
your boots so that they remain dry.

Gaiters come in a variety of heights, from ankle-height to
just below the knee. Some hikers wear the ankle gaiters to

keep dust and leaves from working their way into their boots. Gaiters are also useful when hiking through wet brush, grass, and leaves and poison ivy.

Unlike pack covers and rain suits, gaiters are not essential rainwear for any hike. However, they may make your hikes more comfortable and are worth looking into, particularly for hikes in the snow.

Town Clothes

If you intend to spend more than a week on the trail, and especially if you're going to be long-distance hiking, you may want to consider bringing along "town clothes." All this means is that you stash away one t-shirt that you will wear only when hitching or hiking into a town. Your appearance and your attitude will determine how you are treated when you go to town. Some female hikers carry "scrunchable" gauze skirts. They can pack down small, they're light, and they're supposed to look wrinkled anyway.

Taking Care of Clothing

While backpacking, care of your clothing will be limited to a bit of rinsing here and there. On short trips (unless your clothes get really awful), you can wait until you get home to clean your clothing according to the tags' instructions.

While hiking, I rinse out my nylon shorts every other day (or every day, if I have really sweated). I simply rinse them in a cookpot and hang them to dry on a branch or rock if it's a dry night. If it's wet outside, I take them to bed with me, stuffing them at the bottom of my sleeping bag. If they are not dry by morning, I just wait for body heat to dry them out while I hike (or wet them down again with my sweat).

T-shirts and socks can be rinsed in the same manner and cleaned once a week using a biodegradable soap. Some synthetics require a special detergent to rid them of their perspiration odors. Read labels and know before you go. Never, never wash your clothes in a water source—even biodegradable soaps leave suds and a bad taste. Always dump dirty wash water far from any water source. If you are on a long-distance hike, you will hit an occasional town where you can wash your clothes in a laundromat.

Another method for drying clothes—other than hanging them on a branch or rock—is by using your rope to form a clothesline. Light-weight clothes pins are available at outdoors stores or you can center your rope around a tree, twist it tightly, tie it to another tree, and then pull apart a twist to hold your clothes. You may want to carry a thin, light-weight line just for this purpose.

Vapor Barrier System

The vapor barrier system is a way to get warm the quickest way possible when you're really cold. It involves using an impermeable barrier such as a plastic bag to retain both your body's heat and moisture. Although not exactly comfortable because you stay wet, it is extremely effective.

Vapor barriers can be used in sleeping bag liners and in clothes such as pants, shirts, socks and gloves. I am from the school that believes vapor barriers are just fine when it's freezing cold outside and there is no other way to get warm. I have used plastic bags a number of times to warm up my feet, especially when my boots have failed to dry from the previous days of rain and it is raining again.

Some people believe in using vapor barriers in all cold-weather situations while others would rather die then submit themselves to the agony of the vapor barrier.

Try it before you decide. You may like it or you may decide it's not worth carrying the specially-made garments and that you would rather rely on your Ziploc bags.

Heat Loss

When backpacking, your body is subjected to four kinds of heat loss. Keep these in mind when purchasing backpacking clothes. Do the clothes effectively prevent or produce this heat loss?

Convective Heat Loss: This most common form of heat loss occurs when air and water come into contact, or near-contact, with your body and carry heat away with them. Materials such as pile, down, wool, PolarGuard and Hollofil, and Thinsulate work as a barrier against convective loss—retaining most of your body's heat.

Evaporative Heat Loss: When you sweat, you lose heat through the evaporation of the liquid. This is great in warm weather because it cools the body; but when it's cold and once you stop moving, your clothes remain wet and so do you. This can lead to hypothermia. Fortunately for backpackers, materials such as polypropylene have been designed to wick away the moisture or sweat. These materials work by removing the moisture from the skin before it evaporates.

Conductive Heat Loss: Although this is usually a relatively minor way to lose heat, it can be dangerous in certain

circumstances. Conductive heat loss occurs when the body loses heat to the air, water or fabric that is in contact with the body at a lower temperature. Falling into cold water, for example, you lose all your body heat to the water, a potentially fatal situation.

Radiant Heat Loss: Another minor method of heat loss is when heat radiates out from your body into your clothes. Unless the fabric you are wearing reflects the heat back to you, the heat is lost to the air. Vapor barriers reflect the heat back to your body.

•9•
Backpacks

NEON TONES OF ORANGE, yellow and pink reflected off the dancing porpoises as the sun set beyond the Brickhill River. A cool breeze whispered through the live oaks carrying with it the tangy salt smell of the marshes. Along the mudflats below the bluff, fiddler crabs scurried in and out of the cordgrass and as the last glimmer of gold melted from the sky, the raccoons began their evening feast. Behind us in the maritime oak forest, armadillos rustled among the palmettos, snuffling the fallen oak leaves for insects and small animals. The sounds of nature finally lulled us to sleep.

This experience would have been impossible without our backpacks. Carrying everything you need on your back opens the door to experiences otherwise impossible—from a shared sunrise with a deer atop a Tennessee bald to a bath in the icy water of a stream meandering through a remote Sierra meadow.

The all-important backpack is the "eponym" of the experience just described. Gone are the days of blanket rolls and heavy, shapeless canvas bags. Today, selecting a pack is almost as tough as finding a pair of boots. Dozens of manufacturers offer hundreds of options.

The type of pack you choose is important, whether you're out for a day or for an extended trip. Although the hike is not for the benefit of your pack, you do have to live with it every moment that it's on your back. Advances in technology have made backpacking easier on hikers but as with other types of equipment, you first must choose what type of packing you'll be doing and on what terrain. Fortunately, your choices are limited to internal or external frames—the internal designed for rugged, mountain backpacking; the external for gentle to moderate terrain. (The frameless rucksack is experiencing a comeback as well, and a number of manufacturers offer these packs for hikers who like to travel light.)

External versus Internal Frame

Both frame designs have their pros and cons. The basic differences are: the external frame is designed to distribute weight equally and has a high center of gravity, (perfect for established trails); the internal frame pack is designed to custom-fit each wearer and has a low center of gravity, (popular for off-trail hiking and mountaineering). Also, the external frame is said to be cooler than the internal frame because it is designed to sit away from your back rather than on it like the internal frame. The external frame is better built to carry heavier loads (more than 50 pounds).

External Frame

External frame packs are designed to carry big loads (25 pounds or more). Because you will probably carry about as much for a weekend trip as you would for a longer trip, an external frame needs to have approximately 3,000 cubic inches carrying capacity.

External frame packs come in top-loading, front-loading, and combination models. A top-loading pack works like a duffle bag attached to a frame, whereas, front-loading packs give you easy access to your gear. But most manufacturers

design their external packs with both a top-loaded and front-loaded section as well as front and side pockets.

The most important feature is the pack's hip belt. The hip belt carries the bulk of the weight, so that a properly fitted pack allows you to drop one shoulder out of its strap without a significant change in weight distribution. The hip belt should be padded, well-built and snug-fitting.

Many companies offer optional hip belts that are larger or smaller than the standard adjustable hip belt. If you're planning a long-distance hike, keep in mind that because of weight loss, the hip belt that fits you when you begin may not fit you later in your trip. Hip belts are prone to breaking because of the amount of stress they receive. If this happens, manufacturers are usually great about replacing them free of charge. Keep the manufacturer's telephone number (usually toll-free) handy in case you need to order another hip belt or have one replaced.

Manufacturers of external frame packs boast that the frame keeps the pack away from your body and thus is cooler in the summer. A good external frame pack will have a mesh back band that will allow for circulation of air. This band should be tight and well-adjusted for your comfort.

Features to look for in an external frame pack include:
- A welded tubular frame, preferably of aluminum because it is lightweight and strong.
- A coated nylon packcloth (although not waterproof, it is water resistant—a pack cover is needed to waterproof your pack).
- Thick, padded shoulder straps.
- A mesh backband to allow the air to circulate in warm weather.
- A thick, foam hipbelt with an easy-release buckle.
- Outside pockets on the pack bag.

External frame packs can be purchased from under $50 to $400. Camp Trails, Dana Designs, Jansport, Kelty, Mountainsmith and REI are some of the more popular brands of external frame packs. A complete list of pack manufacturers, from day packs to internal frames, can be found at the end of this chapter.

>>Hiking Tip<<

The best external frame pack won't be worth much to you if the pack bag separates from the frame. Carry extra clevis pins and split rings (approximately six for $2) for repairs in the field or purchase heavy-duty split rings at your local hardware store and replace the flimsier rings on your pack.

Internal Frame

Rather than purchase two packs, many people are turning to the internal frame as their best compromise. Unless you hike easy trails exclusively, an internal frame will suit you well on all trails.

As an example, I had an agonizing time climbing through Maine's Mahoosuc Notch with my external frame pack. The .9-mile stretch of tumbled boulders requires squeezing in and out, over and under. My external frame continually threw me off-balance, leaving me quaking in my boots and near tears. At that moment, I would have done anything for an internal frame. Another thing that irritates me to no end is hitting my head on the frame. Every time I fall while wearing an external frame (I've never met a person who hasn't fallen while backpacking), I bang my head on the frame. Adding insult to injury is the knot on my head.

Internal frames were designed to alleviate these problems. Because they hug your body and have a lower center of gravity, they provide excellent balance and allow more upper-body mobility and flexibility.

There are two basic designs that make up the internal frame—two parallel bars or X-shaped bars. These are sewn inside the packbag. The internal frame is fitted to your body by a number of straps attached to the packbag. The internal frame's major drawback is that because the load is contoured to your body, it is often not as comfortable as a load carried in an external frame.

An average internal frame pack will need a minimum volume of 4,000 cubic inches to be comparable to an external frame pack with a 3,000-cubic-inch capacity. This is because sleeping gear is attached to the frame of an external pack but is carried in a special compartment inside the internal frame pack. Most internal frame packs are top-loading and they do not come with external pockets, another drawback. Internals are the most expensive of all packs.

Internal frame packs are equipped with harnesses, straps, and other adjustments so that the pack may be form-fitted to each wearer.

The hip belt on the internal frame pack is form-fitted and is part of the pack. Although it is adjustable and is offered in several sizes within the pack style itself, it is not optional or easily replaceable. Some pack manufacturers are beginning to make interchangeable parts for internal frame packs.

Things to look for in an internal frame include:

- Contoured aluminum stays to help distribute weight to your hips.
- Thick, padded shoulder straps and hip belt.
- A lumbar pad that will help support a heavy load and enhance ventilation.
- Compression straps to keep smaller loads from shifting.
- A reinforced bottom to resist abrasion.
- A lot of lash points and loops to carry gear outside the pack.
- A slim profile with either outside or add-on pockets.
- Cinch straps at the shoulder and waist to keep the load close to your back.

Internal frames can rarely be found for less than $100 and can cost as much as $500. Camp Trails, Dana Designs,

Gregory, Kelty, Lowe, Mountainsmith, The North Face and REI are popular internal frame manufacturers. The chart on the following page is merely a representative selection of some of the many packs available to backpackers. We neither endorse nor condemn any of these packs.

Frameless Rucksacks
These approximately 2,500-cubic-inch packs are regaining their popularity. For those backpackers who can travel with the bare minimum and don't need the support and suspension of a framed pack, the rucksack is an option. Most manufacturers carry frameless packs ranging in price from less than $100 to $200.

The Overnight or Two-day Pack
Some hikers can live leanly enough to make long trips with the overnight or two-day type pack. The advantages of the two-day pack are obvious—not only do you carry less weight, but stress to your body is lessened. The approximately 2,000-cubic-inch internal frame packs are definitely not for everyone.

Alan Adams regularly hikes with a two-day pack, in which he carries about twenty pounds for each five-day trip. Adams said that by not carrying more than five percent of his body weight, he remains comfortable while hiking.

"Any more than that is work," he commented. Adams keeps his pack weight down by using a two-pound sleeping bag and sleeping under a fly rather than in a tent.

Once again, decide how much you can do without and still enjoy your hike before purchasing a smaller-than-average pack. Two-day/overnight packs range from under $25 to $200. Gregory's "The Two Day" is especially popular.

· Backpacks ·

Pack	Frame	Max. Volume	Weight	Price
CT C.F. Ranger	E	3,330 cu. inch	6lbs.2oz.	$120
CT Wilderness INT	I	4,800	5lbs.7oz.	$180
CT Night Song*	E	2,910	5lbs.8oz.	$135
DD Alpine	I	4,470-5,400	6lbs.	$380
DD The Wind	I	4,100-4,900	5lbs.10oz.	$290
DD Terraplane	I	5,340-6,300	6lbs.9oz.	$390
Gregory Denali	I	7,340	7lbs.13oz.	$420
Gregory Palisade +	I	5,400	6lbs.15oz.	$265
Jansport Sierra	I	5,200	5lbs.9oz.	$180
Jansport D-5	E	3,985	5lbs.8oz.	$165
Jansport Nepali	E	6,750	6lbs.10oz.	$250
Kelty Moraine	I	2,735-3,275	3lbs.1oz.	$100
Kelty Radial Light	E	3,500-5,535	6lbs.9oz.	$200
Kelty Super Tioga	E	4,125-4,745	6lbs.8oz.	$180
Lowe Contour 90+15	I	6,400	6lbs.11oz.	$290
Lowe Contour IV	I	6,400	6lbs.1oz.	$245
Lowe Sirocco	I	5,100	5lbs.6oz.	$235
MH CM LTD*	I	2,000-3,800	6lbs.	$400
MS Crestone I	I	5,000	6lbs.9oz.	$300
MS Frostfire II	I	6,192	5lbs.4oz.	$260
NF Dolomite	I	4,800-5,600	5lbs.	$330
NF Rogue*	I	3,800-4,600	5lbs.3oz.	$260
Osprey Helix	I	5,400-6,900	6lbs.5oz.	$295
Peak 1 TL7000 XPD	E	7,000	6lbs.8oz.	$220
REI Newstar	I	4,504	5lbs.2oz.	$185
REI Wonderland	E	4,093	5lbs.5oz.	$165

* Women's pack referred to for capacity, weight and cost. All packs, except those denoted with an asterisk, refer to men's regular pack size for weight and capacity.

CT-Camp Trails, DD-Dana Design, MH-McHale & Company, MS-Mountainsmith, NF-North Face, REI-Recreational Equipment, Inc.

Daypacks

Most daypacks are made in the same teardrop style, so the important thing to look at is how well the pack is made. Inexpensive daypacks can be purchased at any discount store, but if they are poorly padded and have little support, you won't have hiked a mile before you regret the purchase.

Leather-bottomed packs are the most durable and carry the load better by supporting the weight rather than collapsing beneath it. Make sure the shoulder straps on your day pack are very secure because this is the first place that such packs fall apart. This occurs because you are carrying the weight on your shoulders as opposed to your hips. To prevent ripping, a number of day packs have extra reinforcement where the shoulder straps connect to the sack. Another feature to look for is padding at the back of the pack. The more reinforced this section, the less likely you'll be poked and prodded by the objects inside the pack.

Features to look for in daypacks include:

- Convenient loading through top or front panel.
- Pockets for smaller items (some daypacks feature a special loop to hold keys).
- A waist strap to keep the back from bouncing against your back.
- Padded shoulder straps.
- Lash points for extra gear.

Daypacks are usually less than $100 and most manufacturers feature a variety to choose from.

Fanny Packs

Another way of keeping things handy is using a fanny pack in conjunction with your backpack. Many hikers use these miniature packs in reverse, snug across their bellies with the strap fastened in the small of the back. Cameras, water,

> ❦ *Hiking Secret* ❦
> A daypack can do double duty as a stuff sack for your
> sleeping bag. The daypack will then be handy for sidetrips
> or for slack-packing on long-distance hikes. Slack-packing
> is accomplished by finding someone to meet you at the next
> trail head with your pack so that you can cover a distance
> quickly without the burden of your pack.

snacks, data books, maps, guides, or whatever you need quick
access to can be carried by this method.

Fanny packs are useful on day hikes for the same reasons,
but they are not as comfortable as daypacks because they do
not distribute the weight as well, and often cannot carry as
much as you might like to bring. They can be used along with
a day pack or alone (if you have a partner carrying a daypack).

When purchasing a fanny pack, make sure the belt is well
padded for comfort and the sack is sturdy enough to carry the
load you intend for it. Some fanny packs are designed to carry
only very light loads and will sag if heavy objects are placed
in them. Also, if the fabric is thin, you may get poked and
prodded by the objects inside.

Manufacturers of packs include: Alpenlite, Inc.; Black
Diamond Equipment, Ltd.; Camp Trails/Johnson Camping,
Inc.; Caribou Mountaineering, Inc.; Cascade Designs; Dana
Design; DeFrance Pack; Denali International; Diamond Brand
Canvas Products Co, Inc.; Eagle Creek; Eastpak; Eastern
Mountain Sports; Edko Alpine Design; Famous Trails; Grade
VI; Granite Gear, Inc.; Gregory Mountain Products; High
Sierra; Invicta/Uvex Sports, Inc.; Jansport; Karrimor/Climb
High; Kelty Pack, Inc.; Lafuma USA; L.L. Bean, Inc.; Lowe
Alpine Systems; Madden/USA; Mark Pack Works; McHale &
Company; Millet/Suunto USA; Montbell America; Mountain
Equipment, Inc.; Mountainsmith, Inc.; Mountain Systems;

Mountain Tools; The North Face; Osprey; Outbound; Outdoor Recreation Group; Overland Equipment; Peak One/The Coleman Co. Inc.; Quest; Recreational Equipment, Inc. (REI); Remington Outdoor Products; Ridgeway by Kelty; Rocky Mountain Outfitters; Sierra Designs; Ultimate Direction, Inc.; vauDe USA; Wild Country, USA; Wilderness Experience; Wild Things, Inc.; and Jack Wolfskin.

Pack Construction

Put some mileage on your pack and soon it will begin wearing out. The frame, seams and zippers are especially subject to wear. Frank had a pack whose frame literally exploded off his back when it finally died. I lost an adjustment strap on my hipbelt, a relatively minor inconvenience compared to the number of miles I've put on that pack.

When purchasing a pack, check your pack frame (if you buy an external) for sturdiness and clean welds. Check the seams for even stitching and reinforcements, especially at the stress points. Make sure that there is sufficient room between the stitching and the edge of the seam and fabric because this is a likely place for it to separate. Feel free to tug and pull on the pack as much as you like--better to have it fall apart in the store than on your first trip out hiking. Buy a pack with heavy zippers. They are more durable. Also, if it is a front-loading pack, make sure there are compression straps to take the pressure off the zippers once loaded.

Fit

Before buying any pack, you should test it first. The best method is to rent a pack and try it out on a weekend hike. Some stores even offer rent-to-buy programs. If you can't do that, see if you can't load up the pack you're interested in and try it out in the store. Many stores have sand bags on hand for this purpose.

Also, keep in mind that torso length is more important

than overall height. For example, if a pack is suggested for someone six feet tall, it may also be appropriate for a shorter person with a longer torso--another reason to try on a pack before you buy it.

The hip belt should fit snugly around the top part of your hips and not catch your legs when you're hiking up hill. The belt should be heavily padded for comfort, durability and stability. Most importantly, make sure the hipbelt has a durable, easy-release buckle. There are times when you may have to get out of your pack quickly.

Tips for Fitting an External Frame:
- When fitting your pack make sure that the shoulder straps are level with or an inch or two above the shoulder.
- The mesh back band should fit snugly, but comfortably, against your back and the hip belt should ride on your pelvis.
- Move the hip belt up and down the frame to prevent the lower end of the frame from making contact with your lower back.
- Shoulder straps should not pinch your neck nor should they slide off your shoulders. Mounted too high they put too much of the wait on your shoulders; too low, on your hips.
- If the pack comes with load-lifters, they should join the frame at ear level and attach to the shoulder straps over your collarbone. Weight can be distributed from shoulders to hips with these straps.
- A sternum strap will help hold the pack more closely to your back.

Accessory features in packs include ice axe loops, crampon patches, ski holders, accessory pockets and camera rings. On some packs you will find that these features are standard rather than optional.

Tips for Fitting an Internal Frame:

- Once the hip belt is fastened, make sure that the pack's stays protrude two to four inches above your shoulders. If the stays are less than two inches above your shoulders, look for a larger pack. If they are more than four inches, look for a smaller pack.
- If the padded ends of the hip belt overlap in front, the belt is too big. If they rub your belly, you'll need a larger belt.
- The pack fits you in the shoulders if the shoulder straps join the pack about two inches below the tops of your shoulders. The lower ends of the straps should be a hand's width below your armpits.
- Load-lifter straps should join your frame at ear level to comfortably divert pressure to the front of your shoulders. The buckles for these straps should be positioned over your collarbone. Weight can be distributed from waist to shoulders with these straps, and you should vary the position as you hike for the most comfort.
- If the pack hugs your back like a child holding on for a piggyback ride, you have a proper fit.
- If the waist belt is distorted by the way you cinched your stabilizing belts, the pack needs readjustment. Always make sure the pack is cinched tightly.

How Much to Carry in Your Pack

An easy-to-use rule of thumb is to never carry more than one-third of your body weight. On shorter trips, it is wiser to carry even less—one-quarter of your body weight is about right.

Some hikers swear that you should carry only one-fifth of your body weight, but that can be difficult to do, especially if you are winter hiking or carrying a week's worth of food.

What if you pack your pack and it weighs 60 pounds and you weigh only 120? Unpack and look at everything very carefully. Items like your stove, tent, and sleeping bag are absolutely essential. But what about your clothes? You don't have to wear something different every day.

Another area people overpack in is toiletries. If you must shave, deodorize, shampoo, etc., try to find sample size containers. Don't bring a radio unless it's the compact "Walkman" type. Flashlights that are "hiker-friendly" can be purchased readily these days. A small flashlight that uses AA batteries will serve you just as well as one that uses C or D batteries.

Those are just a few examples. Chapters 8 and 10 also provide suggestions on what to pack. Look objectively at what you've packed: Are you sure you can't live without it?

Packing Your Pack
Once you've bought a pack, where do you put what? You're going to want certain items to be handy. Any system that you come up with will work as long as you know how to get at those necessary items quickly.

Rain gear, for example, will be something that you'll want to be able to lay your hands on immediately. It is not unusual to be caught in a sudden downpour, and if you have to drop your pack and dig through it to get at your raingear, you and all your gear may be soaked by the time you find it.

You will also need a means to carry water so that you can get at it without taking off your pack. Some hikers use holsters for their water bottles while others keep their canteens within easy reach in a side pocket on their packs.

It also is important to distribute the weight as equally as possible. For example, don't put all your food on one side and all your clothes on the other. Believe it or not, food will be a good third of the weight you are carrying.

Packing the heavier stuff toward the top of your pack will keep the load centered over your hips, particularly in an external frame pack. On the other hand, don't follow this rule

> **>>Hiking Tip<<**
>
> If you are going to take your backpack on an airplane remember that the straps and/or frame will make the pack difficult for airlines to handle. To prevent damage in transit, pack your backpack into a large duffel bag before you check it as luggage.

to its furthest possible conclusion because an overly top-heavy pack is also unwieldy.

Sleeping bags are usually secured at the bottom of an external frame pack, strapped to the frame just below the pack sack. In the internal frame packs, the sleeping bag compartment is usually the bottom third of the pack.

Another suggestion: you will probably want your food more readily available than your clothes and cooking gear, particularly at lunch time. Nothing is more aggravating than to have to dig through your clothes just so you can satisfy your craving for Gorp.

Loading Tips:

- On gentle terrain, pack the heaviest items high and close to the back. Because the pack's center of gravity is about at shoulder level, it will take only a slight bend at the waist while hiking to align the weight over your hips.

- If balance is crucial (climbing, off-trail travel, rough terrain), pack heavy items in the center, close to your back. You may have to lean over more to offset the pack's weight, but balance is better because the pack's top-heaviness is reduced.

- If you are carrying anything sharp in your pack, pad it well. The last thing you want is to be stabbed in the back.

- Women have a lower center of gravity and do well to pack dense items lower and closer to the back.

- Color-coded stuff sacks are a great backpacking tool.
- Make sure that all fitting points are properly adjusted to your torso.
- Long items should be lashed to the pack frame.

Pack Covers
Although all backpacks are made of water resistant material, moisture will seep through seams and zippers and saturate your gear if your pack is left unprotected. A pack cover can be anything from a heavy duty garbage bag, which will keep your pack dry when camping (and protect it from the dew at night), to a specially designed cover made for the purpose. These coated nylon or Gore-tex covers, when their own seams are properly sealed, fit over your pack but still allow you to hike. They are usually fitted to your pack by elastic or a drawstring.

No matter what kind of pack cover you purchase (and you do need to buy one), you will still want to carry a heavy duty (BIG) garbage bag to keep your pack covered at night because pack covers are not designed to protect the straps and back of your pack. A plastic garbage bag is indispensable when you are forced to camp in a downpour but don't have room for your pack in the tent.

The poncho-style pack covers work under ideal conditions only. The poncho is designed to be a one-piece rain gear, covering both you and your pack at the same time. Not only do ponchos tend to tear easily, but they work only when the wind is not blowing hard. If the wind whips up, so will your poncho; and both you and your pack will soon be soaked. For added insurance, anything you don't want to get wet can be slipped into a plastic bag before being stored in your pack.

· 10 ·
Other Equipment

WHILE BEING INTERVIEWED on CNN about hiking vacations, Frank and I were asked by a caller what we left at home in order to keep our packs light. The kitchen sink, I thought at the time. But upon later reflection I realized it wasn't such a silly question after all. What we leave behind to keep our packs light is different than what others leave behind.

I do not miss television when I am on a backpacking trip, so it's easy for me to leave mine behind. But there are those who can't live without it and there are now televisions small enough to fit in a pack or even on your wrist. Some people carry guitars while others can't live with out their tapes and portable tape player. I usually carry a book or two and a journal; Frank carries camera equipment. Another of our concessions to luxury is spices. (Trail meals are unappetizing enough without the garlic, pepper and Tabasco.)

While most of us agonize over what to take and what to leave behind, some people go to extremes to cut down on everything in order to reduce the weight they are carrying. They even go so far as to cut the handles off their toothbrushes and the corners off their maps.

In addition to the basics—tent, pack, boots, sleeping bag,

etc.—there are some other articles you will probably want to consider taking along on a hike, especially if you're out for a night or more. Carefully select the equipment you really need and leave at home things that are extra, or even ridiculous. You will be much more comfortable without the added weight.

Toiletries

Depending on the length of your hiking trip, you may want to consider bringing along items such as towel, shampoo/soap, deodorant, razors/shaving cream, toothbrush/toothpaste, eyecare items and toilet paper.

Towel

Most hikers do not carry a towel, per se. We usually carry bandanas and one handcloth for the purpose of washing and/or drying. In warm weather, we let the sun do the job of drying our skin. In cold weather, we use the cloth to hand bathe ourselves with heated water and then dry with a bandana.

For those who need a towel, the super absorbent "Pack Towl" costs about $5 and the manufacturers boast that the towel absorbs up to ten times its weight, as well as dries quickly (which is important because who wants to carry around a soggy, one-pound towel). Most outdoors stores offer this towel and other variations on the "Pack Towl."

Shampoo/soap

Never, ever, wash yourself or your hair in a stream, pond, or other body of water. And never use anything but biodegradable soap. Would you want to drink water that someone had rinsed soap off into? A lot of the water sources along trails provide drinking water for hikers as well as for animals.

Biodegradable soap (at least the widely available Dr. Bronner's) does not work as a shampoo. While you can't beat it for washing your body, it leaves your hair lank and greasy. Before depending on a biodegradable soap as an all-round cleaner, I would suggest testing it on the various things you plan to use it for (ie. hair, body, clothes, pots and pans). There are a number of biodegradable soaps available from outdoors stores, including Mountain Suds, Bio-suds and Sunshower Soap. Soaps average around $3 for a four-ounce bottle.

There is a soap product on the market called NO-Rinse that requires no water for a shampoo and only one quart of water to bathe. N/R Laboratories claims that you simply massage NO-Rinse in and towel dry it out. NO-Rinse Body Bath and NO-Rinse Shampoo are available from Goodman Marketing (P.O. Box 5459, Dept. S, Fresno, CA 93755-5459). The cost is $14.95 plus $4 shipping and handling for one 8-ounce bottle of each.

If your soap doesn't work as a shampoo, most discount department stores (such as Wal-Mart and K-Mart) and drug stores offer trial or sample size products that are great for backpacking. Shampoos are commonly available in sample sizes as are toothpastes and lotions. I've used a variety of shampoos while backpacking but if you can find a biodegradable shampoo you'll lessen your detrimental effect on the environment. As with soaps, though, never wash your hair with shampoo in or near a water source. By the way, even the most hard-core hikers bathe occasionally.

Deodorant

While soap is a necessity, deodorant is considered optional. We use it only on visits to town. Otherwise, there's no one around to smell you but yourself (and other smelly hikers)! You may also want to consider that the less smelly you are, in terms of artificial odors such as perfumed deodorants, the less likely you'll be to scare wildlife away or to attract unwanted insects.

The most natural way to deodorize yourself is by using what is known as a deodorant rock. Composed of natural mineral salts, this crystal-like deodorant supposedly lasts a full year with normal use. My husband and I tried one at home and found that unless you thoroughly cleanse your underarms before each application, your underarm odor builds up very quickly. On the otherhand, this makes it an ideal deodorant for backpacking because you would only use it occasionally, anyway. Deodorant rocks are available at health food stores and through some catalogs. Two of the more popular brands are NATURE'S Pure Crystal Deodorant and Le Crystal Naturel. Deodorant rocks cost approximately $16.

Another relatively natural way to deodorize yourself is to use a baking soda-based powder such as Shower to Shower. My father has used it successfully for years.

If you're not interested in these natural methods of stopping perspiration odor, you can always carry your favorite deodorant in its sample or regular size.

Do keep in mind, especially during the hot and humid days of summer, that you probably reek. The longer you're out on the trail, deodorantless, the more you become accustomed to your body's odor. Which, believe it or not, isn't half as bad as the odor perspiration leaves in your clothes. The clothes you hike in ought to be washed every so often, as well.

People will be more willing to give needy hikers a hitch if they look presentable and smell as inoffensive as possible after spending days or weeks in the woods.

While staying with some friends during one backpacking trip we left a lasting impression on our hostess's olfactory nerves. She later told us that on our first night there she had prowled about the house, sniffing, unable to sleep or to determine the cause of the ungodly smell. Finally she stepped into the entranceway and found the odoriferous source of her nocturnal wanderings—our boots. She quickly banished them outdoors. Embarrassing? You betchum Red Rider. When someone offers you hospitality while backpacking, the last thing you want to do is offend them. If someone invites you to stay, kindly leave your boots outside. Remember, you're used to their smell, but others will find it overwhelming. Most people will be too polite to mention it, so it's up to you to keep your odor under control, at least when you're off the trail.

Razors/Shaving cream
Most men opt to grow a beard when hiking, although some do take the trouble to shave every day or now and then. The same goes for women—many prefer to let the hair under their arms and on their legs grow out while hiking. It's all a matter of preference. I shave at least once a week, using biodegradable soap and a disposable razor, when long-distance hiking because I am more comfortable that way. A battery-operated electric razor is another option.

Toothbrush/toothpaste
Don't brush your teeth near a water source. Dig a small hole to spit into and then cover your spit.

As for toothcare products, there are a variety of options on the market, but a child's toothbrush works great because it is small and lightweight! Toothpaste can easily be purchased in sample sizes or you might want to try using baking soda that you can transfer to a small bottle for convenience.

Eyecare
I am continually amazed at the number of hikers who elect to wear contact lenses during their long-distance hikes. But as risky as it seems, I also wear contacts; although I carry a pair of glasses just in case. The new, daily and extended wear lenses are easy to care for and the cleaning fluid does not add much weight to my pack. Personally, unless I am sitting still,

my body heat raised by the exertion of hiking, fogs my glasses up so badly, they're useless. And, when I'm sweaty they tend to slide off my nose. I remember one night counting three out of six of us wearing contact lenses. Two wore glasses and only Frank had 20/20 vision. Improvements for hikers extend beyond backpacking equipment!

Toilet Paper

Of course you know you need to bring toilet paper. Even day hikers need it occasionally. A good way to pack it is to scrunch it flat and stick it in a resealable plastic bag. By removing the cardboard tube in the center and unraveling the paper from the inside, you will find that your toilet paper crushes down flatter in its plastic bag. Scot toilet tissue seems to have the most paper for the money.

And, while we're on the subject . . . one of the worst sights we saw while hiking through the Great Smoky Mountains were the wads of toilet paper scattered through the woods near shelters. Please take the time to dig a cat hole for your toilet paper and for your feces. A backpacker's trowel weighs a mere two ounces and costs less than $2. That's well worth the "trouble" when you consider how much it will lessen your environmental impact.

Never relieve yourself near a water source. Always find a site at least fifty yards downhill or to the side of a water source. This is for the protection of wildlife as well as other hikers. According to the Centers for Disease Control, beavers living downstream from national parks and forests contract giardiasis (caused by humans) more often than humans pick up the infamous stomach ailment.

A note to women: Urination for male backpackers is as easy, if not easier because there is no seat to lift, as it is in the "real" world. And although some trails offer the occasional outhouse, the chances of your stumbling upon one at the appropriate moment are about nil. Even then, you're likely to find a note requesting you to relieve yourself in the woods because some outhouses are reserved for defecation only.

If you're strong enough and have a good aim, it is possible to pee with your pack on—release the hipbelt, drop your drawers to your knees, bend your knees a bit, lean forward with your hands on your knees for support, relax and go.

Another option is take off your pack and find what Kathleen Meyer, author of *How to Shit in the Woods*, calls the perfect pose. Find two rocks, a rock and a log, two logs, or if necessary, a steep slope and a log or rock. Sitting on one, you balance your feet on the other and avoid the splashed boots that are so common when women try to pee outdoors.

A third option is a funnel, but make sure you purchase one with a long hose. The funnels are designed to slip easily into your pants and transport your urine outside. I never even got up the nerve to try mine, feeling certain that no matter what I did I'd end up with soggy britches.

Menstruation is another problem women face in the wilderness. On most trips, it's going to be "pack it in, pack it out"; so make sure you bring along enough resealable bags to hold your used tampons or napkins. Burning is another option, but the fire must be very hot to completely burn a tampon or napkin. Never burn plastic applicators because they release poisons into the air.

Your best choice is going to be an applicatorless tampon such as OBs. They are compact and produce the least amount of waste all the way around. Once used, wrap them in a bit of toilet paper and seal in a plastic bag until you reach a suitable dumping station. Never drop your tampons or napkins into a latrine nor should you bury them because it will take them years to disintegrate, if animals don't dig them up first.

First-aid Kit

Keeping in mind the fact that it is next to impossible to create a perfect first-aid kit, the following is a list of what makes up a close-to-perfect kit:

- A Ziploc or other brand zipper-lock plastic bag to hold the items in your first aid kit.
- Approximately six, one-inch by three-inch, band-aids. These can be used to cover most scratches, cuts and scrapes.
- Two, four-inch by four-inch, sterile gauze pads that can be cut down or doubled up depending on the size of the wound.
- A roll of athletic tape—one inch by ten yards—has a variety of uses from holding on the sterile gauze to wrapping ankles.
- Tincture of benzoin. Not only does this liquid toughen feet but it helps tape stick better when rubbed on the skin.
- A couple of butterfly band-aids for closing small, gaping wounds.
- An individually wrapped sanitary napkin is great for staunching heavily bleeding wounds.
- Povidone-iodine ointment has a number of uses—disinfects wounds (straight from the tube); dissolves in water for a wash for larger scrapes; and can even be used as a lubricant or to treat water in an emergency.
- Moleskin to treat hot spots and blisters.
- Your favorite painkiller for aches, pains, fever, etc.
- A six-inch-wide elastic wrap (such as made by Ace). These can be used to wrap strains and sprains as well as to hold bandages in place, constrict snake bites, compress heavy bleeding or splint a broken bone.
- A few safety pins always come in handy. They can be used to hold the Ace bandage, drain blisters, repair clothing, etc.
- A few antihistamine tablets such as Benadryl to combat insect bites and poison ivy.

- Pepto-Bismol or some similar tablets for upset stomachs.
- Scissors and tweezers. (You may be able to find a pocket knife with these items. My tiny Victorinox has both and they have come in handy many times.)

Other items to consider, depending on the time of year and the location of your hike, are meat tenderizer or Sting-eze for insect bites, sunscreen, alcohol to help remove ticks (and toughen feet), lip balm, lotion, prescription drugs if you need them, a bee sting kit if you are allergic to insect stings, and DEET repellent for mosquitos and other insects (see Chapter 12). Remember that a first aid kit is a very personal thing. For example, if you have trouble with constipation at home, by all means carry a laxative while hiking.

I use lip balm (Chap Stick works best for me) constantly both at home and while hiking. I can't abide the feeling of chapped lips and always carry several tubes of Chap Stick with me where ever I go. Other good lip balms are Blistex, Carmex and Labiosin. You can find many options both at drug stores and outdoors stores.

Some people have problems with hemorrhoids while hiking and always include Preparation H or Tucks Pads in their kits. Some women may find it necessary to carry birth control pills.

Hiking in the summer, desert or snow might make it necessary for you to carry a sunscreen with a sun protection factor (SPF) in line with your skin's sensitivity to the sun. The higher the SPF number, the less likely you are to be burned. As with lip balms, you can find a wide range of sunscreens to choose from at your local drug, discount and outdoors stores.

Lotion is another product you may wish to add to your kit if you intend to be hiking in hot, dry weather. Some sunscreens combine lotion with the screen or you may wish to carry a sample size of your favorite brand. Remember, though, that baby oil acts as a sun tan lotion as well as a skin softener and could be potentially dangerous if you intend to use it as a lotion. If you will be doing some desert hiking you may want to carry along a lotion with aloe vera that will help soothe any sunburn you might get. If your skin is very sensitive to the sun, a sunburn therapy such as Solarcaine or Ahhh might be worth the extra weight in your first aid kit.

But, unless you have a special need or problem, do not carry too many specific items in your first aid kit. The kit and its contents should be as versatile as possible. It won't matter that you have to cover a two-inch wide wound with a four-inch wide bandage, for example.

Also, remember to repack your first aid kit seasonally or yearly. Medicines expire and may need to be replaced so always check the expiration dates before heading out on any trip. And there is no use carrying insect repellent on a winter trip when there are no bugs around. Your first-aid kit should reflect your personal needs as well as the season and geographic area through which you're hiking.

Most importantly, do not carry anything in your kit that you do not know how to use. For example, a suture kit will be useless to you unless you have been trained in suturing wounds. Don't carry prescription medicines unless you are fully aware of their side-effects and how to use them.

Depending on how safety-conscious you are, there are all sorts of items available to ease your mind while hiking. Everything from dental emergency kits to accident report forms can be purchased for your first aid kit.

Although I've never known any one to use one, some people feel safer if they carry along a snake-bite kit. There are several kits on the market ranging from $5 to $15. The simplest kit contains two big suction cups plus a smaller suction cup for bites on small surfaces such as fingers. The kit also includes a lymph constrictor, scalpel, antiseptic vial and instructions. The $10 Extractor is a double-chamber vacuum pump with four cup sizes, antiseptic, band-aids, a safety razor, instructions and a carrying case. The Extractor is the only recommended first aid for snake bites these days and it is said that even it does little to help.

Outdoors stores offer a variety of first aid kits ranging in price from $8 to $80. Outdoor Research, Adventure Medical Kits and REI are some of the major manufacturers of first aid kits.

Items for Emergencies

When it comes to emergencies, some people like to carry along a mirror, flares and a whistle. I carry a mirror, anyway, because I need it to insert my contact lenses, but you may want to consider carrying a mirror should you need it to signal someone below or above you. If your watch has a reflective surface you can discard the mirror and use it instead. Some compasses have sighting mirrors that can be used for signaling or you can use foil, your stove's windscreen (if it reflects) or even your sunglasses. Signal mirrors, on the other hand, are usually too heavy to be carried by a backpacker.

I've never carried one, but some backpackers feel safer if they carry along a flare or smoke bomb for emergencies. The bombs emit clouds of orange or red smoke that can be seen from both the ground and the air. Flares can be shot up into the air and usually burn for an average of seven seconds. I have seen both smoke bombs and flares available through catalogs—$8 for the bomb, $16 for three flares—and most outdoors stores keep them in stock as well.

For use in both an emergency and as a warning to bears, you can also carry a whistle in your "emergency kit." Just make sure you use the whistle only in emergency situations because in addition to crying "wolf," you'll also be disturbing the other people out there who are seeking peace and quiet.

If you purchase a whistle, make sure the balls inside are made of metal or plastic. Cork, if it gets wet, will ruin your whistle. Survival whistles can be purchased for under $3.

There is a gadget on the market called the Survivo II that includes an accurate compass, waterproof matchcase, whistle, striking flint and signal mirror. It is packed in a 4.5-inch by 1.25-inch case, weighs a mere ounce, and costs only $4.

Sunglasses

There are so many options when it comes to sunglasses that I cannot begin to recommend any one particular brand. If you do carry sunglasses, and I recommend that you do, make sure that the lenses are designed to filter out the sun's harmful rays—both ultraviolet and infrared. Sunglasses are especially essential for desert and snow hiking where the sun reflects off the ground and into your eyes.

Sunglasses can be purchased from $5 to $75. Straps to hold your sunglasses around your neck—Chums, Croakies and others—are worth the extra $5 because they keep you from losing your sunglasses. This is especially beneficial if you just paid $40 for your shades.

There are also a number of other "gadgets" that can be purchased for sunglasses (and glasses, if you wear them) including defoggers and lens cleaners, cases, windguards and clip-on sun shades for eyeglass wearers.

Sunglasses are now manufactured for children, including glasses that filter out ultraviolet and infrared rays.

Sunscreen

Walking in shorts and a t-shirt leaves a hiker exposed to the suns rays for several hours a day. To prevent burning, wear a sunscreen or sunblock. If you have fair or sensitive skin, you will need a sunscreen with a sun protection factor (SPF) of at least 15.

Binoculars

Carrying binoculars is a matter of preference but modern technology has made them both lightweight and tough so the heavy, bulky binoculars of yore are no longer an excuse not to bother.

When purchasing binoculars, there are two things to keep in mind besides weight and durability. First of all, binoculars are identified by two numbers: the magnification and the lens size (for example, 10 X 25). It will be these two numbers that determine the quality of your binoculars.

Magnification—the larger the number, the greater the magnifying power. Numbers greater than 10, though, mean you will have a hard time keeping your hand steady enough to focus on whatever object you've sighted.

Lens size—the second number identifies the diameter, in millimeters, of the objective lens. The objective lens is the lens farthest away from your eye. The larger the objective lens, the more light that reaches your eye and the brighter the image you see. Obviously, the higher the magnification number and the larger the objective lens, the more expensive your binoculars will be.

There are a number of binocular manufacturers including Brunton, Leica, Nikon, Minolta, Swarovski, Pentax, Steiner and Bushnell.

Lighting

Very simply put, it is a good idea to bring along some source of light for evenings at camp and on the trail. From time to time, it will be a relief to have a light to help find things in a dark tent or shelter.

Lanterns

The big, heavy, white gas lanterns have a place in camping but not in backpacking. They are bright and efficient but are far too heavy and bulky to carry along on a backpacking trip.

There are also heavy battery-powered lanterns that weigh even more and are made for family camping.

We started out on our first backpacking trip with a candle lantern, and have continued to use ours, although we have also purchased a flashlight.

Candle lanterns (some of which can be equipped to use gas) are your best bet if you want to carry a lantern. They weigh as little as six ounces (sold by Limelight Productions, REI and Early Winters and at some outdoors stores under the generic—Candle Lantern). One candle will give you as much as eight hours of illumination. The light produced by a candle lantern is not very bright, but it works better than a flashlight for cooking, cleaning, reading and writing when you make camp at dark.

The candle lantern is better than a candle alone because it is safer. It is housed in metal and glass, so you are less likely to start an unwanted fire if it tips over. It is also more economical because it is protected from the wind and, thus, does not burn up as quickly as a candle. You can purchase a candle lantern for $10 to $20 and refills for about 50 cents a piece.

Small oil and gas lanterns burn for up to twenty hours per fill-up and cost about $20 to $25. They weigh the same as candle lanterns, and some can take different grades of lamp oil, including citronella (the insect repellent).

All lanterns are equipped with a hanger and can often be rigged to hang from the apex of your tent by an attached nylon cord. Many tents have loops in the apex that will allow you to fasten a cord. If your tent does not have a loop at its apex, it may be possible to add a loop of velcro or sew on a loop, yourself. Some tents have loops in the corners designed to hold gear lofts from which you can rig a line to hold a candle lantern. Remember to keep the lantern a safe distance from the material of the tent so you won't burn holes in the tent or set it afire.

❦ *Hiking Secret* ❦
Your flashlight can do occasional double duty as a lantern.
Place a Nalgene brand or other translucent bottle over the
end of the flashight to disperse light. Stand the bottle up
on the open end and you have a serviceable lantern.

Flashlights

On our first backpacking trip, we didn't think we'd need a
flashlight because we had a candle lantern. Whether or not
you decide to carry a candle lantern, you will find a flashlight
very handy.

First of all, it's not easy to wake up in the middle of the
night and light a candle lantern just so you won't walk into
briars (or worse!) when looking for a spot to relieve yourself.
Second, if you intend to hike for any length of time, don't be
surprised if you end up walking at night. Whether this
happens intentionally or unintentionally, you'll need a flashlight. Candle lanterns produce good light but are hard to
direct.

The flashlight you take backpacking needn't be really
powerful. Most hikers use the smaller flashlights equipped
with two AA batteries. They are small but adequate. Mini-
mags are popular with hikers because they provide a lot of
output for very little weight.

Flashlights that require two D cell batteries, or more, are
too heavy, and the illumination is overkill for what you'll need
when hiking.

Remember though, if you decide to depend solely on a
flashlight for your light, you will need a steady supply of
batteries. If you choose to use a flashlight rather than a candle
lantern for your light, you may want to look into headlamps
because they provide a light source that does not need to be
hand held.

Headlamps

If you're seriously into night hiking, then you have another good reason to look into purchasing a headlamp. These illuminators are usually on a headband and light the way ahead of you for approximately 250 feet. They are safer than flashlights for night hiking because they leave your hands free.

But headlamps are good for more than just night hiking. They also leave your hands free for cooking, cleaning and setting up your tent. But they, too, use batteries and have a few other drawbacks, as well.

Headlamps are designed two ways—either with the lamp and batteries attached to the headband or with the lamp attached to the headband and the battery unit (sometimes including yet another light) attached to a belt and connected to the headband by wire. The problem with the all-in-one unit is that it tends to be heavy and to induce headaches if you use it for long periods of time. The problem with the latter is that the wires can get caught by branches, arms, etc. The more loose parts you have, the more likely you are to have a short in the wire. A couple of advantages to the two-part system are that it does eliminate headaches and the batteries stay warm when kept on your person.

One important factor to keep in mind when purchasing a headlamp is that battery switches tend to come on while sitting in your pack. The Petzl has a screw-type off/on switch that eliminates this problem. Otherwise, you will probably need a piece of duct tape to make sure your headlamp remains in the off position while packed away.

Depending on your needs, there are a number of functional headlamps available. For three-season backpacking, the Climb High Headlamp, Hartford Headlite, REI Waterproof, REI Cordless, Panasonic Headlamp and Petzl EO3 Micro are your best bets. Except for the Petzl, which uses only

· **Headlamps** ·

Light	Battery	Battery Life at 70 Degrees	Weight	Price
CH Headlamp	2.9V Lithium	20 hours	6 oz.	$25
HES Headlite	4 AAA	6	8 oz.	$25
Petzl EO4 Zoom	4.5V flat	17	11 oz.	$35
Petzl EO3 Micro	2 AA	5	5 oz.	$30
REI Cordless II	4 AA	14	6 oz.	$30
REI Waterproof	4 AA	7	9 oz.	$40

CH-Camp High, HES-Hartford Easter Seals, PS-Panasonic, REI-Recreational Equipment, Inc.

two AA batteries and requires more "fill-ups", the others have decent battery burn times (approximately eighteen hours at seventy degrees).

Major manufacturers of headlamps include Hartford Easter Seals, Petzl, REI and Sylva.

Batteries
When it comes to backpacking, there are only two types of batteries that are worth considering—alkaline and lithium.

Alkaline: These batteries are far more efficient and longer-lasting than standard and heavy duty batteries. They offer as much as double the life yet weigh and cost just a bit more. Unlike carbon-zinc cells, the alkaline battery dies suddenly rather than fades out—a minor disadvantage. Alkaline batteries do recharge themselves a bit and will last for another twenty minutes or so if left to recharge for half-a-day unlike standard batteries that recharge only enough to put out a dim light for another five minutes. Alkalines cost about $2.50 for two AA batteries, $3 for two C batteries, and $3 for two D batteries.

Lithium: Extremely light and efficient, lithium batteries are also expensive (though in ratio to their effectiveness and weight not inordinately so). Unlike alkaline batteries, lithium will work in cold temperatures. Lithium batteries also have a much longer shelf life than alkaline batteries.

As for drawbacks, they are still not widely available. Alkaline batteries can be purchased in almost every supermarket, drug store, convenience store and discount store in the United States. Lithiums are much harder to find but are usually stocked by good outdoors stores. They also require special bulbs and there are restrictions about carrying them on aircraft. It is said that under certain conditions (intense heat or prolonged shorting) lithium cells may explode, although it is more likely that they will release a small bit of sulfur-dioxide gas than explode. Lithiums range in price from $8 for AA to $15 for a C to $20 for a D cell.

Repair Equipment
Even if you're just going out for an overnight hike, it is wise to carry along a few small items to help you out in a pinch. Most problems can be taken care of with these miniature repair kits.

Pack Repair
Pack pins and rings are the most frequent cause of problems. You'll be surprised at the number of rings you'll see littering frequently packed trails. Frank's three-week-old pack lost a ring in the Shenandoahs. Rings, small circles of overlapping wire, are used to keep the pins in place on external frame packs. All those rings on the trail represent pins that are about to work their way loose from hikers' packs, causing

>>Hiking Tip<<

Protect your topographic maps from rain. Coat your maps
with Stormproof, a solution available from many outdoor
retailers. It leaves an invisible water-repellent coating on
your maps without making them stiff. A half-pint treats
ten to twelve USGS Topo maps and costs about $6.

pack bags to sag or hip belts and shoulder straps to spring
loose from the frame. Carrying a couple of extra pins and rings
could save you much discomfort on a hike.

Tent Repair
We always carry a tent repair kit, and boy does it come in
handy—and not just for our tent. I've used it to repair my
sleeping bag stuff sack and Frank's (and Craig Jolly's) rain
pants as well as our tent.

Tent repair kits usually include tent fabric tape (adhe-
sive- backed, waterproof ripstop nylon of two types), a small
amount of duct tape, a needle and thread, a short length of
cord, an aluminum splint for tent poles, and no-see-um
netting. A good kit, manufactured by Outdoor Research, costs
$5 and weighs only 2.5 ounces.

If you're going to be hiking more than two or three months,
you'll want to send ahead some seam sealer. Extensive use is
hard on a tent, and you'll need to reseal the seams every two
to three months, depending on how much you use your tent.

Stove Repair
"Carry a stove repair kit or learn how to build fires," is long
distance hiker Phil Hall's advice. Stoves will break or have
problems when you least expect or desire it. If the manufacturer of your stove offers a kit, it is wise to purchase one.
Packing the extra couple of ounces is well worth the peace of

mind. We use ours, and everyone else we know uses theirs. (See Chapter 4 for more information.)

Repair kits cost about $5 to $10 and weigh approximately two ounces. Not all stove manufacturers offer repair kits for their stoves; some stoves are not designed for field repair.

Clothing Repair

You can purchase a miniature sewing kit, complete with a number of different colored threads, needle, thimble, scissors, needle threader, snaps, and buttons, at almost any drug, discount, grocery or outfitter store. If you're trying to save room, you can throw an extra needle and applicable thread into your tent-repair kit instead.

I carry an entire sewing kit (approximately two by three inches) that weighs about an ounce; and I have used it innumerable times. Dental floss is high strength sewing material if an emergency should strike. For hikes of a week or less, a sewing kit is probably unnecessary.

Boot Maintenance

Boot leather needs periodic waterproofing; and hikes of two weeks or more, particularly in wet seasons, will wear the waterproofing off your boots.

If you intend to be out for more than two weeks, you will need to either carry along Sno-Seal (or whatever you use to waterproof your boots—Silicone Water Guard, Biwell Waterproofing, Aquaseal) or send it ahead. Waterproofers for boots cost from $3 to $8.

Next I discuss two items—one I consider necessary and another absolutely unnecessary—rope and a gun.

Rope

A length of rope, at least ten-feet long and approximately three-sixteenths of an inch in diameter, is absolutely necessary for hiking. As a matter of fact, it would be wise to carry several lengths of rope ranging from a few feet to twenty-feet in length. Rope will definitely prove its usefulness on a hike down any trail.

For instance, many trails are in bear country. Whether protected or hunted, bears love human food. Some national parks provide bear-proof shelters or poles on which you can hang your food. In other areas, rope can be used to suspend a bag containing your food and other "smellables" from a tree to keep them out of reach of bears.

Rope can also be used for hanging your sleeping bags to air and hanging your wet clothes, rigging tents and tarps, lowering or pulling up a pack, hanging a pack from a tree, a belt, replacing frayed straps on gaiters or laces on boots, or for tying to a water bottle when it must be used as a dipper for water.

Keep in mind that if you intend to use a tarp on your backpacking trips you will probably need at least fifty-feet of rope because you never know how far apart the trees, rocks or shrubs will be that you will use to set it up. (Remember, too, that you can tie two lengths of rope together, if necessary.) Also, the tail of each knot should be at least a couple of inches to insure that the knot won't slip.

Most outdoors stores offer several types of rope, but the best for general backpacking is heavy-duty twisted or braided nylon rope ranging in width from one-eighth of an inch to one-quarter of an inch (or three to eight mm). Before using nylon rope, always burn the ends into hard knobs so that the rope does not unravel.

Knots

There are dozens of knots that can be learned, but fortunately only a few you'll need to know. These will come in handy while backpacking.

Double fisherman's knot: This is the most common backpacking and climbing knot because it can be used to tie two pieces of rope together. It is the safest and easiest to tie:

Sheet-bend: This is the simplest way to tie two unequal sizes of rope together and is very strong but the double fisherman is still recommended for climbing ropes.

Tautline hitch: This knot can be used for securing lines from a grommet to a stake or tree.

Clove hitch: You might use this knot when hanging your food for the night or securing your tarp to a tree.

Guns

Firearms are a controversial subject among hikers. Most hikers feel that guns are unnecessary, but a few do pack pistols or even rifles that will break down and fit into their packs.

Carrying weapons into a national park is a federal offense, and firearms are outlawed on other sections of trail as well. The real question is, are they necessary? To find out, we talked to hikers who, collectively, have hiked eighty-thousand miles on the Appalachian Trail as well as thousands of miles on the Pacific Crest, Continental Divide and other trails, including some in Europe. We decided that if the hikers we talked to could walk that far without guns, we could prove a point. The bottom line was this: there was neither a single instance where a firearm was brought out of a pack (if one was carried), nor a case of a firearm helping a hiker out of a jam. None of the hikers we talked to, though some had carried guns, thought that firearms were necessary.

Guns do have a place, but backpacking isn't one of them (unless, of course, it is hunting season; you have a license; and you are intentionally backpacking to a hunting spot). Animals, including humans, don't present enough danger to hikers to justify carrying firearms.

There are a number of additional items that you may choose to carry on your hike, including books, journals, radios, maps, compass.

· 11 ·
First Aid

ARISING EARLY ONE SUMMER MORNING, Frank and I and several other backpacker friends hiked to a picnic area before fixing breakfast. The thought of enjoying our repast at a table (What luxury!) was worth breaking camp at dawn and hiking the couple of miles.

I so enjoyed my first cup of coffee that I asked Frank if there was enough water left for a second.

"Sure," he said, eyeing the pot still simmering on our Whisperlite. He picked up the pot lifter, but before he could pick up the pot, it tipped over and spilled nearly boiling water right into my lap. Quick-thinking Phil Hall immediately doused my lap with cold water from his Nalgene and proceeded to use all the readily available water in the same manner. As soon as I was able, I hurried to the bathhouse and used water-soaked paper towels as compresses until the stinging sensation finally faded. I managed to survive the accident with only one small blister in the groin area. Phil's lightning fast reaction was the result of experience. He had once been burned by boiling water on a backpacking trip.

Whenever you head out into the wilderness, it is essential that you are prepared. We have found that preparation means planning. *Emergency Medical Procedures for the Outdoors* by Patient Medical Associates outlines what to do before you go:

- If you are hiking with one or more people, it is to your benefit to discuss any existing medical problems and knowledge of first aid.
- If any of your party suffers from a chronic illness, such as diabetes and epilepsy, or from serious allergies, list names and illnesses. Also note types of medication, dosages, when the medication is given, and where it is kept.
- If there is no one in your hiking group that knows CPR, the Heimlich maneuver, artifical respiration, or basic first aid, it would be wise to have one of the group take a course that covers these important techniques. If one of your party is trained, he should review the procedures before heading out.
- If you don't have a first aid kit, prepare one. A kit containing the basics is described in Chapter 10. Put the list of names, illnesses, and medications in your kit.
- If children are hiking with you, explain to them how to get help in an emergency.
- Before you leave, inform a close friend or relative of your whereabouts and when you intend to arrive and depart.

It is likely you'll have to contend with nothing more serious than a scratch or two. But even the best-prepared person cannot account for a seemingly stable rock that tips beneath the foot, twisted roots, or even slippery pine needles. No one intends to hurt themselves while hiking. I still bear the scar on my shin from a bad fall I took after slipping on a wet rock. I had walked over hundreds of rocks that day. Why did that one throw me?

Being prepared for backpacking is simply knowing what

you're getting into and what to do when you or someone else is injured. Fortunately, in thousands of miles of backpacking, I have suffered only minor injuries that were easily handled by a basic first-aid kit.

Unfortunately, backpackers cannot carry everything they might need in case of an accident—they wouldn't be able to fit it all in their packs!

In their book, *Medicine for the Backcountry* (by ICS Books), Frank Hubbell and Buck Tilton claim that the first commandment of first aid kits is "Thou shalt find it impossible to put together the perfect first aid kit."

"Go ahead and try," they write, "but eventually, if you spend enough time in the backcountry, you will one day wish for something that is not there."

Because it is impossible to carry everything you might need for an outdoors emergency, your next best bet is knowledge. That is, learn what to do in an emergency. You can carry a first aid or instruction manual with you if you are really worried. Taking a first aid course (wilderness first aid—course and book offered by Outward Bound—is best) is highly recommended to those who spend a lot of time in the outdoors. Taking a course in CPR is recommended for every soul on this planet.

Besides a first aid kit and knowledge of backcountry medicine, it is important to know what you're getting into. Backpacking is more than just a walk in the woods. If you are not prepared to deal with the discomforts that are inherent in carrying a thirty to seventy pound pack on your back as well as the inconveniences involved in a backpacking trip, you need to seriously reconsider getting into the sport. When backpacking, the outdoors is your home. You may have the shelter of a tent over your head at night, but other than that, the sky is your roof and everything beneath it shares its home with you, including poisonous plants (poison ivy), nasty insects (bees, mosquitos, ticks), and rocks, roots, mud, . . . all potential accidents waiting to happen.

I've suffered blisters from new boots, a charlie horse from a slimy puncheon, burns from tipsy pack stoves, mosquito bites and bee stings, scrapes and scratches. Fortunately, all minor injuries that a basic first aid kit easily handled.

But, I am not an expert and I am not going to try to be. I think it is important to list the major categories of medical emergencies that occur and give you some idea of how to prevent them. For the most part, I have listed them in alphabetical order because any other order would imply that one medical emergency is more significant than another. While that is generally not true—one medical problem in the outdoors is just as great as another—two medical emergencies are so important that they need to be mentioned first. If a person is not breathing they will die. If a person is bleeding profusely they may well die. If a person is breathing and they are not bleeding to death, however, you generally have time to react. So, here's the list . . .

Breathing Problems

As I said above, if a person is not breathing they will die. If you do not know how to establish an airway and perform artificial respiration, you should take a CPR course before you head out into the wilderness. Artifical respiration is part of cardio-pulmonary resuscitation and will be taught in a CPR course. There are many instances, particularly in drownings and heart attacks, where CPR has saved lives. Watch the television series Emergency 911 sometime—you're bound to see CPR used several times in every episode.

Bleeding

Unless you have a severe aversion to blood (that is, you get sick or faint at the sight of it), you should be able to handle minor injuries while hiking. (See the section on wounds in this chapter.) But, what if you or a hiking partner slice an arm or a leg while whittling? Knife wounds often demand an emergency trip to the hospital. I know of many hikers, a brother included, who have watched an emergency room doctor stitch their knife wounds together.

How do you stop the bleeding until you or the victim can reach help? If the usual methods don't work—direct pressure and elevation—you have a problem on your hands. A basic first aid course will teach you what to do should a situation like this arise. If you haven't taken a course in first aid, then what you do to stop the bleeding will have to be a judgement call on your part. But, the bleeding must be stopped. Unfortunately, ignoring the problem won't make it go away. People can and do bleed to death. Once again, a first aid course is highly recommended before heading out into the wilderness.

Altitude Sickness
A friend of ours was attempting an ascent of Mt. McKinley when he began experiencing a headache and nausea, as well as unusual fatigue. Suspecting AMS (Acute Mountain Sickness), he retreated (with much regret) to their base camp that was at a much lower elevation. A pal descended with him forfeiting his ascent to help out a friend in need.

Once back in camp, his symptoms faded, but it was too late to attempt another ascent. Fortunately, he was able to leave Denali on his own two feet. Too many people experiencing altitude sickness require emergency help because they let their symptoms go too far.

Although physiological changes (increased respiration) occur at 4,000 feet, complications from altitude sickness seldom occur below 10,000 feet. High altitude is usually considered 8,000-12,000 feet; very high, 12,000-18,000; and extremely high, over 18,000 feet.

Symptoms of altitude sickness usually begin eight hours or more after a quick ascent. Your first symptom will be a

---

>>Hiking Tip<<

The best way to prevent injuries is too avoid pushing yourself. By avoiding extreme fatigue you will keep your reaction time quick and reduce the chance of accidents. As you begin to feel tired, take breaks to catch your breath and give your body a chance to recuperate.

---

headache followed by loss of appetite, nausea, lassitude, and unusual fatigue. You may even vomit and your skin could look bluish or purple.

AMS is severe when you no longer can walk a straight line—heel-to-toe. Edema, or build-up of fluid in the lungs and brain, often kills victims of AMS. Those with edema of the lungs make a crackling noise when breathing that can be heard if you press your ear to their chest. Edema of the brain causes severe headaches, hallucinations, seizures, unconsciousness, coma and then death.

The only way to cure AMS is to descend immediately; the best way to prevent AMS is acclimatize yourself to new altitudes slowly. Never ascend from sea level to 8,000 feet in one day—always spend at least one night at 5,000-7,000 feet first. Once above 8,000 feet, you should spend each night at only 1,000 feet greater than the previous night, even if you climb higher during the day. And, you'll acclimatize better if you spend two nights and days at 8,000-10,000 feet before going any higher.

Blisters

Blisters heal slowly if you continue to hike and keep them aggravated. The best way to avoid this problem is to treat blisters before they occur.

When a part of your foot feels hot or tender, stop hiking. Take your shoes and socks off and inspect the tender area. Cut out a piece of moleskin that is larger than the "hot spot".

Apply the moleskin to the hot spot, change your socks, and put your boots back on. Quick action at this stage may prevent blisters altogether.

If you do get a blister, try to leave the blister unbroken. If it is still small and relatively flat, cover the blister with moleskin and resume hiking. But if the blister gets worse, wash the area with soap and water and make a small hole in the bottom of the blister with a sterilized needle (hold it in a flame until the tip turns red) so that the fluid drains. Once the blister is drained, apply a sterile bandage to prevent further irritation and infection.

If the blister is already broken, treat it like an open wound (cleanse and bandage) and watch for signs of infection. If necessary, quit hiking for a day or two and let your blisters heal.

Bruises

Bruises occur while backpacking when your pack is improperly fitted or when you fall. It's easy to prevent bruising from your pack by using the tips in Chapter 9 to fit your pack to your body. Watching your step may keep you from falling.

If the bruise is severe and it is not helped by elevation and cold compresses and it increases in both pain and size, it could indicate internal injuries or a fracture. Help should be sought.

Burns

Burns are easy to prevent because you need only use a modicum of caution. Sitting too close to a campfire, carelessly lighting your backpacking stove or igniting it in a tent, ignoring the sun and refusing to wear sunscreen, and improperly stablizing your cookpot (on the stove or over a fire) are all sure ways to get burned. With a little extra care and caution you should be able to avoid hurting yourself. But, accidents do happen.

First-degree burns, including sunburn, appear bright red.

Treat these minor burns by pouring cold water over the burned area and applying cold compresses for five to ten minutes. The skin should be allowed to air dry if possible. Sunburn can be prevented by the use of a sunscreen with a sun protection factor of fifteen or more. Continued exposure to sun can cause severe burning and, eventually, skin cancer. Antiseptic burn sprays may be used with first-degree burns, but should not be used with second- or third-degree burns.

Second-degree burns are characterized by bright red skin, blisters, and swelling. Do not break the blisters. Rather, immerse the burn in cold water or pour cold water over the burned area. Quick action will help reduce the burning effect of heat in the deeper layers of skin. Cover the burn with a sterile bandage.

Third-degree burns are highly unlikely on a hike. These burns are distinguished by charred flesh and must be treated in a hospital. If third-degree burns occur, do not remove clothing that may adhere to the burns. If you cannot get to a hospital within an hour, give the victim a weak solution of salt water to sip on. The solution will help replace essential fluids that have been lost because of the burns. Unlike first- and second-degree burns, do not immerse the burn in cold water. Cover the area with a clean cloth and get the victim to a doctor immediately.

Stop, Drop, and Roll

A group of backpackers was sitting around a campfire in Michigan when several flaming limbs tumbled over the rocks of the fire ring. Most of the campers were able to jump back in time, but one unlucky hiker, Jack Lean, caught a flaming branch in his lap that quickly ignited his pants.

Fortunately, he reacted quickly, dropping immediately to the ground and smothering the flame against the earth. His friends helped by dousing his thighs with cold water from their canteens while a couple of friends removed the burned clothing to assess the damage, others high-tailed it to the nearest spring for more cold water. Jack's friends continued to douse his legs with cold water for ten minutes until they were sure that his skin and the tissue beneath it were no longer hot.

Due to his quick reaction and the help of his fellow backpackers, Jack suffered only second-degree burns. It is important that you remember—Stop, Drop, and Roll.

The natural tendency is to run, but this will only fuel the flames. By dropping immediately, flames to the ground, you can smother the fire. By rolling back and forth or in complete circles (depending on the extent of the flames), you will completely douse the flames by denying them oxygen.

Fortunately, burns from campfires are rare. But keep in mind that many of today's synthetic fibers are prone to melting rather than igniting. This can make burns more dangerous because the material melts into your skin instead of ashing and flaking away.

Cold Weather Medical Emergencies

Hypothermia and frostbite are the dangers you face when hiking in cold weather and/or on ice and snow. Humid and windy conditions and wet clothes increase the effects of the cold. If you are fatigued, smoking, drinking alcoholic beverages or under emotional stress, your body is even less resistant. You can prevent injuring yourself when hiking in cold temperatures by keeping these things in mind. If it is really cold, wet and windy, your best bet may be to set up your tent and crawl into your sleeping bag. A little warmth and rest may be all you need to combat the cold.

Hypothermia

It was a rainy day in Georgia, about forty-five degrees, and Ken couldn't wait to get to his planned campsite and make himself some hot tea. A half hour later, soaked to the skin, he arrived at the spring that marked the camping area. Rather than pitch his tent, change into some warm clothes, and crawl into his sleeping bag, Ken decided to pull out his pack stove and make himself the tea he had been longing for.

With numb fingers and a slight case of the shivers, it took Ken several tries to get his stove lit. Cursing, he fumbled open the cap of his nalgene and shakily poured water into his cook pot. Then, apathetically, he sat on the cold, wet ground and waited for his water to boil.

By the time little bubbles began to rise from the bottom of the pot, Ken was shivering so badly that he couldn't control his hand movements. Missing his cup entirely, he poured the hot water all over the soggy ground. Cursing and weeping, Ken stumbled over to the spring for more water. With much difficulty, he was able to get some water in his nalgene; but when he returned to his stove, he was unable to light it, and frankly, no longer cared to.

His shivering was stopping, he was feeling kind of sleepy, and he was enjoying the trees. They were dancing for him. The next morning, two hikers found Ken lying lifeless by his stove.

The first signs of hypothermia—shivering, numbness, drowsiness, and marked muscular weakness—are followed by mental confusion and impairment of judgment, slurred speech, failing eyesight, and eventually, unconsciousness. Death, if it occurs, is usually due to heart failure. Be aware that the most serious warning sign that a hypothermia victim is going down fast is when the shivering stops. It means the victim is close to death.

You are most likely to become hypothermic after you have stopped hiking, especially if you are tired. Movement keeps you warm. Your body's core temperature can drop once you stop.

Fortunately, hypothermia is easy to combat if caught

early. If you arrive at your campsite on a cold, wet day and are experiencing any of the symptoms mentioned above, drop everything and make yourself warm. Strip yourself of your wet clothes and put on dry clothes if possible. Crawl into your sleeping bag and if you're able, heat up something hot to drink—tea, soup, hot chocolate. Anything hot will help raise your internal temperature. Drinks with a high sugar content are best. You may want to carry along a pack of fruit gelatin. It tastes great when heated and contains a lot of sugar. But get your body warm first! Don't take the time to heat yourself something to drink until you've rid yourself of the wet clothes.

If you're with someone else or happen on someone showing signs of hypothermia, try sharing body heat. If you're not too shy, strip down to your underwear or to nothing at all and crawl into a sleeping bag with the victim. Direct skin contact does wonders for transferring heat. Once the victim is in dry clothes, wrapped in a warm sleeping bag, and sipping on something warm to drink, you can try building a fire for added warmth.

Remember to take hypothermia seriously. Most hypothermia victims die in forty- to fifty-degree weather.

Frostbite
Frostbite occurs when crystals begin to form either superficially or in the fluids and soft tissues of the skin. Keep in mind that the effects of frostbite will be more severe if the affected area is thawed and then refrozen. Fortunately, the areas affected by frostbite are usually small. The nose, cheeks, ears, fingers, and toes are the most common areas.

Before frostbite occurs, the area will look flushed and then become white or grayish yellow. Pain is often felt early but usually subsides—if you feel any pain at all.

If you suspect frostbite, the first thing to do is to cover the frozen part and provide the victim with extra clothing and blankets or double wrap in sleeping bags. If possible, bring the victim indoors (a tent will do if nothing else is available) and provide him with a warm drink. Rewarm the frozen part quickly by immersing it in lukewarm water. Continue to keep the water warm. If water is not practical or available, wrap the affected part gently in warm blankets, clothes, etc.

Handle the frostbitten area gently. Do not massage it. Once thawed, the area will swell severely and become flushed once more. At this point, discontinue warming it and have the victim exercise the part if possible.

Cleanse the frostbite with water and soap, and rinse it thoroughly before blotting it dry with clean towels or whatever you have handy that is clean and dry. If blisters have formed, do not break them.

If fingers or toes are involved, place gauze between them to keep them separated. Do not apply any other dressings unless you intend to transport the victim to medical aid. Also, elevate the frostbitten parts and protect them from contact with bedclothes. If toes are involved, the victim should not walk and additional heat should not be applied once the part is thawed. When you are alone and your feet and toes are frozen, do not attempt to thaw them out if you intend to walk to medical assistance.

If you decide to transport the victim, cover the affected areas with a clean cloth, apply temporary dressings, keep affected parts elevated, and continue to give victim fluids.

A note on windchill: When the wind starts to blow, even temperatures in the fifties can be dangerous. The lower the temperature and the greater the wind, the more hazardous the conditions. As I sit here writing this, air temperatures in the teens have the feel of below zero degrees because of the ten to twenty mile per hour winds. The following chart will give you some idea of the temperature your body feels when the winds are blowing:

· Wind Chill Chart ·

Wind (MPH)	Actual temperature in degrees Fahrenheit						
	40	30	20	10	0	-10	-20
	Wind chill equivalent temperatures						
Calm	40	30	20	10	0	-10	-20
5	35	25	15	5	-5	-15	-25
10	30	15	5	-10	-20	-35	-45
15	25	10	-5	-20	-30	-45	-60
20	20	5	-10	-25	-35	-50	-65
25	15	0	-15	-30	-45	-60	-75
30	10	0	-20	-30	-50	-65	-80
35	10	-5	-20	-35	-50	-65	-80
40	10	-5	-20	-35	-55	-70	-85

Drowning

Knowing how to swim is essential for backcountry backpacking. You will often have to cross streams and on really hot days you will be tempted to immerse yourself in streams, ponds, and lakes even if you don't know how to swim. But even Olympic swimmers can have accidents. Between six and eight thousand people die each year by drowning. And, drowning is a distinct possibility in the wilderness where caution is often thrown to the wind and certified lifeguards are nowhere to be found.

I have had two close calls while hiking—both times involved stream crossings after a storm. Once I was nearly pulled beneath a log that I was using for support as I crossed. Another time I was actually flipped over before I could grab a large boulder and keep myself from being swept downstream. Both times I was wearing a backpack.

It is essential to unfasten your hipbelt when packing across a stream, river, etc. Had I not been able to save myself at those moments, I would have been able to shrug my pack off my shoulders and increase my chances for survival. A pack will drag you under. People have died when they couldn't get their pack off their back.

Before heading into the wilderness, make sure that either you or someone else you are hiking with has recently taken a CPR course because once the drowning victim has been removed from the water (and sometimes even before) you may have to perform artifical respiration. If there is no pulse, you will need to use CPR. When dealing with a drowning, always send for help. Without proper care, lung infections and other problems can set in that might lead to death.

Foot and Leg Problems

Extreme pain, and often swelling, characterizes hiking-related problems in the knees, shins, ankles, and feet. Taking a day or two off will often relieve the problem, but if the pain continues (or the swelling increases), only a doctor can tell you if your problem requires medical treatment.

It is not unusual for a hiker to experience some sort of pain every day he is on the trail. As one backpaker put it, "If the pain moves around, you're probably all right; but if it remains in one place, then it is more than likely something serious." Don't wait to see a doctor if there is swelling and continual pain. Nothing is worth causing permanent damage to your body. The doctor probably will prescribe an anti-inflammatory and tell you to keep off your feet for a week or more.

Even if you're hiking long distance, it's not the end of the world. Frank had shin splints while hiking the Appalachian Trail and was forced to take a week off. We still managed to complete the trail in six months—five months of hiking and a month off for various reasons, including the shin splints. But had he not seen a doctor, he could have caused permanent damage to his calves, including gangrene.

One of the most common complaints is knee pain. Fortunately, the tenderness in the joints doesn't necessarily signal a problem. Aspirin or other pain relievers can help alleviate some of the pain. Wearing a knee brace can help prevent knee problems or aid in support once a problem develops. If you have a history of knee problems, it is a good idea to carry a brace just in case.

Strains and sprains
A strain is simply a pulled muscle (something weightlifters do on purpose to increase muscle bulk). A strained muscle should be treated with cold if the pain appears suddenly, with warmth if the pain sets in gradually. After a couple of days, heat should be used in most cases. The muscle can be used, but if it hurts, don't do it.

A sprain, on the other hand, is a more serious injury. A sprain occurs when a joint and the ligaments that hold it are damaged. Unless treated properly, a sprain can stay with you the rest of your life.

When I was a child, my brother, sister, and I would play Batman by jumping off my top bunk onto the trundle bed. One day, I missed the trundle and hit the floor; my foot rolled and there was searing pain. My father had a clothful of ice on my ankle before I'd completed my first wail of pain. (My brother wasn't so lucky—on a separate occasion, Batman missed the trundle and broke his collarbone.)

My father's quick reaction saved me later pain. After my ankle had been thoroughly numbed, it was wrapped with an Ace bandage and I was forced (or should I say "bribed" with peppermint candy) to stay on the sofa with my foot elevated for awhile.

A sprain can be as simple as overstretching the ligament or as complex as tearing the ligament. Unfortunately, sprains don't hurt as much as they should and are often not treated until the awful swelling is noticed many hours later (and too late).

Treating a sprain is relatively simple, even in the backcountry. Take all pressure off the sprained body part immediately. Let's assume it's your ankle because that is the most likely thing you'll sprain while backpacking. Lie down and elevate your leg (that means make sure it's higher than your heart). A cold compress can be made by soaking a bandana or t-shirt in cold water—the evaporation will help cool the injury. Once numbed, let the injury re-warm for ten to fifteen minutes. An Ace bandage (there should be one in your first aid kit) is used to wrap the sprained ankle. After applying a gauze pad over the swelling on the sprained joint, use "figure of eight" winding to wrap the joint. Be careful not to wrap too tightly because you don't want to impair circulation.

Continue to use cold compresses on the injured joint for the next several days, and as soon as the swelling begins to recede, begin exercising the injured part. Never overdo it. If it starts to swell and ache again, retreat and begin the process over again. It is important that you exercise the sprain so that the muscles do not atrophy. And keep in mind that it will take a good two months before your joint is back to normal again.

Fractures
Fractures are serious injuries and will require evacuation from the backcountry. When someone has a possible fracture, your first move should be to look for swelling, discoloration, asymmetry, and severe pain. If you're not sure, assume it is a fracture.

Never try to set the fracture or straigten the injured part unless the limb is bent under the person and you are several hours from help. And in that case, move the limb very gently. Wet clothing should be cut away so that the victim may be kept warm.

If the fracture is of the collarbone, upper arm, elbow, forearm, wrist, finger, ankle, or foot, you may be able to splint it. Use heavy sticks or tent poles for splints and bandanas or clothing for padding. Splinting should immobilize the joint above and below the injury unless the break is isolated in a joint. If the victim is able to walk, get him to help as soon as possible.

If the fracture is not in one of the places listed above, you should have the victim lie as quietly as possible. Protect and immobilize the injured area by surrounding it with sleeping bags, clothing, and other appropriate materials. Make sure the victim remains warm and go for help.

Hot Weather Medical Emergencies
The three hot weather ailments described below are serious problems. The best advice is to avoid them by taking a few precautions in hot weather.

First, when you are hiking in the heat, try to maintain a consistent intake of fluids. Dehydration can lead to these more serious hot weather ailments. Second, if the heat starts to get to you, take a break. Sit down in the shade, drink some water, and give your body time to cool off. For more information on dehydration, see Chapter 2.

Heat Cramps
Heat cramps are an early sign of heat exhaustion, especially if the victim is dehydrated. Cramps occur first in the muscles of the legs and abdomen. If you're experiencing heat cramps, sip salt water (one teaspoon of table salt per quart), drinking sixteen ounces over a period of an hour. Massaging will help relieve the cramped muscles according to the American National Red Cross book on first aid.

Heat Exhaustion

If the heat cramps are not treated and lead to heat exhaustion, you will find that the body temperature is nearly normal. The victim's skin is pale and feels cool and clammy. It is possible that the victim will faint, but lowering his head will help him to regain consciousness. Weakness, nausea, heavy sweating, severe headache, and dizziness are symptoms of heat exhaustion.

As with heat cramps, the victim needs to drink a diluted solution of salt water. Lay the victim down, loosen his clothing, and raise his feet eight to twelve inches. Applying cool wet cloths will also help relieve heat exhaustion. If the victim vomits, stop the salt water intake. At this point, medical attention should be sought. If you experience heat exhaustion on a hike, it would be wise to take a day off or even cancel the remainder of the hike.

Heat Stroke

Treatment of heat stroke should be immediate. You will know when a hiker has heat stroke because his skin will be hot, red, and dry. His pulse will be rapid and strong, and he will probably lapse into unconsciousness.

Undress the hiker and bathe his skin with cool water or place him in a stream or other cold body of water if possible. Once his temperature lowers, dry him off. If cold water is not available, fan him with whatever you have on hand. If his temperature rises again, resume the cooling process. Never give a hiker with heat stroke stimulants such as tea.

In the case of heat stroke, the victim should receive medical attention as soon as possible. Heat stroke is a life threatening situation.

Lightning

While playing Trivial Pursuit one night, our team was asked what natural disaster claims the most victims each year. We thought about it—floods, earthquakes, tornadoes, tsunamis. We finally decided on floods because of the number of people killed during monsoon season. We fell out of our seats when we learned it was lightning. We hadn't even considered it. Really? Lightning?

Sure enough. Lightning kills between one hundred and three hundred people each year, particularly between May and September. An encyclopedia informed us that lightning strikes a hundred times a second worldwide with as much as 200 million volts, 300,000 amps, and 8,000 degrees Centigrade. Ouch! Fortunately, when you're outside during a lightning storm, it is usually just a matter of luck that you are not hit.

Lightning can strike three ways—within a cloud, cloud-to-cloud, and cloud-to-ground. Cloud-to-ground lightning can injure you in four different ways: by direct strike, when the bolt hits you directly; by the splash or side flash, when lightning hits something else but flashes through the air to hit you as well; by ground current (the most common method of injuring humans), when the lightning strikes a tree, for instance, and the current runs through the ground or water and into you; and by the blast effect, when you are thrown by the sudden expansion of air caused by a strike. Some people get lucky when the ground current charge passes over and around them without entering their body. This is called the flashover effect.

There are a number of types of injuries a lightning victim can receive—traumatic, respiratory, neurologic, and cardiac injuries, as well as burns and everything from loss of hearing to vomiting. Treatment is for the type of injury the victim has sustained. Knowing cardio-pulmonary resuscitation will be invaluable to you in a lightning case because most victims can be revived by this method. Never assume that a lightning victim is all right. Always go for help.

Lightning can strike from a mile away, so once you see your first flash begin counting—one one-thousand, two one-thousand, etc. If you hear the thunder when you reach five one-thousand, you are within range (one mile) of the storm. That's when you need to find a safe spot. Storms move quickly, it's doubtful you can outrun it.

So what's safe? Not much. Avoid bodies of water and low places that can collect water. Avoid high places, open places, tall objects, metal objects, wet caves, and ditches. Your best bet is a small stand of trees. Sit on a sleeping pad (unless it has metal in it) with your knees pulled up against your chest, head bowed, arms hugging knees. If you're in a group, spread out but make sure you can all see at least one other person in case any one gets hit.

Rashes
While camping in the Los Padres National Forest in California, my family had one of its worst experiences ever. As we sat eating dinner at our picnic table, we watched as another family gathered wood for their campfire. After a while, their roaring fire began sending streamers of smoke our way. Coughing and waving our hands, we were eventually forced to flee our dinner table.

While gathering wood for our own fire, my father made a disconcerting discovery—the other family was burning poison oak. Unlike poison ivy, poison oak (even though it has leaves of three) is hard to recognize. We had been playing in the poison oak all day.

By the next day, we were absolutely miserable and covered from head to foot in a light rash (fortunately, it was an

Posion Sumac (top right), Posion Ivy (bottom left), and Poison Oak.

early rash for me—poison oak, ivy and sumac get worse each time you get it). Our throats ached and itched from the smoke we had inhaled.

The best thing to do once you realize you've had one-on-one contact with the poisons—ivy, oak, sumac—is to take a cool or cold bath and completely cleanse yourself with soap. After that, use Calamine or other poison ivy-specific lotions. Cortisone creams help some (I've had poison ivy so bad I've needed cortisone shots). Antihistamines such as Benadryl also offer some relief. Prophylactics are available, although how well they prevent you from getting rashes from poison plants is debatable.

Your best defense against poison ivy, sumac and oak is to be able to identify and steer clear of them. As the saying goes—leaves of three, let them be.

Poison ivy isn't the only rash you're likely to get while hiking. Rashes caused by friction, heat, and humidity are also common, especially in the crotch area. One way to deal with this problem is to apply vaseline to the areas that rub against one another. If heat is the problem, try to keep the area as cool as possible. Shorts with built-in liners will keep you drier than shorts and underwear because they are made to allow moisture to escape. If the rash gets to be a real problem, try sleeping nude at night to allow the area to dry as thoroughly as possible. Powder will also help keep the problem area dry. If the rash begins to look fungal, there are a number of over-the-counter products, such as Desenex, that will clear it up.

Hip belt rashes—when the hip belt is too loose and rubs the hiker's hips raw—are common. This happened to me in the heat of the summer, and the combination of the hip belt rubbing through my cotton shorts and the sweat soon caused a mean wound across my lower back in the shape of the hipbelt. It bled and scabbed and bled and scabbed and left me nearly frantic with pain. Changing to a pair of nylon shorts

> **>>Hiking Tip<<**
> Don't step on anything you can step over; don't step over
> anything you can step around.

solved the problem—the material was slick enough to keep
the hip belt gliding rather than rubbing against my hips. I
already had the smallest hip belt available for the pack so that
wasn't an option.

An opposite problem many hikers develop are swollen and
bruised hips caused by the pressure of a heavy load on the hip
belt. Other than lightening your pack, there is really no way
to avoid this. Fortunately, every day you're on the trail the
pack gets lighter until you resupply again. The welts on our
hips usually disappeared a day or two after we settled an
especially heavy load on our backs.

Wounds
It is not unusual to experience minor and sometimes major
wounds—abrasions, incisions, lacerations, and punctures—
while hiking. Avulsions, though rare, are also possible.

I still bear the scars of some of my falls, most of which
involved slipping on leaves, roots, or rocks. Sometimes it
doesn't matter how careful you are, you're just going to fall.
Any backpacker can relate a major fall story. Our favorite is
a fall that I wish I could have captured on video. It was really
a very minor slope, but somehow I slipped (on a rock or slick
leaves) and my feet went flying out from under me. Soon I was
rolling down the hill. Although Frank laughed at me, he soon
found himself in the same predicament. It wasn't long before
we were entangled and rolling down the slope together. It
must have been a comic sight. Fortunately, neither of us
suffered more than a few bruises. We picked ourselves up,
dusted off, and headed up the trail.

When someone is injured to such a degree that there is a flow of blood from the wound, you need to do three things: 1)stop the bleeding, 2)prevent infection, and 3)promote healing.

Here are two methods, described in order of preference, that should be used to stop bleeding:

1) With a dressing or a cloth, apply direct pressure over the wound. In most instances this will stop the bleeding and the thick pad of cloth will absorb blood and allow it to clot. Once the blood clots, leave it alone. If blood should soak the pad before clotting, do not remove the pad but add another layer to the already soaked cloth and increase your pressure on the wound. If you need both your hands to help the victim, apply a pressure bandage with a strip of cloth. Place it over the pad on the wound, wrap it around the body part, and then tie a knot directly over the pad.

2) Elevate the wounded part, unless there is evidence of a fracture, above the victim's heart. This will also help reduce blood-flow. Wounds of the hand, neck, arm, or leg should be elevated and direct pressure should be continued.

These methods will stop most bleeding, but taking a course in first aid will teach you other options (too technical and risky for discussion here) to use if the bleeding doesn't stop with direct pressure and elevation.

Preventing infection goes hand-in-hand with proper cleansing of the wound. Your first step is to wash your hands and to avoid contaminating the wound further. That is, don't breathe on it, cough or sneeze on it, drool on it, throw dirt on it, etc. Cleaning means cleansing around and sometimes in the wound. You can make an antiseptic wash by using the povidone-iodine in your first aid kit or soap and water or just plain water if that is all you have.

Cleanse around the wound with a sterile gauze pad and in the wound only if there is foreign material in it. Always rinse everything, even the antiseptic wash, from the wound before you dress it. You can irrigate the wound with water from a plastic bag that has a pin hole (to direct the stream of water).

If foreign matter remains in the wound after irrigation, you may try using sterilized tweezers (sterilize by holding them to a flame until red hot or by boiling them in water—make sure they cool down a bit before you apply them to the wound). If you can remove all foreign objects and have stopped the bleeding, allow the wound to air dry a while before dressing it. If you can't remove the foreign objects or the wound is big, keep it moist until you can get to a doctor. If it is a gaping wound, apply a butterfly bandage after bringing the folds of skin together. Some first aid books do not advocate the use of butterfly bandages because it is felt that the bandages promote infection. Do as your conscience sees fit.

When dressing a wound, do not touch the sterile dressing except at the edges where it will not come in contact with the wound. If possible, the dressing should extend at least one inch past the edges of the wound.

The dressing should be bandaged snugly but not too tight. Remember to check it often and never apply tape on the wound. Also, if you use tincture of benzoin on the healthy skin, the tape will stick better; but don't get the benzoin in the wound because it will hurt and encourage infection.

Abrasions
Most of the wounds you'll suffer when hiking will be abrasions, which occur when the outer layers of the protective skin are damaged, usually when the skin is scraped against a hard surface.

Although bleeding is usually limited, danger of contamination and infection still exists. Simply cleansing the wound, applying an antiseptic, and keeping it clean until healed will avoid serious problems.

Incisions

An incision occurs when body tissue is cut with a sharp object. When hiking, most incisions are the product of poor knife handling. People can never seem to remember that they are supposed to cut away from their body. I've seen a number of hikers forced to head off for emergency help because they sliced their hands while whittling.

An incised wound often bleeds heavily and rapidly, and if deep, can damage muscles, tendons, and nerves. Incisions need immediate attention, even if small, because they can easily become infected. Whether a deep or shallow cut, the bleeding should be stopped immediately. If the wound is large, you should also treat for shock.

Punctures

The most likely puncture wound you will receive while backpacking is a splinter. But if you walk around barefoot, you're asking for all manner of foot wounds. Keep shoes of some sort on at all times.

When several layers of skin are pierced by a sharp object, you have a puncture wound. Although bleeding is usually limited, internal damage can result if tissues and muscle are pierced. Infection is likelier because there is no flushing action from blood. Cleanse the wound; and if there is a foreign object (such as a splinter) that is easily removable, do so with a pair of sterilized tweezers or needle. Objects imbedded deeply in the tissue should be removed only by a doctor.

Amputation

If tissue is forcibly separated or torn from the victim's body, seek help as soon as possible. Bleeding will usually be quite heavy and should be stopped before transporting the victim, if possible. Send the avulsed body part along with the victim to the hospital. It can often be reattached.

Getting Help

The above was a list of some of the more common emergencies you might face on a backpacking trip. There are a host of others—everything from abdominal pain to diabetic shock to spinal injuries. All of these take a knowledge of first aid that cannot be encompassed in this book. Taking a first aid course will introduce you to these problems and what to do about them.

While talking to a couple of rangers on a mountain trail in Washington, a friend of ours took a step backwards while saying farewell and stepped off a cliff. The rangers quickly sent for help, but it took a major evacuation effort before she could be reached and her injuries assessed. Even two rangers, knowledgeable in wilderness first aid, were forced to make a judgement call on how to handle this outdoor emergency.

I can't tell you how to evacuate a person who has just fallen off a cliff, but if I had to make that decision, there are a number of questions I would have to consider. How far is help? Is the person already dead? Is there someone around more qualified to deal with the situation? Can the victim be reached? Is the temperature detrimental (too hot or too cold) to the victim? Is the victim breathing or bleeding? And so on.

In emergency situations that require evacuation you will be faced with many choices. But unless you're trained in wilderness rescue, you would be best advised to go for help rather than trying to evacuate the victim yourself. I can't put it more simply. Never evacuate the victim yourself. Let professionals handle it. If you try to evacuate the victim yourself, you may injure him further. And unfortunately, that means you can be sued. The world is in a sad state when good Samaritans are sued for trying to rescue someone, but it happens all the time.

If something has happened and someone(s) need to be evacuated, send for help as soon as possible. In the meantime, there are a number of things you can do to make the injured

---

❦ *Hiking Secret* ❦

In emergency situations that require the use of distress signals, try using a space blanket as an emergency flag. The reflector-like silver coating of the lightweight blanket will be highly visible to aircraft when attached to a tall tree.

---

person more comfortable. According to *Emergency Medical Procedures for the Outdoors*, you can:

- Set up a shelter and protect the victim from direct contact with the ground if possible.
- Cover the victim with a shirt, jacket, sweater, etc. to retain body heat.
- Leave or provide food and water.
- Make sure victim is comfortable.
    If it is an extreme emergency and time is of essence, you may want to try using distress signals:
- Standard ground-to-air signals: one rectangular shape means "require doctor—serious injuries," two rectangular shapes, side by side, mean "require medical supplies." Build these symbols as large as possible by digging in sand or snow or earth. You can also use tree limbs, rocks, clothing, or whatever else you might have on hand to represent the image. The most important thing is to make sure the image is clearly visible from above and that it contrasts with the ground color as much as possible.
- Universal distress signals: a series of three sights or sounds and can include shouts, whistle blasts, high-frequency beeps, gunshots, and flashes of light.
- SOS Morse Code distress signal: a series of three dots, three dashes, three dots (...---...) means SOS or Help! They can be made by blows on a whistle, high-frequnecy beeps, or flashes of light—three short blasts, beeps, or flashes—three long and three short.

- A large flag at the top of a tree, the brighter the better.
- A mirror or other shiny object can be flashed across the sky several times a day to attract planes.
- Flares.

If you must leave the victim, alone or with others, it is important to mark your trail (unless it is already clearly blazed). You can do this with branches, cairns (rock mounds), arrows carved in the dirt or snow, grass tied in bunches, sticks dug into the ground at the side of the trail, torn pieces of cloth tied to branches, or whatever you can think of to ensure help can find its way to the victim.

It's a dangerous world out there and the Boy Scouts had the right idea when they chose as their motto the succinct, "Be prepared." Basically, if you plan on surviving on this planet that is predominately water; in a world where every day you face the spectre of death in automobiles and lunatics with guns; and within an environment where even fresh air and clear water carry potential hazards—you need to be prepared. It's easily done! Courses in CPR, first aid, and self-defense are offered in nearly every county, parish, and township in the United States. So, before you head out into the backcountry, be prepared. Or hike with someone who is.

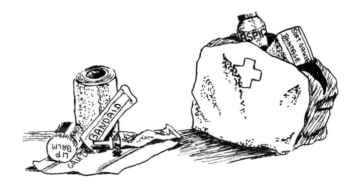

· 12 ·
Problem Animals

THE SUN HAD SET and Laurie and Kevin Turner were dozing off in their tent when they were startled out of imminent sleep by the gentle snuffling of a large animal. Camping in Yosemite National Park, they expected bears to invade their camp and had carefully strung their food bags more than ten feet off the ground between two trees. What they hadn't expected was what they were soon to term "Kamikaze Bears." Cringing inside their sleeping bags, they listened to the bear claw its way up a tree. Peeking out of their tents, they were treated to a most unusual sight.

Launching itself from the tree, the bear was attempting to dive bomb the food bag. It worked! The rope snapped and the food bag and the bear tumbled to the ground. Our friends watched, dumbfounded, as the bear opened up the bag and began to munch its way through their week's supply of food.

Bears, raccoons and other animals are ingenious when it comes to parting backpackers from their food. When the recommended methods don't work, you're left with no other option than to hike backward or forward to restock your supplies. Fortunately (or maybe unfortunately), you rarely find these street-smart animals outside of state or national parks.

Bears

The Black Bear has a commanding presence and can summon an ominous "woof" to warn backpackers to stay away; but a face-to-face encounter will probably end with the bear ambling, if not scurrying, away. Bears are hunted in national forests and so they are usually wary of humans; but in national parks, bears can be conniving and aggressive when it comes to looking for food. Bears are also notoriously unpredictable and can be very vicious.

The National Park Service offers some tips for how to handle bear encounters as well as how to prevent them from getting into your food and pack. The following list is based on those recommendations:

- If you stop to take a break, keep your pack nearby. If a bear approaches, throw your pack on, pick up whatever you have out, and leave the area. Bears have been known to bluff hikers into leaving food behind. Don't fall for this ploy, but on the other hand, don't take your time getting out, either. Avoid trouble at all costs. Bears seldom attack, but when they do they can cause plenty of damage.
- If the bear continues to approach, loosen your hip belt in case you have to drop your pack. Keep your face turned toward the bear and slowly back away from it.
- If a bear charges, don't run. Like many animals, bears react to running as if it is "food" trying to escape. Don't bother trying to climb a tree, either; bears are adept at climbing trees, and can probably do so faster and better than you can. They also can outrun you.
- If the bear is a lone black bear, you can try and fight back by screaming, yelling and kicking at it. That is often enough to scare it away. You may also want to try dropping your pack to distract it. If these ploys don't work, react as you would with a grizzly or mother with cubs (following page):

- If you are charged by a grizzly or a mother with cubs, your best bet is to lie on the ground in the fetal position, arms drawn up to protect your face and neck. Most bears will leave you alone if you do this or content themselves with a scratch or two.
- Never, ever look a bear (or any animal) in the eye. Direct eye contact is perceived as aggressive.
- If, while backing away, you lose sight of the bear, move downwind of the bear and continue on your way. Keep an eye out for the bear until you are positive the bear has not followed you.
- Never, under any circumstances, try to feed a bear or leave food to attract one. Once a bear has tasted human food, he will continue to search for it, which means trouble for the bear as well as for humans.
- When making camp for the night, stash your food in a bag (a heavy-duty garbage bag may mask the smell of your food) and make sure it is securely tied off the ground and between two trees. The bag should be approximately ten feet off the ground and ten feet from the nearest tree. In areas where there are a lot of bears, bearproof means of storage are often provided for hikers. For example, in the Smoky Mountains, chain-link fences keep bears from getting into shelters (although bears have been known to keep humans from getting into the shelters when the door in the fence has been left open). In other places, the park service provides bear poles—tall, metal poles with four prongs at the top from which food bags can be suspended. A gaff is provided to lift the food to the top of the pole.

A special word about Grizzlies: Edward Abbey once said, "If people persist in trespassing upon the grizzlies' territory, we must accept the fact that the grizzlies, from time to time, will harvest a few trespassers." But what if you're not willing

to sacrifice your life to the Great Griz? Fortunately, when hiking in griz country, there are some precautions you can take to avoid meeting up with one of these legendary creatures.

When hiking, stop and listen every five minutes or so, especially if it is windy. Grizzly bears are loud, particularly when they are not yet aware that their territory has been invaded.

Keep your head up. It is very likely that you can spot a grizzly before it spots you and thus avoid a potentially dangerous situation. If you've got your headphones on and are just hopping it to your next campsite, chances are you won't make it there. If you're hiking in griz country your life may depend on your alertness.

I once left a sign on the trail that spelled out in rocks, "Get water here." I used sticks to make arrows to point at a spring. We had found out the hard way that once we'd made camp (at an established site) that it was a good quarter-mile trek back to the spring for water. Only one out of eight hikers saw the sign! But that was nothing compared to the time that a fellow we were hiking with was oblivious to the 16" by 20" painting of the Pope that was propped against a trailside tree. I still don't know how he missed it. And, if you can't spot a garish painting of the Pope, you'd better reconsider any trip into grizzly country.

Whether or not to walk into or with the wind depends on who you're asking. Grizzly expert Doug Peacock says that he walks into the wind for the most part, confident in his ability to spot grizzlies before they spot him. Peacock does say he does this only when he's heading toward potential bedding sites that he cannot otherwise get around. The government says you ought to walk with the wind so that grizzlies smell you before you spot them and disappear before you arrive.

While hiking in grizzly territory, you do not have to be unnecessarily loud to scare off the bears. A normal, conversational tone interspersed with some singing and a yell or two will suffice to alert bears of your impending presence. If you feel as if you must make lots of noise (bang pans, clang bells, etc.) just to feel safe, forget it and hike somewhere that is safe.

Be on the look out for cached carcasses (if you're downwind of it, you'll smell it) because it probably means there is a grizzly nearby. If you see a carcass, freeze and look around to see if you spot any grizzlies. Then retreat slowly without turning around.

Avoid bedding areas whenever possible (grizzlies like to sleep in cool places such as thickets, under deadfalls, next to trees). If you spot such an area walk around it or, at least, make a little noise.

Always, always, always sleep in a tent in grizzly country and keep a knife (for cutting an escape hatch in the tent), flashlight and firestarter handy. Although often illegal, camp away from established areas and any area where a bear is likely to travel. If you bushwhack into the brush a hundred yards or so off a trail (check for bear beds, food and trails), you'll probably be safe.

Don't bother bringing a gun, it'll only make the bear mad. And never drop your pack. Grizzlies are inteligent animals and we don't need to teach them that they can find food in backpacks. Bear repellents are iffy at best and are better left at home. Never travel at night. If possible, travel in groups because bears rarely attack a group of four or more.

If you actually come in contact with a grizzly, don't panic. Young (not baby) grizzlies can probably be scared off—stand your ground, act a bit aggressive and you'll probably send the young adult scurrying. On the other hand, if you run into cubs, there is probably a mother griz nearby. If you're within a hundred feet to a hundred yards of her precious babies, you are probably within the mother bear's critical distance, that is the distance in which she will violently defend her young'uns. I'd like to reiterate this—never, ever run from any bear. As I said before, they run faster than you and will probably chase you if you flee.

The first thing to do when you encounter any adult griz is to speak quietly, hold your arms out at your sides and avert your head. Avoid direct eye contact but do keep an eye on the bear to continue to gauge its mood. Unless the bear flattens its ears back and looks directly at you, begin to retreat—slowly. If it does flatten its ears, freeze and wait and then slowly begin to retreat.

Never make sudden movements or loud noises. Don't try to climb a tree—it takes too long and grizzlies can knock down some trees or possibly shake you out of your perch.

If you should be attacked, play possum but—in this case—don't expose your vitals. Draw up into a fetal position. Use your pack and hands to protect your neck and skull and as painful as it might be, try to stay still. It might be your only chance to save your life.

Finally, don't worry too much about sex or menstruation. Bears are not drawn irresistibly to those human odors. Keep yourself as clean as possible. You don't have to avoid back-packing trips into grizzly country just because you might be menstruating, but if you can delay your trip by a day or two, it may make you feel a bit safer. The same goes for sex. While a griz may not notice the sounds and scents of your coitus outdoorsus, do you really want to take that risk?

Snakes

In the wild, snakes lie in wait along a path for small rodents or other prey. Coiled along the edge of a trail waiting for food to pass by, the patient reptiles test the air with their flicking tongues for signs of game.

This image of the snake lying in wait just off the trail is a cause of concern among some hikers; but what about the snake's view of things? The snake is aware of its place in the food chain; it must watch for predators as well as prey. A hiker making a moderate amount of noise will usually be perceived as a predator and the snake will back-off or lie still until the "danger" passes.

To avoid confrontations with snakes, remember to make a little extra noise when you are walking through brush, deep grass, or piles of dead leaves that block your view of the footpath. This will warn snakes of your approach. By kicking at the brush or leaves slightly, you will make enough noise to cause a snake to slither off or lie still.

Many species of poisonous snakes prefer areas near rocky outcrops and can often be found among the boulders that border rocky streams as well. Generally, coral snakes appear in the south and southwest, water moccasins in the wetlands of the south, copperheads throughout the east, and rattlesnakes throughout the country. Poisonous snakes do not occur in the far north where the temperatures remain cool or downright cold most of the year. When in doubt, avoid all snakes. But keep in mind that more people die each year from insect bites than they do from snake bites.

Rattlesnakes
Rattlesnakes are heavy-bodied and can be from three to five feet long, although large rattlesnakes are increasingly rare. Rattlesnakes have large blotches and crossbands (though these are not hourglass-shaped). There are two color phases (i.e. the background color)—a yellowish and a dark, almost black phase. Sometimes their overall color is dark enough to obscure the tell-tale pattern.

The real giveaway is the prominent rattle or enlarged "button" at the end of the snake's tail. Rattlesnakes usually warn predators with a distinctive rattle; but this can't be relied on because they may also lie still as hikers go by.

Rattlesnakes are frequently seen on trails both in the west and in the east, although their presence has been greatly reduced by development encroaching on their terrain. Although found throughout the U.S., cases of rattlesnake bites are almost unheard of; and when quick action is taken, they will almost never prove fatal, except among the very young or old. Even so, rattlesnake bites are extremely dangerous and more potent than the copperhead and water moccasin because of the snake's size.

Copperheads

Copperheads are typically two to three feet in length. They are moderately stout-bodied with brown or chestnut hourglass-shaped crossbands. The background color is lighter than the crossbands, anything from reddish-brown to chestnut to gray-brown. The margins of the crossbands have a darker outline. This pattern certainly helps the copperhead blend in among dead leaves. Other, nonpoisonous snakes (e.g., corn snake) have similar patterns, but the hourglass shape is not so prominent.

Copperheads prefer companionship; if you see one copperhead, there are probably others in the area. In the spring and fall they can be seen in groups, particularly in rocky areas. Their nests have the strong and distinctive odor of cucumbers. Copperheads avoid trouble by lying still and will quickly retreat as a last resort.

The bite of the copperhead is almost never fatal. Rarely has someone weighing more than forty pounds died of a copperhead bite. While not fatal, the bite is dangerous and medical attention should be sought immediately.

Copperheads can be found from Massachusetts south to North Florida and westward to Illinois, Oklahoma and Texas.

Water Moccasin or Cottonmouth

One of the largest poisonous snakes in America, the cottonmouth's head is diamond-shaped and very distinct from the neck. Water moccasins are dull olive to brownish in color and a bit paler on their sides. Their sides also sport indistinct, wide, blackish bands. The body is very stout in proportion to length—they can be as long as five feet. With an abruptly tapering tail and eye shields, the cottonmouth is a very sinister-looking snake. It is also the most aggressive poisonous snake in the U.S.

Water moccasins, as the name implies, can be found in swamps and along streams, ponds, lakes and rivers from Southern Virginia (sometimes) south to Florida and westward into Eastern Texas. They range northward up the Mississippi as far as Illinois and Indiana.

Coral Snake

Also called the Harlequin snake, the brightly banded coral snake rarely reaches a yard long. When it comes to recognizing the coral snake, just remember, "red on yellow will kill a fellow." Broad bands of red and blue-black are separated by narrow yellow bands. Other snakes imitate the coral snake's colors but not its pattern.

Although small and rarely known to bite, the coral snake is the most venomous of the poisonous snakes inhabiting the U.S. An antivenin is needed to counteract the poison of a coral snake, which unlike the venom of the three pit vipers above, is a neurotoxin. Most coral snake bites occur when the snake is being handled because it has small fangs and needs direct contact.

The coral snake can be found from northern North Carolina to the Gulf of Mexico and westward through Texas. A smaller, less venomous species, occupies parts of Arizona.

Treating poisonous snakebites

The reaction to the bite of a poisonous snake will be swift. Discoloration and swelling of the bite area are the most visible signs. Weakness and rapid pulse are other symptoms. Nausea, vomiting, fading vision, and shock also are possible signs of a poisonous bite and may develop in the first hour or so after being bitten.

It is important to know that tourniquets can cause more damage to the victim than a snakebite. If improperly applied, the tourniquet can cause the death of the infected limb and the need for amputation. The cutting and suction methods called for in snakebite kits also are not recommended.

The best treatment is to reduce the amount of circulation in the area where the bite occurred and seek medical attention immediately. Circulation can be reduced by keeping the victim immobile (which isn't easy if the bite occurs five miles from the nearest road); by applying a cold, wet cloth to the area; or by using a constricting band. A constricting band is not a tourniquet and should be tight enough only to stop surface flow of blood and decrease the flow of lymph from the wound. The constricting band should not stop blood flow to the limb.

The Extractor, which I discuss briefly in Chapter 11, is state-of-the-art, so to speak, in snake bite kits because it uses mechanical suction (rather than mouth suction) and it does not involve cutting the bite with a razor or knife. It is also said to remove approximately thirty percent of the venom if used within five minutes of being bitten.

Treating nonpoisonous snakebites
By making a little extra noise in areas where snakes may be hidden from view, you should avoid any chance of snakebite. If a bite should occur, proper treatment is important.

The bite of a nonpoisonous snake can be dangerous. If not properly cleaned, the wound can become infected. Ideally, the victim should be treated with a tetanus shot to prevent serious infection. Although, all backpackers should have a current booster before heading out into the wilderness. Nonpoisonous snake bites will cause a moderate amount of swelling. If large amounts of swelling take place, the bite should be treated as if it were caused by a poisonous snake.

Poisonous Lizards

There are only two poisonous lizards on God's Green Earth and both of them can be found in the United States, but not in the woods and forests. The Gila Monster and the Mexican Beaded Lizard occupy the deserts of the Southwest and will bite if picked up or stepped on. You must come in direct contact with these critters because their jaws must clamp down on you for them to be able to drool venom into the wound they make with their primitive teeth. You may even have to heat the underside of their jaws with a flame before they'll let go. The bite should be treated as you would treat a snake bite.

Boars, Moose, Elk and Other Beasts

Boars, which are not indigenous to the United States (they were brought here from Europe for hunting purposes), can be found in the Southern Appalachians and throughout the deep South. They are rarely seen, and like most animals, will disappear if they hear you coming. If you happen upon a boar, try to avoid direct confrontation; just continue hiking.

Male moose and elk should be avoided during rutting season because they may mistake you for a rival and attempt to chase you out of their territory.

Females of any and all species should be avoided when they have their young with them. The instinct for protecting their young is strong and you cannot predict what a mother will do if she feels her children are threatened.

Birds are especially vicious. You may not see the grouse and her babies but she'll spot you and let you know that she is not pleased with your presence.

Only the very lucky will catch glimpses of other wild animals—wild cats, wolf, coyotes, big horn sheep. Chances of confrontation are slim.

Pests

Backpackers often attract rodents and other small mammals. These creatures are searching for food and can do much damage, especially if you do not take care to protect your belongings. It is never wise to leave your pack, and particularly your food, out on the ground for the night. Food, and sometimes whole packs, should be hung where these animals cannot reach them.

Porcupines

These nocturnal creatures love to gnaw on anything salty. Outhouses, shelters, and particularly hiking boots and backpack shoulder straps are all fair game to the porcupine. That may sound strange, but they are after the salt from your sweat. So hang your packs and boots when you're hiking in porcupine country, and take particular care in areas that are known to be frequented by porcupines.

Direct contact is necessary to receive the brunt of the porcupine's quills. Although it is unlikely for a hiker to be lashed by a porcupine's tail, it is not unusual for a dog to provoke a porcupine into defending itself. Porcupine quills become embedded in the flesh of the attacker, causing extreme pain. If the quills are not removed immediately, they can cause death.

Skunks

Skunks can be found nationwide but are usually only a problem in high-use areas. Dogs, on the other hand, can provoke skunk attacks just about anywhere. Although we've only seen a few skunks, we've been aware of their presence (that telltale odor!) on many a trip.

During the night at Ice Water Springs Shelter north of Newfound Gap in the Smokies, a brazen skunk wove around our legs as we warmed ourselves in front of the campfire. It was very pleasant, scrounging for scraps of food on the

> ## >>Hiking Tip<<
> If your pack is not in your tent with you, leave the pack pockets open at night. Mice, chipmunks and other rodents have a way of finding packs, particularly at frequently used campsites. If the pockets are open, rodents won't have to chew their way into your pack to search for food.

shelter's dirt floor and along the wire bunks. The skunk occasionally stood on its hind legs and made a begging motion, which had no doubt been perfected on earlier hikers. We didn't give in to the skunk's pleas for food, and it eventually crawled back up under the bunks as we sighed in relief.

We heard of another skunk encounter in the same shelter, perhaps with the same skunk, a year earlier. Two British hikers, who were unfamiliar with the animal, tried to chase the skunk away by throwing a boot. They were given a quick course in skunk etiquette!

Mice
Mice are the most common pests to be found in the outdoors. If you leave your pack sitting on the ground beside your tent, don't be surprised the next morning if mice have gnawed their way into your pack (if you neglect to hang it) and have helped themselves to a mouse-sized portion of your food or clothes. While we were hiking in Virginia, I decided to change into a warmer shirt, and was shocked to find that mice had gnawed several holes in the shirt's collar. On another trip, I discovered holes in my socks. Mice use the fibers they gnaw from clothes in their nests.

A few hikers carry along mousetraps, but this is a little controversial. Some hikers feel that the mice have a place in the "trail ecosystem."

Raccoons

Raccoons are also a widespread nuisance. They, too, will invade your pack searching for food. Camping along Ontario's Bruce Trail, Doug Hall was awakened one dawn by a rustling sound outside his tent. Quietly unzipping his tent fly, the beam of his flashlight soon found the culprit. Atop his pack sat a portly raccoon contentedly munching on a piece of pemmican. Several pine cones had to be lofted at the raccoon before it decided it was time to leave its comfortable perch.

Dogs

Some dogs encountered on the trail are hiking companions and others are strays or property of people who live along the trail's route. If they are strays, they can be very friendly as well as hard to get rid of. They can also be aggressive, especially if they are hungry. Other dogs can be agressive if they feel they are defending their territory or their masters.

Fortunately, most of the dogs you'll meet while backpacking are friendly, but we have also had bad experiences with dogs. In Kathmandu, we were befriended by a friendly mutt while hiking in the hills north of Swyambunath. As we passed through a small village, we were soon surrounded by a circle of vicious dogs, all eager to get their teeth into the stray, who suddenly chose to use us as its bodyguards. With hiking sticks we were able to chase all the dogs (including the stray) away and were careful not to befriend any more dogs while visiting that country.

How to Avoid Troublesome Dogs

As with bears and most other animals, don't run. Don't look directly into a dog's eyes. If it is necessary to defend yourself, use your hiking stick or small stones. Sometimes just picking up a stone and holding it as if you're going to throw it is enough to dissuade a dog. Throw the rock only if it's absolutely necessary.

Rabies

While hiking in Kathmandu we were horrified to read of a sudden outbreak of rabies in the capital's surrounding villages. After our experience with the stray dog, we were even more determined to steer clear of the animals when we heard this awful news.

For those of us who enjoy backpacking, it is wise to keep in mind that ninety-six percent of the carriers of rabies in the U.S. are wild animals. Skunks are the chief carrier followed by raccoons, bats, cattle, cats and dogs. Wolves, bobcats, coyotes, groundhogs, muskrats, weasels, woodchucks, foxes, horses and humans can also host the disease.

Transferred through saliva, death from rabies is very rare in the U.S. because treatment is available. Symptoms appear anywhere from three weeks to a year after being bit and include headache and fever, cough and sore throat, loss of appetite and fatigue, abdominal pain, nausea, vomiting and diarrhea.

If you have been bit by a mammal and are experiencing any of these symptoms, get to a doctor immediately. The rabies vaccine (a series of five shots in the arm--no longer the painful abdominal shots) may be recommended and has so far always been successful.

When bitten by any mammal, it is best to thoroughly cleanse the wound and see a doctor. You may need nothing more than a tetanus or antibiotic shot.

Please don't take the risk and forego seeing a doctor. Rabies is an incredibly painful and unpleasant disease, and past a certain stage—fatal.

Insects

You can't escape them. They're everywhere. Even in the coldest reaches of the Arctic and Antarctic, it is not surprising to stumble upon a bug. Mosquitos, bees, hornets, wasps, fire

```
❦ Hiking Secret ❦

Marines on South Carolina's Parris Island, where sand
fleas abound, mix Skin-So-Soft with alcohol (roughly half
and half) and put it in an empty pump spray bottle to make
their own DEET-free repellent.
```

ants, scorpions, ticks, chiggers, blackflies, deer and horse
flies, gnats and no-see-ums are among the millions of insects
out there that torment the human soul . . . and skin.

They invade our lives both indoors and out, and to be
perfectly honest, I find insects much easier to deal with in the
out-of-doors than inside my home or car. They may be demons
outside, but they are Satan incarnate when trapped somewhere they do not want to be. So, because you can't live with
them and you can't live without them, how do you handle
insects, especially those that like to feast on human blood?

No-see-ums
These are the smallest of our tormentors and perhaps those
most likely to drive us insane; the tiny midges and gnats that
tend to swarm otherwise happy campers. But there are ways
to avoid that which you cannot see. First of all, camp away
from running water and make sure the no-see-um netting on
your tent is a very fine mesh, otherwise they will torment you
all night long. If hiking through a swarm, use DEET (more on
this miracle repellent later) and wear a long-sleeved shirt
buttoned up to your throat and closed at the cuffs. For those
of you who are really irritated by no-see-ums, you can purchase headnets made out of no-see-um netting. The covering
fits over your head and is secured by a cord around your neck.
Be careful not to pull it too tight.

If you are bitten, grin and bear it because there's not much
you can do to stop the fortunately brief pain. On second

thought, don't grin because no-see-ums are not averse to flying in your mouth.

Bees, hornets, wasps
I've only been stung once by a yellow jacket in thousands of miles of hiking. Mostly, these insects will try to avoid you but they are attracted to food, beverages, perfume, scented soaps and lotions (including deodorant) and bright-colored clothing. Also, they nest anywhere that provides cover—in logs, trees, even underground.

Yellow jackets are the most obnoxious of the bunch, often stinging more than once and without provocation. By keeping your camp clean and food and drink under cover, you should avoid these stinging pests.

If stung by one of these insects, wash the area with soap and water to keep the sting from becoming infected. Apply a cool cloth for about twenty minutes to reduce swelling and carry an oral antihistamine to reduce swelling as well.

Check your damp clothing and towels before using to make sure one of these stingers has not alighted on it. And remember, bees, hornets and wasps kill more people each year than snakes.

Numerous stings can induce anaphylactic shock, which can be fatal. Those who know they are allergic to bee stings should carry an Anakit (available by prescription) with them into the backcountry. These kits carry an antidote for anaphylactic shock--epinephrine (adrenalin). More on anaphylaxis following fire ants.

Blackflies, deerflies, horseflies
Most abundant during late spring and summer, these flies produce a painful bite as well as leave a nasty mark on your skin. They sponge up the blood produced by their bite which is why the wound is often so big. Deerflies, in particular, seem

to prefer to dine on your head. When swarmed by the monsters, I have covered my head, Arab-style, to avoid their nasty bites. If bitten, wash with soap and water and use an oral antihistamine to reduce swelling and itching.

Fire ants

So far these nasty little creatures are found only in the South. But both Frank and I have experienced first hand their tenacity and painful bite. Frank found one little ant clinging stubbornly to his foot hours after he stepped in a fire ant bed. These ants are very aggressive, consider your passing a provocation, and will sting you repeatedly. They build distinctive foot-high mounds but you don't necessarily have to kick one to be the brunt of their anger. Water-borne fire ants will attack you as viciously as those defending their territory, which often appears to be the entire universe. Treat a fire ant bite as you would a bee sting.

Anaphylactic Shock

Bees, wasps, yellow jackets, hornets, ants and black flies can all cause an extreme allergic reaction in some people that is referred to as anaphylactic shock. If you know that you are susceptible to anaphylaxis, then it would be wise to carry an Anakit whenever you go backpacking. The kit contains a couple of injections of epinephrine and antihistamine tablets. Your doctor should be able to prescribe one for you. If you must use the injection, always get to a hospital as soon as possible in case the anaphylactic state returns.

Anaphylactic shock occurs when the body produces too much histamine in reaction to a bite or sting. The reaction turns your skin red and itchy hives appear; and your airways begin to close down and will eventually shut completely, causing asphyxiation.

If you are presented with a first-time case of anaphylaxis,

give the victim antihistamine tablets if they can swallow. You should be carrying Benadryl or some similar antihistamine in your first aid kit. Seek help immediately.

For those not allergic to bites and stings, Sting-eze is supposed to be a superior product when it comes to relieving the pain and itching caused by most insects. It is said to combat infection from poison oak, cuts, burns, and abrasions, as well.

Scorpions

Scorpions hide under rocks, logs and other cover during the day; and although they pack a powerful wallop when they sting, only one species is potentially fatal. You'll rarely encounter scorpions in the woods, but keep a look-out for them in the desert where they may crawl into your boots, clothing or sleeping bag during the night. Make sure you inspect your boots and clothing before putting them on and shake out your sleeping bag before crawling into it. Once again, wear shoes around camp, and if you are building a fire ring, be careful. My brother, Tom, was stung a few times while gathering rocks for a fireplace in central Georgia.

If stung by a scorpion, treat the wound as you would a wasp sting. If the scorpion that stings you is about one-half to three inches long and yellow or greenish-yellow and you are in Texas, Arizona, New Mexico, southern California or northern Mexico, seek help immediately. It may be the one exception to the rule, the potentially deadly Ceturoides sculptuates. If unsure and if it's possible, kill the scorpion that stung you and show it to the doctor.

Chiggers or Red Bugs

Although reputed to burrow beneath your skin and to retreat only when full or suffocated, chiggers actually cause that red, itchy irritation on your skin when secretions are released during feeding. Treat chigger bites as you would bee stings.

Mosquitos

As monsoon season approached in Kathmandu our room was suddenly invaded with all manner of insects, but the most annoying were the mosquitos. They would buzz around our heads nearly driving us insane. Likewise, when camping, there is nothing worse than a mosquito caught in your tent with you. They always seem to vanish, mysteriously, when you turn your flashlight on. Only the females bite, but there always seem to be plenty of them around.

Most of the time it is impossible to avoid mosquitos, but if you camp in open, breezy areas away from still water, there's a good chance your sleep will be mosquito-free. Go for light-colored clothing that is too thick for mosquitos to penetrate. If they are really bad, wear long-sleeved shirts and pants and use DEET.

Wash mosquito bites and use an oral antihistamine to reduce swelling. A paste of baking soda and water also often helps reduce the itching of mosquito bites.

Ticks

A relative of spiders (another insect that leaves nasty bites), the tick has become a serious health threat. It is the carrier of both Rocky Mountain Spotted Fever and Lyme disease. Rocky Mountain Spotted Fever is carried by the wood ticks (west), lone star ticks (southwest), and dog ticks (east and south). Lyme disease is carried by the deer tick, which is about the size of a pinhead.

Whenever you are hiking in tick country—tall grass and underbrush—make sure you check yourself afterwards for ticks. Wearing a hat, long-sleeved shirt, and pants with cuffs tucked into socks will also discourage ticks. This can be very uncomfortable in hot weather. Using a repellent containing permethrin will also help, as will keeping to the center of the trail.

Like mosquitos, ticks are attracted to heat, often hanging around for months at a time waiting for a hot body to pass by. Wearing light-colored clothing will allow you to see ticks. After a hike on Cumberland Island, my husband arrived back at camp with his sock literally covered in tiny seed ticks. We quickly removed the sock and proceeded to send the ticks on to their next life. If a tick attaches itself to your body, the best way to remove it is by grasping the skin directly below where the tick is attached and removing the tick along with a small piece of skin. Once removed, carefully wash the bite with soap and water.

It takes a while for a tick to become imbedded. If you check yourself thoroughly after each hike—every mole and speck of dirt as well—you are more likely to catch the tick before it catches you. Tick season lasts from April through October and peak season is from May through July. But in warmer climates, tick season may last year 'round if there has been a warmer than average winter.

Lyme Disease

More than 21,000 cases of Lyme disease have been reported in forty-five states since it was first identified in 1982. The cases are almost doubling each year, with 4,574 reported in 1988; and 7,400 in 1989.

Among the symptoms of Lyme disease are fever, headache, pain and stiffness in joints and muscles. If left untreated, Lyme disease can produce lifelong impairment of muscular and nervous systems, chronic arthritis, brain injury, and in ten percent, crippling arthritis.

Lyme disease proceeds in three stages (although all three do not necessarily occur):

The first stage may consist of flu-like symptoms (fatigue,

headache, muscle and joint pain, swollen glands) and a skin rash with a bright red border. Antibiotic treatment wipes out the infection at this stage.

The second stage may include paralysis of the facial muscles, heart palpitations, light-headedness and shortness of breath, severe headaches, encephalitis and meningitis. Other symptoms include irritability, stiff neck, and difficulty concentrating. Pain may move around from joint to joint.

The third stage may take several years to occur and consists of chronic arthritis with numbness, tingling and burning pain, and may include inflammation of the brain itself. The disease can also lead to serious heart complications and attack the liver, eyes, kidney, spleen and lungs. Memory loss and lack of concentration are also present.

Although antibiotics are used for treatment in each stage, early detection and diagnosis are critical. If you suspect you have Lyme disease, see a doctor immediately.

Repellents
DEET is the hands-down winner when it comes to repelling insects. Short for N, N-diethyl-meta-toluamide, DEET is found in some percentage in most repellents—lotions, creams, sticks, pump sprays and aerosols.

This colorless, oily, sightly smelly ingredient is good against mosquitos, no-see-ums, fleas, ticks, gnats and flies. Although it can range in percentage from five percent to ninety-five percent, the longest lasting formula contains approximately thirty-five percent of DEET.

Repellents containing DEET in the thirty-fifty percent range are (in ascending order): Deep Woods Off! lotion, Deep Woods Off! Towelettes, Cutter's Stick, Cutter's Cream, Cutter's Cream Evergreen Scent, Cutter's Cream Single Use Packets (35%), Muskol Ultra Maximum Strength, Repel and Kampers Lotion (47.5% and includes suntan lotion).

Avon's Skin-So-Soft is a highly recommended deterrent against no-see-ums and some bigger bugs such as sand fleas and black flies. It appears to work differently on each person. I have better luck with it than my husband, for example.

During a trip to the low country of South Carolina, I was glad I packed the Skin-So-Soft. My daughter, Griffin, was bitten only on the head (where she was still greatly lacking in hair)—the only place I couldn't slather her with the stuff. I received only one bite, my husband quite a few more.

· 13 ·
First Hikes

IN FICTION, THE HEROES always seem to be able to sling on a pack and hike fifty miles at a four-mile-an-hour pace. Knowing better, I smirk and wonder if I should enlighten the author. I'm not saying you're incapable of hiking fifty miles nor am I saying that a four-mile-an-hour pace is impossible. But add a thirty-five to fifty pound pack to the natural ruggedness of trail and try to keep up that kind of pace for twelve-plus hours. As the old hiker joke goes, "How long is two hours?" The answer, "About five miles."

A lot of people assume that a four-mile-an-hour pace is standard. Well, it is if you're walking around a track or on a level stretch of road. But even the most seasoned hiker finds it next to impossible to keep a four-mile-an-hour pace on tough terrain. A two- to three-mile-an-hour pace is average for a hiker in peak condition.

The best advice when it comes to your first hike, is: don't bite off more than you can chew. It is very easy to run yourself into the ground, and it takes a lot longer to hike ten rugged miles than you would think. Before you head off into the wilderness, you've got to get your pack on your back . . .

First Things First

Getting your pack on your back is surprisingly difficult at first, but it gets easier with practice. There are two basic ways to get it on your back:

- Settle your pack on your right knee if you're right-handed, left if you're left-handed. Insert your arm through the pack strap and swing the pack around your back. Finally, insert the other arm in the arm strap, tighten your hip belt and sternum strap, and you're on your way.
- Sit down with your back against your pack, insert your arms through the straps. Roll on to your knees and stand up. This may sound easier, but it's actually a bit more difficult.

Once you get your pack on your back, it's time to hike. The next question is . . .

How Far and How Fast?

Don't plan on more than ten miles a day when you first start hiking. A five-mile day hike is a good choice. It will allow you plenty of time to enjoy the scenery without overextending yourself.

For an overnight hike, plan on a ten- to twenty-mile, two-day trip. After several smaller hikes, you may decide that you can extend your backpacking trips without ruining the fun. You don't have to be in great shape to backpack. But if you're not in good shape, you should allow yourself time to adjust.

When you first start hiking, don't count on more than a one-mile-per-hour pace with a full pack. Allow yourself ten hours to hike ten miles. Your actual walking pace will probably be faster, but your body will crave frequent breaks.

It won't take long before you can easily walk two miles per hour. A good rule of thumb for planning your trip is to allow an hour for every two miles of trail plus one hour for each one thousand feet of elevation to be gained. So, for a hike that will cover fourteen miles and have an elevation gain totaling

> ❦ *Hiking Secret* ❦
>
> By tilting your head sideways (so your eyes are perpendicular to the ground), you can improve your perception of an impending climb. Normally a slope will look easier or harder than it really is; this trick will put things in perspective.

three thousand feet, you should allow yourself ten hours.

Phil Hall had a novel idea for training for his first hike: "I carried around a seventy-pound bag of birdseed on my shoulders for ten miles over a ten-day period," he said. "From this, I got a tired and sore neck but discovered a clever way of hitching rides easily."

Phil realized the folly of his plan and chucked the bag of birdseed and took the direct approach. "I then decided that I would just start out slowly and do however many miles I could." He had the right idea. The only way to adjust to backpacking is to backpack. Unfortunately, there is no other way to prepare yourself. Being in good cardiovascular condition helps, but it takes the body time to accustom itself to the strain of even a light pack.

We trained for backpacking by taking up running and including an incredibly steep hill in our mile. We figured that when we could run a mile (including the hill) in eight minutes, we would be in good cardiovascular shape. But running up that hill was nothing compared to some of the climbs we faced with 40-pound packs on our backs. Unfortunately, nothing prepares you for backpacking except backpacking.

Taking Breaks

When we first started hiking, we took what we called a pack-off break every two miles and pack-on breaks after almost every hill. A pack-on or bend-over break is accomplished by leaning over and holding your knees so that your back supports all the pack's weight. Try it; it really helps when you first start hiking. By the time we had hiked five hundred miles, we could hike for hours without any breaks at all.

Uphill and Downhill Techniques
Taking breaks does slow down your overall pace. One way to avoid frequent stops is to use the rest step when ascending mountains. Perform the rest step by pausing for a moment with all your weight centered on your downhill leg, which should be kept straight. Then step forward and pause again with your weight on the opposite leg, which is now the downhill leg. Vary the length of the pause as needed. This step will not only get you up a steep slope faster but will get you up a mountain with less effort. The idea is to use this step on extremely tough sections of a hike by pausing slightly with each step—continual movement instead of vigorous hiking separated by a number of breaks.

Hiking downhill is as tough on your body as an uphill climb. Whereas an ascent places cardiovascular stress on your body, a descent takes its toll on your feet and knees. To lessen the impact, try pausing with your weight on one foot between each step; this will relieve some of the strain. Also, spring forward with each step, flexing your legs as you put weight on them. This is the fastest and safest way to get downhill.

Where Permits are Needed
Permits are needed only within the national park system. The heavy use of trails in these areas has created a need to limit the number of hikers staying overnight in the parks. The permits are free and are used only to control the number of campers.

Guidebooks

Guidebooks, if you choose to use them, can be purchased through supervising trail groups and at your local outdoors stores. They usually consist of a point-by-point description of the trail you're hiking (from the author's point of view, of course). That is, keep in mind that what the author might call a moderate slope, you may consider difficult or easy. Some guidebooks include a history of the area as well as what is available at road crossings and access to different points along the trail.

Maps

Topographic maps (also called contour maps) are best for hiking because in addition to roads, trails, rivers, etc., they also show the altitude changes with contour lines. These lines note how far above (or below) sea level points are. These maps from the U.S. Geological Survey are available from most outdoors stores or from the Geological Survey—east of the Mississippi at U.S. Geological Survey, Washington, D.C., 20242; west of the Mississippi at U.S. Geological Survey, Federal Center, Denver, CO, 80225. The best maps are those called the 7 1/2 minute maps. Index maps that show what maps are available for each state are free upon request.

Compass

Compasses are not absolutely necessary on all trails but there are some places where they are indispensable. Before doing any backpacking, you should become familiar with using the compass. The book *Be an Expert with Map and Compass* by Bjorn Kjellstrom is a classic and we recommended it highly.

Also, it is very important to keep in mind that compasses do not work by true north but rather by magnetic north— which is about one thousand miles south of the north pole. The difference between the two is called declination and you

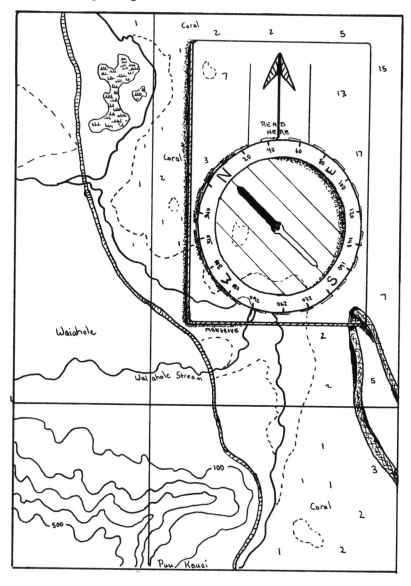

need to know this difference for the area you'll be hiking or the compass may confuse the situation. For example, while the declination for Maine is 20-22 degrees west, the declination for Oregon is 22-23 degrees east. Eastern Tennessee, on the otherhand, has a 0 degree declination. A compass can be set for the area's declination.

From the simple to the complex, pack-weight to pack-train weight, and cheap to inordinately expensive, there is a wide range of compasses to choose from. When purchasing a compass, make sure it is going to do everything you want it to do. Sturdiness is probably the most important quality for a backpacking compass but there are other features to consider as well. For example, some compasses feature sighting mirrors, clinometers and straight-edges.

Compasses range in price from $6 to $200. Also available for about $16 are wrist compasses. Manufacturers of quality compasses include Brunton, Silva and Suunto.

When hiking, you can use a map and compass to orient yourself by setting your compass to north and then aligning the map's north indicator with north as shown on your compass. Once you have accomplished this, you should be able to determine landmarks, such as mountains, that are indicated on the map. Unfortunately, this will not work if you're in a gap surrounded by forest or if you are enveloped in fog. But it is a good way of surveying the surrounding area when you are at a viewpoint.

Stream Crossings

In high use areas you are likely to find a nice little bridge to help you cross a stream, but the further you advance into the backcountry, the more likely it is you're going to have to cross a stream using your own initiative. I've crossed streams on logs and stepping stones, ankle-deep and waist deep, and all

---

>>Hiking Tip<<

For a rough estimate of how long you have until sunset, hold your hand out at arm's length and line your fingers up with the horizon. Each finger that you can fit between the horizon and the bottom of the sun represents about fifteen minutes. If six fingers separate the sun and land, the sun should set in about one and a half hours.

---

very safely. I've also crossed streams during and just after rainstorms when they become very dangerous.

Following an amazing thunderstorm and torrential downpour, we came upon a stream in the throes of a flash flood. The stream was neither very wide (about six feet) nor very deep (thigh-deep on a man, waist on me), but it was moving very rapidly and carrying all sorts of debris in its wake.

Although there was a log, which under normal circumstances might have made a nice bridge, it was too slick at this point to cross over standing up. We walked up the stream and down the stream looking for another option. There was none. The place we had intended to camp was under several inches of water and we had just passed a tree that had been struck and knocked over by lightning. We were soaked and our only thought was to get to higher ground and a road.

We tried crossing the log sitting down but the current tried to pull our dangling legs beneath the log. Our only option was to cross the stream using the downed tree as a brace. Frank made it across successfully and I was within arm's reach of Frank when I lost my footing and my right leg was pulled painfully beneath the log.

With Frank grasping my arm, I was off balance and unable to regain my footing. I was slowly slipping beneath the log. He finally, reluctantly, let go. Using both arms to hold on to the tree, I was able to pull my leg loose and Frank quickly pulled me out of the water.

All of this happened within seconds. I neither had the time to remove my pack nor harness myself with rope, which I should have done earlier in this very dangerous situation. I was lucky. Many are not. Crossing flooded streams kills more people than any other hiking-related accident.

If there is neither a dry log nor stepping stones, you must think carefully before crossing any stream. Take a good look at it. How fast is the current? How deep is it? If it is deeper than about eighteen inches, be especially careful. I've been knocked off my feet in knee-deep water. Using a rope will not prevent you from falling but it may help you in the rescue if you do fall. Keep these factors in mind when looking for a place to cross:

- The narrowest point in a stream may be the most tempting, but is probably the most dangerous point to cross because the current is more powerful there. The widest part is probably the safest. At any rate, going for the slow and deep is usually safer than shallow and fast.
- Always release your hip belt when crossing in case you are knocked off your feet. This way you can easily rid yourself of the pack if you are washed downstream. It could save you from drowning, and it is better to lose your pack than your life.
- If you are trying to cross a snow-fed river near the end of the day, consider waiting until morning. Pitch camp and spend the night there. The stream's flow will be reduced during the cool evening and will be easier to cross before things heat up during the day. Had we waited a few hours, our flash-flooded stream would probably have eventually subsided. Hindsight being 20/20, the area suffered several more downpours that night, but that is rare.
- Long pants have more drag on you than shorts. Cross in shorts or even nude or in underwear. Once across, you can warm up by redonning your clothes.
- Some crossings are safe enough to do barefoot, but why

take chances? Wear your boots or camp shoes, if you have them. A number of companies make water socks—scrunchable shoes with a rough sole made for gripping rocks and stream beds.

- When crossing rapids, face upstream and move sideways like a crab. Using a hiking stick or pole will help you maintain your balance.

Using a Hiking Stick

A hiking stick can take some of the impact on the downhill and will keep you steady on rough sections of trail. If this was all they were good for, they would still be worth carrying. But hiking sticks also can be used to fend off stray dogs, keep your balance crossing narrow bridges or fording streams, flip small branches out of the path ahead of you, and more.

Some people simply pick up a different stick every time they hike, whereas others purchase a ski pole for the purpose. Some people swear by ski poles, noting that they are very strong, lightweight, and have a device at the tip that prevents the pole from burying itself in mud or rocks.

The Human Factor

Problems with other humans while hiking are rare and following these few guidelines will help:

- Avoid camping near road crossings.
- Do not tell strangers exactly where you intend to camp for the night.
- Take any valuables (e.g., wallet) with you; do not leave anything valuable in your car at the trailhead.
- If you get a bad feeling about someone you meet up with, move on to another campsite.
- Do not leave your pack alone in frequently traveled areas because there are people out there who will steal packs.

·14·
Long Distance Hikes

Where are we going? I don't quite know. What does it matter where people go? Down to the woods where the bluebells grow. Anywhere, anywhere, I don't know.

—A.A. Milne

GETTING LOST IN NATURE is one of the best reasons I know to get into backpacking. As I said in the introduction, there are things you see only when long-distance hiking. Heading off into the "woods" for a week or more provides you with opportunities that the day and weekend hiker may never experience.

Long-distance hikers are a special breed of people. Backpacking is far from easy, but hiking more than a hundred miles at a time has its advantages. Anyone who has backpacked for a month or more at a time picks up a totally new outlook—a special regard for the simpler things in life. It's a very refreshing philosophy that is often at war with today's materialistic society. Many hikers coming off a long-distance trip rethink and subsequently change their lifestyles.

Each year a thousand or so people set out to hike the

length of the country's major long-distance trails—the Pacific Crest, Continental Divide and Appalachian are the most popular. If you are thinking about hiking an entire trail in a year, you may want to consider this first: only two hundred to three hundred of the thousands who try make it the whole way in a single year; the others must leave their dreams by the wayside.

This happens for a number of reasons, but mostly because long-distance backpacking turns out to be more than they bargained for.

There are many long-distance trails that can be back-packed by just about any person. Others—the Pacific Crest and the Continental Divide, for example—possess too many physical challenges for some people. There are easier trails (the Florida Trail and the Appalachian Trail, for example), that many people have the physical ability to complete the entire trail. Long distance trails have been backpacked by the young, the old, the handicapped, and everybody in between.

But physical ability is not all it takes. We sometimes romanticize backpacking as an easy walk in the woods. It is almost never easy, and it is never just a walk in the woods.

What it Takes to be a Long-distance Hiker

"Finishing the trail was all-important," said Sondra Davis, who hiked the Appalachian Trail with her husband, Craig. "But enjoying the trail was reason enough."

"I started with the intention of finishing," explained Doug Davis. "I think a lot of the quitters only committed themselves to giving it a try. As I went along I would try to imagine finishing. It was hard. I also tried to imagine not finishing. It was impossible."

Davis sums up the way most long-distance hikers feel. It takes determination and goal orientation to finish the trail you have chosen. Flexibility is the key.

Phil Hall said, "It takes determination, flexibility, and endurance. Without all three, you probably won't make it that far."

Before you begin planning your hike, ask yourself these questions:

- Will completing my hike be worth being wet/cold/hot day after day?
- Can I wear the same dirty clothes for days on end?
- Can I go without a bath or shower, sometimes for as long as a week?
- Can I withstand the physical pain that often accompanies backpacking?
- Can I stand being away from my home/relationship for a month or more at a time, sometimes as long as six to eight months?
- Is the idea of backpacking this entire trail my all-consuming desire? Am I willing for it to be?

- Am I afraid of the outdoors—insects, animals, sleeping outdoors night after night?

Some of these questions may seem trivial, but all of them point to reasons that people quit their long-distance hike. Obviously, severe physical injuries and emergencies at home also are a factor, but these have nothing to do with the determination, flexibility, and endurance it takes to hike an entire long-distance trail.

What do we mean by flexibility, endurance, and determination? Consider this experience penned by Cindy Ross in her book, *Journey on the Crest*, about her hike on the Pacific Crest Trail.

"We're aiming for a reservoir that the guidebook suggests we camp by, where we can go for a delightful swim. The idea has been on our minds all day. When we spot the blue speck below, Todd takes off in a trot, hollering like a madman. He kicks up the chocolate brown dust and chases all the cows, who run away in their own frightened cloud. I lag behind, giggling at the sight.

When we arrive, we stare in disbelief. The "lake" is four inches deep! It's a slime-covered mud hole! The water level is very low, so that the rocks that no doubt normally lie submerged are exposed. We step on them to get out in the water. Muddy ooze squishes from the pressure of our weight, disturbing billions of mosquitos breeding in the slime. Immediately they cover our ankles and begin sucking blood. Take a swim in this? Todd begins the laborious project of filtering water. He takes a sweaty bandana and drapes it over a water bottle opening, putting a shallow dip in the cloth to help the liquid through. I swat bugs off him as he collects a gallon. We look at each other. 'Let's get out of here!'"

Cindy and Todd did not enjoy their problems, but they also didn't think about quitting. Every hiker has at least one day like theirs, usually many more. It's just something you have to keep in mind when you intend to hike long-distance. Like four to six months in the "real" world, something is bound to go wrong occasionally.

Why People Hike Long-distance

There is no one reason that draws people to hike an entire trail, but there does seem to be a common denominator. Most are at some period of change in their lives—divorce, graduation from college or high school, retirement, marriage, or an anticipated change of careers. These are all typical times that hikers take to some long-distance trail to follow it from end to end.

"One might conclude," said Bill Foot, "that the trail is a great place to figure out where to go or what to do with the rest of your life."

Unhappy with our jobs at a daily newspaper, we decided to hike the Appalachian Trail and search for a solution to our problem—what are we going to do for the rest of our lives? The six-month trip confirmed the fact that we wanted to continue with writing and photography but on our own terms.

As Henry David Thoreau once said:
"I go forth to make new demands on life. I wish to begin this summer well; to do something in it worthy of it and me; to transcend my daily routine and that of my townsmen . . . I pray that the life of this spring and summer may ever lie fair in my memory. May I dare as I have never done! May I persevere as I have never done!"

It is with that spirit that many backpackers seek the solitude and simple life of long-distance hiking—to be dependent on no one but themselves for four months or so; to be one with nature day after day after day; and to have no other worry but where to camp and where to get water.

When and Where to Start

Obviously, where and when to start depends on what trail you're hiking. The shorter long-distance trails (75-400 miles) give you a bit more leeway. Longer trails—such as the Appalachian, Continental Divide and Pacific Crest—are very limited as to when you can start.

The majority of backpackers begin the Appalachian Trail between March and May and hike northward from Georgia. A few choose to begin in Maine during the summer months and hike southward.

Most Continental Divide Trail hikers begin in the north in July at the Canadian border and hike south to Mexico; and those hiking the Pacific Crest Trail usually begin at the Mexican border in June and hike north to Canada. The latter two trails are often hard to complete in one year due to weather conditions.

Smaller trails—those from approximately 75 to 400 miles- - are also considered long-distance but take much less time to hike. Because backpacking trips will range from a week to a month for the shorter trails, the hiker has more options as to when to start. It is up to the backpacker to contact the supervising trail group and find out when and where are the best times to start the trail they have chosen. While it might be folly to hike the Ice Age trail in the winter, this is probably the best time to hike the Florida Trail.

Where to Hike

The Appalachian, Continental Divide and Pacific Crest are the best known and most popular of the super long-distance trails. Another trail, the American Discovery, will soon be the

---

>>Hiking Tip<<

For more information on long-distance trails and long-distance hiking, you can contact the Appalachian Long Distance Hikers Association, the nation's only group for long-distance hikers. Their annual Gathering of Long Distance Hikers meets Columbus Day weekend each year and features workshops and slide shows from trails all around the country. Their address is in Appendix 3.

---

first American coast-to-coast trail. Although the route has been flagged, it is not yet a fully completed trail. Chapter 1 lists National Scenic and Historic long-distance trails, including the four above. Many of these are nearing completion and can be hiked from end to end; others are still in progress.

Shorter long-distance trails abound in the fifty states. Some of the more popular trails are Vermont's Long Trail, the C&O Canal Towpath Trail in Maryland and West Virginia, the John Muir Trail in California, the Chilkoot Trail in Alaska, the Grand Canyon trails in Arizona, the Horseshoe Trail in Pennsylvania, Isle Royale trails in Michigan, the Long Path in New York, the Ozark Highlands Trail in Arkansas, and the Pacific Northwest Trail in Oregon and Washington.

There are hundreds of short long-distance trails in the U.S. and many more in Canada and Europe. England is especially famous for its paths, which criss-cross the country. The Pennine Way is said to be England's Appalachian Trail.

Flip-flopping

Some hikers find that they are not going to be able to make it to their destination before the weather gets too rough to permit hiking. Others find they have arrived at a section of trail that is still snowed in. Instead of calling off your hike, try flip-flopping. This is not even an issue on most trails, but on the Continental Divide Trail and the Pacific Crest Trail, in particular, many hikers consider the flip-flop or hiking a trail in two sections rather than in one continuous journey.

You leave your north/south-bound hike, and travel to the opposite end of the trail. Here, you begin a north/south-bound hike back to where you left off, thus completing the trail in one year.

For example, a hiker begins the Appalachian Trail at Springer Mountain in Georgia. When he reaches Harpers Ferry, West Virginia in August, he begins to worry that he won't make it to Mount Katahdin in Maine before the park closes on October 15. He then decides to travel to Mount Katahdin and hike south to Harpers Ferry so that he can complete his hike in one year.

Some hikers set out to flip-flop the trail because they feel it gives them more time, or because they cannot begin their hike until mid-summer and do not wish to hike entirely south or north-bound. A good friend of ours started the Appalachian Trail from Harpers Ferry in June so that he could hike with that year's thru-hikers. After making it to Mount Katahdin, he returned to Harpers Ferry and hiked to Springer Mountain in Georgia.

Blue-blazing

Before you begin your hike, you should make an important decision. What is the goal you are pursuing? Is it to hike the entire trail or is it merely to spend several months hiking in the Sierras, Rockies, Appalachians, etc.? You should ask yourself this question because opportunities will arise to cut off sections of the trail to make it shorter, easier, or to provide faster access to towns.

The term for taking these shortcuts is blue-blazing. The name comes from the fact that many of the side trails you will intersect are marked with blue blazes. While the Appalachian Trail has one set route and hikers who stick to this white-blazed trail think of themselves as purists, most other trails offer "official" alternative routes. Both the Pacific Crest Trail and Continental Divide Trail have variable routes because the weather changes so drastically on those trails.

If you decide ahead of time how "pure" you want your hike to be, you will have less trouble deciding later. We discovered that once you begin to blue-blaze it is harder not to do so again. An example of an extreme case of blue-blazing would be taking the Tuckerman Ravine trail down from Mt. Washington in New Hampshire to turn a 12.9-mile hike across the Northern Presidential Range into a less than five-mile hike downhill.

So you can see that making a distinction before you leave home will help you choose which trail to follow once you're hiking. Whatever choice you make for yourself, remember that you are hiking for your own reasons, with your own goals. Allow others the same courtesy. Don't view another's hiking style as wrong; it is only different.

Section Hiking

An alternative to hiking a trail end-to-end in one year is to hike it in sections. This means completing an entire trail over a period of two, or perhaps more, years. If you are unable to take four to six months off for one long hike, you can break the trail up into smaller sections to be hiked over several years.

The completion of a trail over many years is just as meaningful, if not more so, as hiking the trail in one long hike. But it means a longer commitment and it is a logistical nightmare when it comes to getting to and from the trail each year.

How Much Does it Cost to Hike?

How much do you want it to cost? A good rough estimate is $1 a mile, not including any equipment you may need or transportation to and from your selected trail. This is not going cheap, nor is it extravagant. If you are careful, the trail can be a very inexpensive four to six months.

Your only big cost is food. Another expense is fuel for your stove. From there, what you spend is optional. Most hikers will splurge on restaurant meals when they go into town or might pay for a night in a motel.

Other expenses might include:
* laundry and detergent
* entertainment (more batteries for your Walkman, movies, dancing, books, magazines, etc.)
* replacement of gear (if you haven't already set aside a fund for emergencies)
* doctor bills (also an emergency fund item)
* miscellaneous items (batteries for your flashlight or headlamp, stamps, stationery, etc.)

Alcohol

There is something that is missing from the above list, and it's something that hikers tend to spend a lot of money on—alcohol. We don't intend to preach because, personally, nothing tastes better to us than an ice-cold beer on a hot summer's day. Unfortunately, during the past decade, the drinking of alcoholic beverages on trails has gotten out of hand. The result is that hikers are no longer allowed in certain places.

One hiker nearly died of hypothermia atop New Hampshire's Mount Mariah after drinking a fifth of Vodka. Too drunk to know where he was, he stumbled off the trail and passed out. Fortunately, he was spotted by other hikers and a search-and-rescue team was able to save him in time. A hiker in Pennsylvania was forced to shoot another hiker in self-defense when that hiker attacked him with a shovel during a drunken rage. Some hostel owners we know came close to closing their hostel (which was adjacent to their bed and breakfast) when some drunken hikers began using their front yard as a urinal.

Tales like these abound. Please don't add your name to the list of those who have destroyed good situations for other hikers. Keep your consumption of alcoholic beverages moderate, especially if you are hiking alone. Alcohol can be life-threatening in the wilderness (and in town, for that matter). Fortunately, most hikers are considerate; but remember that it is always the few who ruin things for all.

Money
Hiking with a thousand dollars in cash is a bad way to test your trust in your fellow humans. Most hikers choose the safety and convenience of traveler's checks. Traveler's checks can be cashed almost anywhere. We haven't heard of any store, no matter how small or out-of-the-way, that wouldn't cash a traveler's check. By buying the checks in denominations of $20 as well as $100, you can assure that you won't be caught carrying a large amount of cash at any one time. For added peace of mind and to help you stay on budget, it is a good idea to split your traveler's checks up into two or three groups send some ahead to your mail drops.

Automated Teller Machines have made their way to many towns and have become a reliable way to receive money. With credit cards or bank cards that are part of a nationwide network, such as Cirrus, hikers can obtain money in an emergency or as part of a scheduled withdrawal.

Whether or not you intend to use your credit card for cash withdrawals, bring it along. A major credit card can be a lifesaver if equipment breaks or medical problems arise. Telephone company credit cards are helpful in reaching

family and friends from the trail and can be used to contact
equipment manufacturers in an emergency.

Shelters

A very few trails—the Appalachian and Long Trail, and those
in Smoky Mountains National Park and the White Moun-
tains--offer hikers some sort of shelter as an alternate to tent
camping. Very few shelters are available on western trails.
You may find a few along the Pacific Crest or Continental
Divide trails but they may not be in excellent condition.

Hostels

A hostel can be as simple as the floor of a church or barn, or
as elaborate as a hot shower, warm bed, laundry facilities,
and food. Hostels range in price from free (although a donation is always appreciated) to $20 or more a night. They are
run by the American Youth Hostel (AYH) group, churches,
trail clubs and private citizens.

If you intend to stay in hostels during your hike, count on
leaving at least a small donation (especially if they don't ask
for it). Some hostels will let you work off your stay, but all
appreciate a helping hand, even if you're paying. If the hostel
is a business, you need only to be courteous and may stay as
long as you are willing to pay for a room or bed; but if it is run
by volunteers, help out. It is a good idea to limit your stay to
a night or two (unless it's an emergency) if the hostel is run
by volunteers on a donation basis. Prove that hikers are not
the socially irresponsible crowd a lot of people think we are.
Try to clean up behind other hikers as well as yourself. A good
attitude goes a long way toward improving relations along
any trail.

AYH hostels require membership in their group before
you can stay in one of their hostels. The group was created to
provide inexpensive lodging for travelers. Be sure to look into
this before counting on a stay at a particular hostel. For more

information on AYH, write: AYH, Data Processing Department, P.O. Box 37613, Washington, D.C. 20013. They will send you membership information. Upon joining AYH, you will receive a handbook that includes a listing of AYH hostels in the U.S.

The time to plan on staying in hostels is before you hike. It is up to you to look into whether there are any hostels available along the trail you plan to hike. The local trail club will be able to give you this information.

Trail Registers/Trail Names
Along some trails, you may find "trail registers." They are anything from a sign-in sheet in a national forest to a notebook or diary at the shelter or in specially-built boxes along the trail.

Started as a safety measure to pinpoint the whereabouts of hikers, trail registers have become an important link in a vast communications network. Trail registers offer hikers the chance to make comments to those behind them, and to get to know, sometimes intimately, those ahead.

A little common sense should be used when writing in trail registers. Profanity should be avoided because families hike the trail and read the registers; don't write anything you wouldn't want a second-grader to read.

With that said, remember how important other's entries can be to you. If you have something on your mind, don't be afraid to share it. After a tough day of slogging through the rain, a read through the register can be entertaining. On the other hand, entries that ramble on for more than a page often go unread.

To fulfill the registers' initial purpose of keeping tabs on hikers should an emergency occur, always give the date, the time of day, your name or trail name, and where you are headed next.

Along the same vein, "trail names" can become an important identifier even if you hike on the trail only a few days a year. Trail names are the nicknames used by hikers to identify themselves in registers. For some reason, trail names are much easier to remember than given names. They are more interesting and often give you some idea of the person who bears the name. For example, when Ed Carlson began hiking, he was under a lot of stress and very high strung. He decided to take the name of Easy Ed, hoping that he would change to suit the name. In his case, it worked.

Names involving characters from the Tolkien novels are popular as are those playing off the slowness of turtles. The Grateful Dead have inspired numerous trail names while some people choose an aspect of their name or personality to draw upon.

Sending food ahead

If you intend to keep to a strict schedule and do not mind planning what you are going to eat weeks or months in advance, sending all your food ahead is a viable alternative. On a number of trails, it may be your only choice.

Said Bill and Laurie Foot, "We sent ourselves large boxes every eight to ten days. When we picked them up, we would pack what we needed for four or five days and put the remainder into a smaller package, and send it to a post office five days ahead. This way, we knew our schedule better and avoided problems with arriving in a town when the post office was closed."

Frank and I agreed that post office drops in expensive or poorly stocked towns are an immense help. Also, sending yourself "care" packages filled with goodies such as candy and nuts makes sure you'll have a high-calorie treat when you finally arrive at the post office. You can also send yourself dehydrated foods to add variety to your diet.

Mail Drops

Even if you don't intend to send your food ahead, you should plan a few mail drops. Sending hard-to-buy items such as film, guidebooks and maps, Sno-Seal and seam sealer is just one use for a mail drop. Friends and family can be given a list of post offices where you plan to check for mail. This usually produces a variety of letters and packages, making all your planning worthwhile.

Packages should be addressed to you, General Delivery, with the city, state, and zip code of the post office. By having the letters and packages marked "Hold for North-bound (or South-bound) (Name of Trail) hiker," you will ensure that the post office will hold them much longer than customary. Post offices that are frequented by hikers generally hold mail until that year's group of hikers stops coming by, then returns them to sender. Zip codes for post offices near the trail and distances from the trail to the post office can be received through the conference in charge of the trail you are hiking.

As nice as receiving mail can be, remember that mail drops can also be a nuisance. If you come in to a town after noon on Saturday, you will probably have to wait until Monday morning for mail. If the mail drop is not essential, you can send or leave a forwarding card and let the mail catch up to you later. Using a number of mail drops for food or any other essential (e.g., money) will mean that you will have to schedule your hike around getting to town when the post office is open.

Spacing your post office pick-ups about 150 to 200 miles apart should be sufficient if you don't use them as your only source of food. Distances between post offices will vary according to what trail you are hiking. You will find fewer roads and towns on the Continental Divide Trail than you will on the Appalachian Trail, for example.

Mailing Gear Ahead

One way to use the mail system to your advantage is to send equipment further down the trail instead of home.

"One of the most helpful things I did for myself about a third of the way through my trip was to have a box that I continually sent ahead of myself," said Rob White. "I used the box to carry excess equipment up the trail for me. And when I decided to get rid of my tent and use the tarp, I sent the tent about a week ahead before I sent it home."

This technique can be used for extra food, contact lens solution, clothing, soap, resealable plastic bags, and more. The postage costs can add up, but if you're thinking of doing without some piece of equipment, this is the best way to try living without it.

How often do you resupply?

How often you resupply depends on what trail you are hiking. Study the trail carefully. Some trails, like the Appalachian, afford resupply points on the average of once a week. Others, like the Pacific Crest and Continental Divide often force the hiker to carry as much as two week's food.

Figure out what is best for you. Some people have no problem continually carrying two week's worth of food on their back, whereas others strain under the weight of a week's worth. Know your limits. We often carry only a few day's worth when we know we'll be able to resupply more frequently.

An alternative to buying or sending food is burying food canisters along the trail you plan to hike. The method is seldom used because it is time-consuming and risky. Hikers must bury their food along the trail before their trip, and it is possible that the food will be found in the meantime. Relocations of the trail may cause you to lose some caches, not to mention the possibility of your markers disappearing.

Insurance

Setting out to hike a long-distance trail without medical insurance is folly at best, though many hikers, ourselves included, take this route. Relatively low-cost, short-term medical insurance is available through many companies. The short-term policies are designed for people between jobs and typically last no longer than six months. This type of policy is nonrenewable but allows enough coverage for the duration of a long distance hike. As with any policy, the higher the deductible, the lower the premiums will be.

The Afterlife

Once you've hiked an entire long-distance trail, you will find that things will never be quite the same again. The trail's effect is different on each hiker, but no one is left unchanged.

"Too many things hit you," said Todd Gladfelter, who has hiked both the Pacific Crest and Appalachian Trails, "Bills, phone, cars, appointments."

After hiking the Pacific Crest Trail, Todd's wife, Cindy Ross, had so much trouble readjusting that she camped out in her backyard for awhile upon her return home and walked around sniffing sage from her mother's spice cabinet because it reminded her of the desert. These changes often lead to a change of lifestyle, and sometimes a change of career. Cindy and Todd have since built their own log cabin, grow their own vegetables, and do whatever it takes to be their own bosses.

Many others have settled down near a trail so that they can continue to be a part of the lifestyle they love so much. Teaching is a favorite career taken up by long-distance hikers because it allows them to hike during the summer months. Others have chosen jobs that allow them to work for awhile to raise enough money for a long-distance hike and then take off for four to six months. Folk singer Walkin' Jim Stolz has accumulated thousands of miles of hiking experience while maintaining his lifestyle by singing about his journeys.

· 15 ·
Special Hikes

THE SNOWFLAKES PATTERED SOFTLY against my tent and I slowly drifted awake to the soft blue light. Snuggled up and warm in my sleeping bag, I reluctantly withdrew an arm to unzip the tent and its fly. There were three inches of snow on the ground!

It was dawn and the snow picked up and reflected every glimmer of light. The forest, caught between the paleness of snow and clouds, hung suspended in an unearthly glow.

I quickly pulled on pile pants and top over my longjohns. Boots, gaiters and rain suit followed and I stepped out into this rare Southern world.

Walking through the forest that morning was like getting a glimpse of the imaginary world in "Silent Snow, Secret Snow" by Conrad Aiken. It was a quiet place of softly falling snow and the almost silent crunch of footsteps.

Camped just off the summit, I climbed up to its rocky outcrop to survey the valley below. It glittered like a scene in a magic egg—the snow shone like sugar, a stream was a ribbon of black licorice and a barn was a gingerbread house topped with a layer of thick white icing.

I returned to my tent for a warm breakfast and then

carried my cup of coffee back to the summit. As the sun burned its path through the sky, the clouds disappeared. In the valley, the snow sparkled like diamonds as the crystals slowly melted away. Trees that only recently blossomed with bolls of snow began to lose their icy flowers.

Twisting its way through the snow-covered pastures and fields, the stream was soon swollen with the meltoff. Rows of cornstalks marched out of the snow while shingles of snow began to slide from the roof of the barn.

With a sigh, I returned to my camp and began to pack up. I had retreated to the woods that weekend for a bit of solitude. I left having been part of a fairy tale.

Experienced hikers have learned that pleasurable backpacking need not only be found during the spring, summer and fall. Winter camping is possible in many parts of the U.S. and provides much more solitude. It is a way to experience the Earth during its darkest season—to discover a new world both physically and mentally.

Even in the south, where contrary to popular opinion, it does get cold, and even, occasionally, snow, you'll find the trails much less crowded. By the same token, you can find snowy places throughout the country where you can hike and camp in peace.

Before you throw on your pack and snow seal your boots, keep in mind that winter backpacking requires a little more forethought as well as preparation.

Winter Backpacking

First, you must decide whether you intend to hike in boots with or without crampons, on snowshoes or on cross-country skis. If the snow is not deep or if it is hard-packed, boots will probably suffice. A pair of gaiters and well-sealed boots will make the trip more comfortable. The hard, plastic, cold-weather, mountaineering boots which were designed for technical climbing are impractical for backpacking.

If you plan a trip in snow that will be knee-deep or more, you will want to opt for snow shoes or cross-country skis to get you to your destination.

Crampons and Snowshoes
Some backpacking requires the use of crampons. Simply put, crampons are used for hiking on ice and hard snow. While not necessary for most backpacking trips, there are areas along both the Pacific Crest and Continental Divide Trails (among others) where it would always be wise to carry a pair.

Crampons, usually twelve-pointed, strap onto your boots. They must be fitted properly—loose crampons being as, if not more, dangerous than hiking crampon-less across slick ice or snow. For backpacking, flexible crampons are a must. Consult an outdoors store that features climbing equipment when choosing a pair of crampons.

When hiking with crampons, an ice ax is another useful piece of equipment. It will help you cut steps in ice or snow and can be used as a brake to stop yourself should you fall. The purchase of an ice ax should be discussed with your local outfitter.

If you're going to be doing a lot of backpacking in soft snow—the kind you can sink up to your waist in—it would be wise to look into purchasing a pair of snowshoes. Remember, though, that even with snowshoes, four hours a day is about all most people can manage to backpack in the snow.

The traditional snowshoes of wood and rawhide are still available but are giving way to technologically superior frames of aluminum and thongs of nylon and plastic. A good pair can be purchased for approximately $125.

When purchasing snowshoes, there are five qualities you should look for:

1) Flotation—the surface area of the snowshoe. A backpacker will need more surface area because of the added weight of his pack.
2) Traction—depending on how much climbing you will do, your snowshoe will need more traction.
3) Tracking ability—the shoe should be heavier in the tail than in the toe, and your boot toe should fit through the toe hole and dig into the snow.
4) Traversing ability—a narrow design of ten inches or less is best.
5) Weight—the lighter they are the better. There is an old saying that "a pound on the foot is equal to five on the back." That is very close to the truth.

When it comes to purchasing snowshoes, there are five basic designs to choose from: 1) Green Mountain Bearpaw, for mountainous, wooded terrain; 2) Cross Country, similar to the Bearpaw but with a ten-inch tail; 3) Michigan, for trail and sparse-forest travel; 4) Alaskan, for open country and deep snow; and 5) Ojibwa, similar to the Alaskan--for open country and deep snow.

A pair of ski poles are supposedly invaluable to the snowshoer (many backpackers use ski poles as hiking sticks as well). There are a number of books on the subject, including *Snowshoeing* by Gene Prater (from The Mountaineers).

Cross-country skis

Depend on the expertise of your salesman when choosing the right cross-country skis. In some areas of the country, it is possible to rent both snowshoes and cross-country gear from local outdoors and ski-gear stores.

Basically, you have a choice between waxable, waxless and climbers. The waxable skis are the most common and can be found in both wood and fiberglass, although fiberglass is much more popular than wood these days because of their speed. If you're looking for a ski to backpack in, you'll need one with the following characteristics: durability, maneuverability, good flotation and light weight.

When purchasing skis, make sure you inform the salesman that you are interested in a touring or mountaineering ski, particularly a ski with a hickory base and lignostone edge (if you're interested in wood) or polyethylene base and ABS sidewall in fiberglass skis. These are the most durable. Mountaineering skis should have metal edges.

Maneuverability means your ski should have a flexible tip, a midsection strong enough to support your weight but flexible enough to grasp the snow, and the tail should be less flexible than the tip but more flexible than the midsection. The ski should also have an arc (called a camber) as you look at it from the side. It should also be narrower at the waist than at the tip.

For the best flotation, you will need a waist width of 52 to 60 mm for skiing in hilly, forested areas; and a waist width of greater than sixty for above timberline.

Once you find all these qualities in your ski, your lightest weight will be about five pounds for the touring ski, six pounds for the mountaineering.

Because waxable skis require a different wax for different snow conditions, some people prefer to purchase waxless skis. Although these skis are not as fast as the waxable, they are great for those people who anger quickly because they require less maintenance. Waxless skis can ice up easily and require a de-icer in changing temperature conditions.

Waxable skis have bases which feature either a negative or positive pattern. The positive pattern skis are the most popular because they seem to work better. Among the designs are Trak's patented fishscale and the mohair strip. Negative pattern skis use bells, diamonds, crescents and steps.

Climbers are used only when you intend to do, obviously, a lot of climbing. They can only be used on mountaineering skis because they are designed for widths greater than 62 mm. Both mohair and woven-plastic cord treads are available for mountaineering skis.

After purchasing your skis, you will have a choice of pin or cable bindings. If you purchase pin bindings, make sure they are made of heavy-duty aluminum. Cable bindings should have a safety heel release to prevent broken legs.

Your next purchase will be touring boots. Make sure that they rise over your ankle and that they are not the lighter racing boots. Also look for leather uppers and buy them a bit large to accommodate warm socks—try them on that way! Touring boots should be used with gaiters to avoid wet feet. If you have purchased mountaineering skis, you can use your hiking boots or the heavier ski mountaineering boots that have felt or leather inner boots.

Finally, you will need ski poles. High quality aluminum or

fiberglass poles are your best bet. Make sure that the poles have adjustable wrist straps and that the baskets at the bottom of the pole are 4 to 5 inches in diameter. Most importantly, make sure that they are the right length. How to tell? Standing in stockinged feet, the pole should fit snugly in your armpit.

Once you determine your method of transportation, you must pack your pack. If you're heading out into the snow, you'll need a four-season tent, preferably one that offers a cook hole in its floor. In the deep South, a three-season tent will probably suffice since the temperature rarely drops below twenty degrees Fahrenheit.

A freestanding, four-season tent is the best choice because other types of tents need special pegs to keep the tent anchored in the snow. Even these don't always work. You will also need a tent with a waterproof floor.

Some four-season tents offer cookholes: a zippered or gathered hole in the bottom of the tent that can be flapped or pulled back so that you may cook directly on the ground. A cookhole is preferable to cooking on the floor of your tent, which can catch fire easily should the stove tip.

When pitching your tent in the snow, make sure you level the area and pack the snow down. If this is not done, it is very likely you will wake up when the tent collapses on your head. Leaving your pack on while you stamp the ground flat will give you some extra weight that will make the job go more quickly. If you make the base wider than necessary, you'll be able to walk around your tent without snowshoes or skis, which will be especially useful should nature call in the middle of the night.

Special tent pegs for snow camping can be purchased from most outdoors stores. Once your tent is pegged, try pouring some water on the pegs. Once it freezes, the pegs really won't move.

There is more information on pitching a tent in the snow in Chapter 5.

When camping during the winter, you will also need a sleeping bag with a low comfort rating—a zero-degree bag will do for most situations. If you don't want the expense of two sleeping bags, consider using a liner to make your three-season bag warmer. It should go without saying that you will need a mummy-style bag for winter camping. It will keep you the warmest and if the temperature really drops, you can tighten the hood until nothing but your nose is showing. Some sleeping bags are available with extra insulation in the foot of the bag to combat cold feet.

Since the bottom of your tent may be on top of snow, you will want some good insulation between the bottom of your tent and yourself. While a three-quarter sleeping pad may do for three-season camping, if your feet get cold easily you may want to consider a full-length pad for winter camping. Bags, liners and pads are discussed in detail in Chapter 6.

Remember that layering your clothing is of utmost importance when backpacking during the winter. Beginning with a layer of long underwear, you may want to add a warm shirt and pants or a pile or fleece shirt and pants set. You can top these off with a layer that includes a warm parka and waterproof, insulated pants if it is really cold or a rain/wind suit if the temperature is only reasonably cold. Don't forget that you can add greatly to your warmth by donning a hat or balaclava.

If you are sufficiently bundled, the exertion of hiking should keep you warm. If you start feeling hypothermic, stop immediately, change into dry clothes if yours are wet, crawl into your sleeping bag and heat yourself some warm liquid. Make sure the stove you bring will light (as well as boil water) in frigid weather.

Cold-related hazards are discussed in detail in Chapter 11. Remember that when hiking on open snow, it is wise to wear sunglasses because the sun reflecting off the bright, white snow can burn your eyes. Snowblindness can occur even on overcast days. If you don't have sunglasses, cut eye-slits in anything (a bandanna, for example) that can tie around your head. Should someone become snowblind, cold compresses, a painkiller and a lightproof bandage are needed. Between 18-20 hours later, the blindness should fade.

All the equipment needed for winter camping--warm clothes, four-season tents, sleeping bags, tent pegs, snow-shoes or skis—is available through outdoors stores where you will also find information on how to use the equipment.

A good reference book for camping in extremes such as snow and heat is *Harsh Weather Camping in the '90s* by Sam Curtis. The book is published by Menasha Ridge Press.

Desert Backpacking

The sun was sliding behind the mountains to the West. Stretching and yawning, Peter and Janet hoisted their packs on their backs and hit the desert trail.

Having taken a siesta during the worst heat of the day, they were now ready to put in a few more miles before night settled in too deeply.

A full moon and millions of stars lit the path that lay before them, and as the sky was painted from brilliant orange to midnight blue they began looking for a good place to camp.

A rocky outcrop looked promising and using a flashlight, Peter checked for poisonous snakes. Given the all clear, Janet pulled on her wool sweater and unrolled sleeping pads and bags while Peter fired up the stove for some herbal tea.

Sipping the relaxing liquid, Peter and Janet listened to the scurrying of night creatures and the occasional howl of a coyote. The theater of the sky above their heads played on—the man on the moon smiled down on them as stars twinkled, planets glowed and comets flared against the backdrop of the Milky Way.

Janet named her cactus sentinels while Peter pointed out the constellations. The night air had grown cool but their sleeping bags were warm and it wasn't long before they drifted off to sleep with an alarm set for 4 a.m. and some pre-dawn hiking in an effort to beat the desert's vicious heat.

> "In the desert, one is sensible of the passage of time. In that parching heat, a man feels that the day is a voyage towards the goal of evening, towards the promise of a cool breeze that will bathe the limbs and wash away the sweat. Under the heat of the day, beasts and men plod towards the sweet well of night, as confidently as towards death."
>
> —Antoine de St. Exupery

If you hike the Pacific Crest, Continental Divide or the Grand Canyon, three of the most popular trails, you will find yourself hiking in the desert. There are also hundreds of lesser known desert trails throughout the Southwest.

Many hikers enjoy taking backpacking trips into the desert because, like winter camping, there is more solitude and an awesome beauty few people have the chance to experience.

Because of the intense heat in the desert, there are several problems you face immediately—dehydration, hyperthermia and sunburn. Dehydration is discussed in detail in Chapter 3, hyperthermia in Chapter 11.

Sunburn is a potential problem, even in cold weather, because it can do extensive damage to your skin and constant burning can lead to skin cancer. Burned skin can also retard

> **>>Hiking Tip<<**
> When backpacking in the desert, dowse your clothes with water every chance you get. The continual evaporation will keep your body cooler.

sweating. If you do not want to hike in loose but body-covering clothes, use a sunscreen (discussed in Chapter 10). Also wear sunglasses. The bright light of the desert can burn your eyes as well as your skin.

Fortunately, there are ways to avoid these problems. If you intend to do a lot of backpacking in the desert, you may want to use an external frame pack as opposed to an internal frame pack. Why? Because the external sits away from your body, allowing more air to circulate on your back thus promoting evaporation of sweat and the cooling of one of the sweatiest places on your body.

Obviously, the best time to camp in the desert is during the winter. Avoid the summer months, if possible. If you must desert-hike in the summer, keep in mind that the sun often rises about 5:30 a.m. and does not set until almost 16 hours later. Three or four hours after sun rise temperatures peak and do not fall until evening.

By rising just before or at dawn, hiking until the temperatures peak and resting throughout the hottest part of the day, you can save yourself a lot of grief. Try to find some shade, if possible, under a tree or rocky outcropping. You may also want to try setting up a tarp, but unless your tent is highly ventilated I wouldn't suggested pitching it because it will heat up like a furnace. Hiking in the early evening, when it's cool, is also a possibility. Use a flashlight, head lamp or if you're lucky, a full moon.

Sun block is necessary no matter what part of the day you're hiking. The Arabs know what they are doing when they cover their bodies and heads with long, flowing material. Take a cue from them and wear, at least, loose, long pants and a loose but high-necked and long sleeved shirt. When it comes to desert backpacking, clothes made of cotton are your best bet because they get the wettest and the evaporation will cool your body. Keep in mind that the more area you leave uncovered the more sunscreen you will need to use. Don't wear black out in the sun unless you want to be baked. On the other hand, bring along some warm clothes for night because the desert cools down in the evening except for the hottest part of summer.

Wide-brimmed hats and sunglasses that block the ultra-violet rays are mandatory. For more information on sunscreen and sunglasses, see Chapter 10.

To keep from getting dehydrated, you must drink at least a gallon of water per day, and unless you have very reliable sources, don't count on just anyone's word for where you'll find water.

Although heavy, it is safest to carry your own water. And, like they say, don't put all your eggs in one basket. If you carry a one gallon jug and it breaks or leaks, you've lost one entire day's water supply. Spread the water around by carrying it in one- and two-liter bottles.

You can also get water in an emergency by memorizing the following method of distilling water in the desert:

Solar Water Still
- Dig a hole two feet deep by three feet wide.
- Set wide mouth bottle or pot in bottom of hole.
- Fill area around bottle with any plant material you can find.
- Cover hole with plastic (clear or translucent, if possible)
- Weigh down edges of plastic around hole so that it is "sealed."
- Place a light-weight, insulated rock in the center of the

plastic so that a funnel shape is formed over the mouth of the bottle. Water will then drip from the "funnel" into the bottle. You can insulate the rock with a bandana or piece of paper.

After three hours, the still will produce about a pint of water.

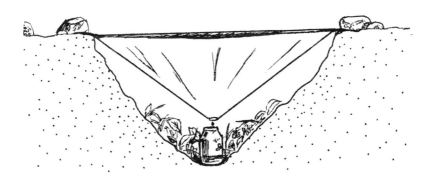

Also keep in mind that your appetite drops some in the desert, so you don't necessarily have to carry a cook kit. Cold foods will do you just fine; besides, who wants a hot dinner in the desert heat unless it is eaten in the middle of the night?

Some desert food could include tuna and hard-cheese-stuffed pitas, fruit leathers, peanutbutter, candybars, pemmican, beef jerky and so on. Remember, though, that while hiking in the desert, it is better for your digestion to eat a bunch of small meals rather than one big meal.

Backpacking with Children

Some of my best memories of childhood are of hiking and camping. We spent a lot of time hiking around California's Lake Shasta. I remember a hike in which we found a clear pool, almost perfectly circular, filled by a small waterfall—icy meltoff from the snowy mountains that towered above us.

On another trip, we stumbled on a ghost town and camping nearby set the perfect stage for ghost stories that night.

Then there was the time we were caught in a hailstorm on a sparsely treed hillside . . . my siblings and I concocted musical instruments from nature's bounty and held a concert for my parents . . . or a hike through head-high (on a 9-year-old) weeds that tripped us all so continually that we ended up soaked with dew and busting a gut laughing at our completely innocent Keystone Kops imitation.

Should you take your children on a backpacking trip?

Why not? Most children love the outdoors. I have vivid memories of it that have led me to continue my love affair with nature.

I discovered my daughter's love for the outdoors when she was three months old. While attending a conference in San Diego, I found that Griffin fell asleep more quickly when I carried her around outside than she did when I walked her in our room. Maybe it was all those long walks I took trying to induce labor when she was two weeks overdue, but she blossoms when the wind caresses her face and the sun shines on her head. She even loves the sprinkle of rain and overcast skies! Since the conference and a subsequent tour of Muir Woods, she has graduated to a backpack and absolutely loves her new vantage point.

From carrying a child in a pack, one can advance to having the child carry a pack, increasing the pack size and weight carried as the child grows.

Infants

The younger the child is, the more difficult the packing (except for ages four to six months when they have not yet learned to crawl). Younger than four months they don't yet fit in a pack and after six, they take off as soon as they touch the ground. If it's possible to set up your tent before you put your child down, you have a handy playpen to hold the child until you've set up camp.

Until the child is toilet-trained, you must carry diapers--disposable or otherwise. You'll have to pack them in and out. Cindy Ross suggests cloth diapers which she and her husband, Todd, dry on the back of their packs so that they are lighter to carry. When the child has a bowel movement, you can simply bury her poop as you would your own, fold up the diaper and carry it in a sealable plastic bag.

Because one person is carrying the child, the amount of extra stuff that person can carry is limited. This means the length of your trip is shortened but there are ways to get around that.

One option is to use the cache system and bury or hide extra diapers, food, etc. along the trail you plan to hike. Another option is to plan a hike where you know you'll be able to stop at stores often enough to pick up the items you'll need—more food and diapers. Yet another option is to send extra items to post offices along the way if you have steady access to them. Finally, there is the option of a support crew that meets you at road crossings with the extra things you need.

As for food, once the child is started on solids, it will make your trip a bit more difficult until she can eat what you eat without mashing, smashing, etc. If you plan meals that your child can partake of, too, then you can bring along a hand-grinder. Also, some health food stores offer dehydrated baby foods. Jars of baby food are a heavier option and will keep only a few days (less if it really hot outside) once the jar is opened.

If your child is still breastfeeding but not yet on solids, you're in a perfect situation for backpacking because you don't have to carry formula and bottles. Although difficult, formula-feeding is not impossible. Bottles can be heated on your cook stove the same way they would be heated on your stove at home--by warming them in water in your cook pot. As for clothes, you know your child. Griffin tends to stay on the warm side so we don't have to carry a lot of warm clothes for her when backpacking. Other babies stay cool and consequently the parents must bring extra layers of clothing for their child's comfort. Children can be layered as easily as adults. There are a lot of layering options for children. Many catalogs even offer miniature rain suits.

Since my child was due in the winter, I was anxious to find some warm clothes in a newborn size. I'll admit there wasn't much available but I was able to find some red, cotton long johns. Less than twenty-four hours after Griffin's home birth, I dressed her in those very long johns for her first trip to the doctor. It was twenty degrees outside and the long johns were layered with a blanket sleeper and finally a fleece baby bag.

Keep in mind that there are many things infants under six months of age cannot do—such as wear sunscreen or insect repellent. If you are hiking in the sun, they need a wide-brimmed hat or a screen on their backpack. If your infant will wear them, there are sunglasses available in infant sizes. While still an infant, Griffin successfully wore the Flap-happy Hat sold by Biobottoms of California. The baseball-style cap had a wide front brim and a protective "flap" of material that covered her delicate neck. Patagonia makes a similar hat for infants and children.

When it comes time to bed down for the night, where do you put your infant? When Griffin was younger, I shared my bag with her but she is now too big for that. I have yet to find an infant-sized sleeping bag although some companies make bags designed to keep an infant warm that can work as sleeping bags. You may also want to try designing your own with a child-size down comforter or several blankets.

Some children, like Griffin, have no trouble falling asleep in a dark tent while others who wake to total darkness will freak out. I always keep a flashlight handy should I need to comfort Griffin with a little light. Others may find the confining walls of a tent disconcerting and fuss, but usually they get used to a tent after a night or two.

Keep in mind that a two-man tent is too small for the three of you, while a three-man tent will suit you for a long time.

I am only mentioning one child at this point because unless your second, third, etc. child(ren) can carry their own pack or hike entirely on their own, your backpacking will be limited to day hikes.

Toddlers

While you have basically the same concerns while backpacking with a toddler as you do with an infant, there is one major difference—they can walk.

This means that they'll be eager to escape their pack and hit the ground running. Unfortunately, running for a toddler means two entirely different methods of movement: 1) Literal running which usually ends up with the child on her face, especially on unlevel trails; and 2) Walking a few steps and then stopping to explore, walking a few steps then stopping to explore, walking a few . . . .

Both of these methods can result in frustration for the parent but are absolutely necessary for the sanity of your child. As much as Griffin loves her pack, she still needs to get out of it every once in a while to stretch her new walking legs.

Once the child is out of the pack, though, they demand at least one set of eyes on them constantly. The outdoors is great for growing minds but also poses certain dangers, especially if the child is still teething since everything she picks up is likely to end up in her mouth. She needs you to keep her from eating poison ivy, snails, deer droppings, etc.

Most packs for child-carrying will hold your toddler until he reaches thirty-five to forty pounds. After that, you will begin backpacking with . . .

Children

This will be a difficult stage, no doubt about it. Your child—even packless—will walk a hundred yards (if you're lucky) and then start complaining, weeping, wailing that he is tired. Remember that this is the same kid who can easily run the length of three football fields while playing with his friends.

When your child is at this stage, it is best to take frequent breaks until you reach your destination. You are thus limited as to the number of miles you pack each day. No problem—just tone down your trips for awhile.

Your child can start with a fanny or daypack and carry his own toys and clothing. As your child gets older and stronger, you can move on to bigger packs and add food and sleeping bag to the gear he is carrying.

Gear

Sleeping bags can be purchased for children up to forty-eight to fifty-four inches. From $40 to $100, you can purchase your child a fifteen-degree or higher bag in the backpacker's mummy design.

There are also packs designed especially for children as well as for parents to carry children. Tough Traveler, Gerry and Kelty all make superb packs to carry your infant or toddler. Designed to hold kids up to thirty-five or forty pounds, all include a pocket to carry diapers and other essentials for your baby. An optional rain/sunscreen can be purchased with the Tough Traveler as can extra pockets. Child carriers cost from $50 to $120.

Children's packs are made by a number of manufacturers but the most commonly available is from Camp Trails, who also designs a child's pack for REI. The pack costs $50 and adjusts to the growth of your child.

Manufacturers offer children's hiking boots, too! Both Vasque and Hi-Tec make hiking boots for children starting at about children's size 10. You can even find little boots for toddlers, but make sure they can actually walk in them before you purchase them for your child—they may be absolutely adorable but too rigid for a toddler's intrepid step.

Motivating Children

How can you make backpacking fun for your children and avoid the "how much farther" syndrome? The following are a few suggestions:

- Revel in nature. Stop to point out interesting flowers, clouds, trees, mushrooms, etc. Enjoy water by throwing pebbles, floating sticks and leaves. Play in sand or mud or snow. Watch frogs hop, squirrels and chipmunks scuttle from tree to tree, insects going about their business, a deer standing stock still, a hawk drifting on air currents . . .
- Teach your children geologic and natural history—that Indians once hunted in these woods, that they are walking on what was once hot lava, the intricacies of the glacier that molded this valley . . .
- Answer your child's questions—Why is the sky blue? Are there still Indians in these woods? Will the volcano erupt on us? . . .
- Get out the toys and a treat. Give your child a break with some fruit leather or a muffin and his or her favorite toy.
- Promise a celebration when they have attained a certain goal—some juice and a piece of candy or if health-conscious a fruit-sweetened cookie when you reach the top of the mountain or the next stream.
- Play games that keep you moving. On slight inclines play Runaway train by running wildly to the bottom of the hill (only if your child is capable of doing this without falling on his face); continue the train theme by pretending your family is a train and by making the appropriate noises while walking. Try some other vehicle—airplane, ship, racecar, truck.

- Tell stories. The parents can tell stories of past but true events, make up stories or even invite the children to tell a story. Asking questions of a child can also prolong their stamina.
- Sing songs. Let the child choose or take turns choosing.
- Play animals. Pick an animal and tell about it, makes its noises, etc.
- Give them gorp. A handful of gorp for every 5, 10, 15, 20 steps (or whatever they're capable of) will keep them going for awhile.

At some point or another your child will pull the "I can't take another step without collapsing" trick. When the parent falls for this ploy and the child is carried to your destination, they usually experience a miracle upon arrival. The child's eyes spring open and she's off and running while the poor, exhausted parents later have to beg her to crawl into her sleeping bag.

On the other hand, children do not recognize fatigue and will drop from exhaustion before they show any true signs of tiring. Children are tough but not super-human. Don't push them too hard. Chances are, if you're tired, so are they.

Limitations

Unless one partner is capable of carrying most of the gear (or in the case of a walking child, the parents can split most of the gear) you will have to put off any major backpacking trips until your child is old enough to take care of himself.

A single parent will have to limit his or her backpacking trips to dayhikes unless they intend to camp extra light (which is not really wise if you're hiking with children) by not carrying a tent, cookstove, etc.

You should be aware of your own limitations. If you can't regularly carry a 60-pound pack, don't think that you can do it if you have a child. If you normally carry a forty-pound pack and your child weighs twenty pounds, carry no more than twenty pounds extra. Remember, you have a life on your back now. Don't endanger it.

Introducing your child to the outdoors early does not necessarily mean they'll become avid backpackers later on, so don't be disappointed if they eventually lose interest.

Dogs as Hiking Partners

Although dogs can make wonderful hiking partners, most hikers we have talked to said they prefer not to hike around people who are hiking with dogs. Unless you have complete control over your animal, you are going to make a lot of people unhappy, especially if you intend to stay in a shelter. Two of the biggest complaints that we've heard from backpackers were about wet dogs climbing all over their sleeping bags and other gear, and dogs who tried to eat their food.

Peter Keenan has had a positive experience with his dog, Bobo, even though other hikers have occasional complaints. Bobo, who started hiking the Appalachian Trail as a puppy, only knew about life on the trail. She had a way of lifting spirits on cold and wet days with her boundless energy, and she was always ready for a game of fetch—even after twenty miles.

We mention this only because there are two ways of looking at hiking with dogs. Obviously, things are going to be a lot different if the dog is your hiking partner: you'll probably be indifferent to your wet dog lying on your sleeping bag or your hungry dog begging for your food.

Keep in mind, if you plan to take a dog, that dogs usually are not welcomed by other hikers and do not have priority when it comes to shelter space. Dogs often are not allowed in state or national parks. Be sure to check the regulations before you hike.

Dogs tend to scare up trouble. They have been bitten by rattlesnakes, swatted by porcupines and are keen on rolling in dead animals—not a pleasant odor. If you choose to hike with a dog, you won't see much wildlife.

If you do bring a dog on the trail, make sure you keep it under control. We were chased by some dogs in New Hampshire who, a few minutes later, bit another hiker. The dogs were on a day hike with their owners.

Other reasons not to bring a dog include the rough-rock scrambling on many trails and the intense heat of summer hiking. We witnessed the death of a dog who had overheated in 90-plus-degree weather on a day hike in Pennsylvania. The owner, though well-intentioned, had neglected to bring enough water for his pet. Consider the kindness of leaving your dog at home, especially when you intend to long-distance hike.

If you do decide to hike with your pet, you will need to look into purchasing a pack for your dog unless you intend to carry all its food yourself.

Both Wenaha and Caribou make packs for dogs. Packs are designed to hold the dog's food. Like humans, dogs will need more food because they will be expending more energy while backpacking. The packs fit over the dog's back like a saddle and is secured across the dog's sternum (and sometimes its chest) with easy-release belts. Packs range in price from $20 to $50, and come in different sizes.

Make sure your dog gets enough water. Dogs dehydrate too. Don't let them get to the stage where they refuse drink. I have given up my last canteen of water several times to dogs who were on the verge of hyperthermia. Even if the dog has to carry it, always make sure you have extra water for your pet.

· 16 ·
Hiking Green

It began to be noticed that the greater the exodus, the smaller the per capita ration of peace, solitude, wildlife and scenery, and the longer the migration to reach them.

—Aldo Leopold

As Aldo Leopold wrote years ago, it is getting harder and harder to find solitude. Even wilderness areas seem to overflow with humanity at times. Backpacking is a way to get away from the mass of people and be alone (or at least among the noble few who will respect your wish for solitude). But, are we as backpackers destroying the last vestiges of wilderness in our selfish quest for peace and communion with nature?

Like Kermit the Frog says, it's not easy being green. Backpacking is not really the greenest form of recreation. Although we revel in the environment, do we trade price, nutrition, quality and convenience for environmental quality? Are the products we buy and use dangerous to the health of people and animals? Do they cause damage to the environment during manufacture, use or disposal? Do they consume a disproportionate amount of energy and other resources during manufacture, use or disposal? Do they cause unnecessary waste, due to either excessive packaging or a short useful life? Do they involve the unnecessary use of or cruelty to animals? And, finally, do they use materials derived from threatened species or environments?

These are all questions John Elkington, Julia Hailes and Joel Makower say should be asked when deciding whether or not a product is "green". In their book, *The Green Consumer*, they agree that it is difficult to find a perfectly green product. But when purchasing equipment, you may want to take some of these factors into account. Fortunately, backpacking gear already has one major factor in its favor—minimal packaging! Most backpacking gear comes as is: sleeping bags and tents packed in stuff sacks; packs purchased off the rack; stoves in environmentally sound cardboard cartons.

In the book, *Shopping for a Better World*, by C.E.P., manufacturers are rated on how green they are. Criteria used to determine the rating include: how environmentally clean the company is, if animals are tested, and if the company is associated with South Africa or nuclear weapons. The book focuses on manufacturers of food, personal care products and other items typically found in a grocery store. To find out about the manufacturers of boots, backpacks, tents and other backpacking equipment, contact the company and question them about your concerns.

There are a number of companies these days involved. Some outdoor businesses are involved in the Outdoor Industry Conservation Alliance (and help out the environment by providing grants to grassroots conservation organizations) that have become ecologically and environmentally involved. Other businesses are helping to purchase land for the Nature Conservancy and other groups. Chevrolet, Coleman, ACG (Nike), AT&T, Canon, Duofold, Kodak, Merrell, Mountainsmith, Nalgene, Nature Valley Granola Bars, Nike Hiking, REI, Spenco, Trek, Wild Country USA and Yakima are corporate sponsors of the new American Discovery Trail.

Recycled Gear

One of the biggest changes taking place in the 1990s is that manufacturers of backpacking equipment are making gear using recycled products. One example is Patagonia's recycled Synchilla fleece jackets made from recycled plastic soft drink bottles. They contain 80 percent recycled polyester (including post consumer plastic) and 20 percent virgin fibers.

Other products using recycled materials include Nike boots, which use reground rubber in the soles, and Reebok, which includes pigment-free leather and recycled plastic soft drink bottles in their lightweight Telos hiking boot's uppers. The Telos also have outsoles, 75 percent of which are manufactured from recycled car tires.

Other manufacturers are joining the "Green" bandwagon with decreased packaging and increased use of recycled materials in both their packaging and in the products themselves.

Minimum Impact Camping

There are ways we can control our impact on the environment through our purchases of hiking gear. But backpackers also have to make a conscious effort to make as small an impact on the environment as possible when hiking. In recent years, "minimum impact camping" has become the catchphrase for responsible outdoors behavior.

Groups such as the Boy Scouts, who once espoused techniques like trenching your tent to prevent water from running under it, have adopted low-impact techniques. Minimum impact camping is a philosophy once summed up by the National Park Service as "Take nothing but pictures, leave nothing but footprints." The following are measures you can take to eliminate any trace of your presence along the trail.

Carry Out All of Your Trash

This includes everything, even organic trash. Orange peels, apple cores and egg shells may strike you as natural trash, easily biodegradable, so why not toss it into the brush? It takes five months for an orange peel to rot and become one with the earth. If you don't want to carry it, at least bury it!

Also, there is nothing worse than heading back into the woods to relieve yourself only to discover a trail of paper proving you weren't the first to have this idea at this spot. Soggy, used toilet paper is probably one of the uglier reminders of human presence.

I've followed trails littered with candy bar wrappers and cigarette butts. If you want to smoke, that's your prerogative, but you shouldn't think of the outdoors as one big ashtray. Not only is the litter of cigarette butts ugly, but it only takes one stray spark to start a forest fire that will turn the woods into a huge ashtray.

If you smoke, munch on candy bars or snack on fruit while hiking, keep a sack handy to store your waste in. Pack it in, pack it out and you're already one giant step toward improving the environment you've supposedly escaped to.

Carry Out Trash Left by Others

If your trip is a long one and there aren't many stops available to drop off trash, it is perhaps understandable (but not excusable) that you carry no more than your own trash. Unfortunately, the enviro-conscious do not outnumber the users and abusers of America's trails, and we have to make up for their ignorance and sloth by picking up after them.

A friend of mine who maintains a section of trail in Virginia once disgustedly told me of the miles of string he had to pick up when that section of trail was being measured, and the measurer neglected to clean up after himself. The trails abound with trash. For some reason, people who wouldn't dare throw trash on the ground at home do so freely in the outdoors. You can make the outdoors an even better place by stopping occasionally to pick up other people's trash. You don't have to be ridiculous and carry out nasty toilet paper or rotting organic material. But, you can take a minute to cover it with leaves, moss, dirt and twigs. Pick up trash, you'll find you'll feel a lot better about yourself.

Cook On a Stove Rather Than Over a Fire

It is now illegal in many forests to build fires—and for good reason. If not cared for properly, they can start forest fires. They are also damaging to the environment. Scars from fire rings last a long time. Blackened earth and rocks are messy and far from aesthetically pleasing to the eye. Using a cook stove puts less wear and tear on the environment.

If you build a fire, do not burn or leave trash in the fire pit. This is even uglier than finding trash alongside the trail. Once you've started something burning, you'll have the tendency to leave it in the pit whether it is fully burned or not. Do not put tinfoil-lined packages in fire pits because they will not entirely burn up. The easiest thing to do is to avoid this problem altogether by packing out all your trash.

If you do decide to build a fire, use only downed wood. Breaking branches from trees or chopping dead or live trees for wood should not even be considered a possibility. Killing plant life for atmosphere is inexcusable. Obviously, rules change for just about anything if a life or death situation is involved. Once again, if you do intend to build a fire, do so only in designated fire pits. As I said earlier, fire pits deeply scar the earth. If there is a pit already available, use it.

Limit Your Group Size to Ten or Less

Any time you have ten or more people camping in one spot, you're going to have a major impact on the environment. You've got ten people using the surrounding area as a toilet,

> **>>Hiking Tip<<**
>
> Looking for a little solitude? By camping in little-used areas, you'll not only find peace and quiet, you'll spread out the impact humans make in a given area. Ask park rangers and others familiar with the area if they know of any infrequently used campsites.

ten people beating down the ground to set up tents. The environmental impact a group of ten or more can have on a campsite is shocking. Obviously, not all large groups are detrimental to the outdoors, but enough are that they make a bad impression on those who are environmentally conscious. If you become involved with a group that is interested in backpacking trips, make sure that you divide yourselves into groups of ten or fewer before you set out.

Camp in Designated Sites or Well Away From the Trail
Similarly, when camping on a backpacking trip, make sure you camp in designated areas only. The spaces are chosen because they are more resistant to constant use. If you should feel it is too dangerous (in griz country, for example) to camp in a designated area or if one is not available, camp well off the trail. Trails already receive a lot of impact and camping away from the trail will cut down on its wear and tear.

When you leave a campsite, take a long, hard look at it. It should look better than when you found it. If you camp off the trail, it should look as if you had never been there. It can be done. We've even gone so far as to rescatter leaves and fluff up grass so that you could not tell where our tent had been pitched. It only takes a few minutes and your efforts are more than compensated for with peace of mind.

Stay on the Designated Trail (Don't Cut Switchbacks)
The switchbacks are there for a reason. They slow down the

erosion of trail on steep climbs. Sure, it may seem easier to scramble up the hillside the ten yards or so to the next section of trail, but if too many people do that, rain will start using the newly exposed earth as a watercourse—washing away both trail and mountain in its wake. Stay on the designated trail. You may curse the person who blazed it and those who attempt to keep it passable for you, but remember that just about any trail you hike was built and is maintained by volunteers.

Don't Use Soap in or Near Streams

As discussed in both Chapters 2 and 10, there are a number of reasons to avoid the use of soap in or near a stream. Unless you are using a biodegradable soap, you could poison the water for any animal that drinks from it, including yourself.

Streams are often water sources when backpacking. Even if you do have biodegradable soap, do you really want to drink water that has any type of soap in it? If you need to wash your body, your hair or your dishes, use stream water, but carry it well away from the stream before using it.

One method for washing your hair is to get it wet while at the water source, and with a pot-full or waterbag of water, walk about 150 feet away from the water source. You can then wash your hair and rinse it with the water in your pot or bag. If you have a waterbag with a shower attachment, you can hang the bag from an appropriate tree and rinse your hair out that way.

The same goes for washing clothes and dishes. Carry the water away from the water source. You can wash both dishes and clothes out of your largest cooking pot. For more information on cleaning up after meals, see Chapter 3.

Solid Waste Management

In other words, how to dispose of your excrement. Kathleen Meyer has written a book, which she calls "an environmen-

❦ *Hiking Secret* ❦

Try blending environmental self-education into a trip. While you don't want to burden your pack with various field guides to flowers, birds or trees, you can take a moderate approach. Take a flower hike one spring weekend and bring your guide along, or take a bird hike or a tree hike on another weekend. Look up species you are likely to encounter ahead of time and refer to the book as you hike to broaden your enjoyment of the outdoors.

tally sound approach to a lost art." To learn about the fine details of relieving yourself in the woods, Meyer provides plenty of advice in *How to Shit in the Woods*, which is available from Ten Speed Press.

Disposing of your feces when backpacking is absolutely necessary. Always, always, always (I can't say it too many times) dig a hole. More importantly, make sure you're at least 150 feet from the nearest water source. If you're hiking in a canyon through which water runs, climb up. If it's winter and snowing and you can't dig through the frozen snow and ice (if you can, make sure you dig into the earth as well), pack it out. Yes, it sounds horrifying but if it's cold enough, it can be done. Just line the hole in the snow with a plastic bag, do your thing and then tie-twist or zip it shut, and pack it out. Otherwise, when the snow melts, your feces will end up on the ground surface and make an unwelcome sight (not to mention odor) for any springtime hikers. There's more to being green than just packing out your trash. Disposing properly of your solid waste will keep the wilderness much more appealing.

Trail Maintenance
One of the biggest ways you can give back to the trail and the hiking community is by becoming involved in trail maintenance. I don't know offhand of a trail that isn't maintained by volunteers.

Maintaining a section of existing trail or helping out regularly with the blazing of new trails is a good way of paying back the outdoors for the good times you have received from it. Trails are beginning to criss-cross the entire country, and there is sure to be a new or old trail somewhere near you. Contact your local trail clubs to see what you can do to help out. A list of trail-related clubs and organizations appears in the back of this book.

The late Henry Lanham would often speak of the users and the givers—those who used the trails, selfishly, with no thought of even a day's work to help what had given them so much pleasure; and the givers, those who paid back many times over all the joy the trails had given them by spending hours working on the trail. Henry was a giver. Active in the Natural Bridge Appalachian Trail Club for years, Henry died in 1991 while cutting new trail in Idaho.

What Else Can You Do?
There are a number of little things you can do to decrease your environmental impact:

- Reuse your zipper-lock bags. Not only can they be reused during a trip but once home, you can wash and dry them to use on your next trip. Don't reuse bags that carried raw meat or human and animal waste.
- Buy hiking equipment (tents, backpacks, etc.) in environmentally eye-pleasing colors such as forest green, grey, light blue, tan and brown.
- Purchase environmentally-sound toiletries by manufacturers such as Aubrey Organics, St. Ives and Tom's of Maine. Catalogs from The Body Shop, The Compassionate Consumer, Ecco Bella, Seventh Generation and others offer environmentally safe products. *The Green Consumer* supplies lists of both catalogs and manufacturers.
- Always change into a pair of lightweight, soft shoes when you make camp to lessen your effect on the site.

This chapter is not a list of rules; it is a way of living that is becoming increasingly important to adopt. If these techniques are not used by everyone (and currently they're not), the trail will lose its natural beauty.

Nature is resilient but its ability to fight back is limited. It takes a long time for a campsite to recover from a single overnight stay by an inconsiderate group of hikers.

But a little bit of help goes a long way toward improving the world we're escaping to. If everyone pitches in—even just a little bit—we'll be able to enjoy our backcountry experiences even more.

Remember, Earth, despite her condition, will be here forever. It is the human race that needs saving. If we can't preserve our environment, we can't preserve ourselves.

· Appendix 1 ·
Equipment Checklists

Equipment for a Day Hike
(This list assumes you are already wearing comfortable clothes and good walking shoes)

Day pack or fanny pack
One-liter (minimum) Nalgene-style bottle
Rain gear
Food for the day
Lighter or waterproof matches
First aid (bandages, moleskin)
Toilet paper, trowel
Map and/or guidebook*
Camera and film*
Binoculars*
Gloves and knit cap†
Extra shirt†
Bandana*

Equipment for an Overnight Hike
Light- or mediumweight hiking boots
Internal or external frame pack
Sleeping bag
Sleeping pad
Tent/tarp and groundcloth
Stove and fuel
Cooking pot and eating utensils
Knife (pocket)
Water purifiers (or plan to boil your water)
More than adequate food for length of hike
Spices*
One-liter (minimum) Nalgene-style bottle

Drinking cup
Rain gear including pack cover
Gaiters*
One pair of shorts
One pair of loose fitting, long pants+
One to two short sleeve shirts
One long sleeve shirt or sweater
Knit cap
Balaclava†
Down or synthetic fill parka†
Two pairs liner socks
Two pairs socks
One or more bandanas
Long johns†
Underwear (2 pair)*
Toilet paper, trowel
Biodegradable soap and washcloth
Deodorant*
Toothbrush and toothpaste
Shaving kit*
Nylon cord (at least 10 feet)
Maps, guidebooks
Compass
Flashlight with new batteries
Watch or clock*
Sunglasses*
First Aid kit (including moleskin)
Space blanket
Swimsuit and towel*
Extra shoes*
Repair equipment (for pack, tent, and stove)*
Camera and film*
Radio with headphones*
Insect repellent†

Sunscreen/lotion†
Hiking stick*

Additional Equipment Needed for Longer Hikes
Repair equipment for pack, tent, stove, and clothes
Trash bag (a small one for your own trash)
Long sleeve shirt or sweater
Long johns
Film mailers*
Reading material*
Journal*
Crampons and ice ax†

*Optional
†Seasonal

· Appendix 2 ·
Suppliers of Backpacking Equipment

The following list of manufacturers and distributors of backpacking equipment includes most of the major and minor suppliers in the country. Some of the more significant products that the manufacturers sell are listed in parantheses. Not all equipment offered by these manufacturers is listed.

Adidas America, 541 N.E. 20th Street, Suite 207, Portland OR 97232. Phone: (800) 423-4327. (Lightweight boots, outdoor clothing)

Alico Sport, P.O. Box 165, Beebe Plain, VT 05823. Phone: (514) 937-2320. (Lightweight boots)

Alpina Sports Corp., P.O. Box 23, Hanover, NH 03755. Phone: (603) 448-3101. (Boots)

Asolo/Nordica USA, 139 Harvest Lane, Williston, VT 05495. Phone: (800) 862-2668. (Boots)

Basic Designs, Inc., 5815 Bennett Valley Road, Santa Rosa, CA 95404. Phone: (707) 575-1220. (Sleeping pads)

Bibler Tents, 5441-D Western Avenue, Boulder, CO 80301. Phone: (303) 449-7351. (Tents, sleeping bags, butane stove)

Black Diamond Equipment, Ltd., 2084 East 3900 South, Salt Lake City, UT 84124. Phone: (801) 278-5533 (Packs, tents)

Camping Gaz/Suunto USA, 2151 Las Palmes Drive, Suite G, Carlsbad, CA 92009. Phone: (800) 543-9124. (Butane stoves and lanterns)

Campmor, P.O. Box 997, Paramus, NJ 07653-0998. Phone: (800) 525-4784. (Distributor of a wide variety of hiking equipment, including Campmor brand products.)

Camp Trails/Johnson Camping, Inc., P.O. Box 966, Binghamton, NY 13902. Phone: (800) 848-3673 (Packs)

Caribou Mountaineering, Inc., P.O. Box 3696, Chico, CA 95927. Phone: (800) 824-4153. (Packs, sleeping bags)

Cascade Designs, 4000 First Avenue South, Seattle, WA 98134. Phone: (800) 531-9531. (Packs)

Climb High, 1861 Shelburne Road, Shelburne, VT 05482. Phone: (802) 985-5056. (Boots, packs, butane/propane stoves, sleeping bags)

Coleman Footgear, 9341 Courtland Drive N.E., Rockford, MI 49351. Phone: (800) 253-2184. (Boots)

Columbia Sportswear Company, 6600 North Baltimore, Portland, OR 97283-0239. Phone: (800) 622-6953, Customer Service Phone: (503) 289-8736. (Sportswear)

Dana Design, 1950 North 19th Street, Bozeman, MT 59715. Phone: (406) 587-4188. (Packs)

Danner Shoe Manufacturing Company, P.O. Box 30148, Portland, OR 97230. Phone: (800) 345-0430. (Boots)

Diamond Brand Canvas Products Co., Inc., P.O. Box 249, Naples, NC 28760. Phone: (800) 258-9811. (Packs, tents)

Eastern Mountain Sports, One Vose Farm Road, Peterborough, NH 03458. Phone: (603) 924-6154. (Distributor of a wide variety of hiking equipment, including EMS brand products.)

Eastpak, Inc., 50 Rogers Road, Ward Hill, MA 01835. Phone: (508) 373-1581. (Packs)

Edko Alpine Designs, P.O. Box 17005, Boulder, CO 80308. (303) 440-0446. (Packs)

Envirogear, Ltd., 127 Elm Street, Cortland, NY 13045. Phone: (607) 753-8801. (Sleeping bags)

Epigas/Taymar, Inc., 2755 South 160th Street, New Berlin, WI 53151. Phone: (800) 776-7189. (Stoves)

Eureka!/Johnson Camping, P.O. Box 966, Binghamton, NY 13902. Phone: (800) 847-1460. (Tents)

Expedition Trails, P.O. Drawer G, Haleyville, AL 35565. Phone: (800) 221-7452. (Sleeping bags)

Explore by Modan, 453 R Hartford Turnpike, Vernon, CT 06066. Phone: (800) 755-1797. (Packs)

Fabiano Shoe Company, 850 Summer Street, South Boston, MA 02127. Phone: (617) 268-5625. (Boots)

Feathered Friends, Department B, 2013 Fourth Avenue, Seattle, WA 98121. Phone: (206) 443-9549. (Down sleeping bags)

Five Ten, P.O. Box 1185, Redlands, CA 92373. Phone: (909) 798-4222. (Lightweight boots)

Foam Designs Consumer Products, Inc., P.O. Box 11184, Lexington, KY 40581. Phone: (606) 231-7006. (Sleeping pads)

Garuda, P.O. Box 24804, Seattle, WA 98124-0804. Phone: (206) 763-2989. (Tents)

General Ecology, 151 Sheree Boulevard, Exton, PA 19341. Phone: (800) 441-8166. (First Need brand water purifiers)

Georgia Boot, Inc., P.O. Box 10, Franklin, TN 37065. Phone: (800) 251-3388. (Boots)

Gerry Baby Products, Company, 150 East 128th Avenue, Thornton, CO 80220. Phone: (800) 525-2472. (Children's packs and child carriers)

Gold-Eck of Austria, 6313 Seaview Avenue, N.W., Seattle, WA 98107. Phone: (206) 781-0886. (Sleeping bags)

Grade VI, P.O. Box 8, Urbana, IL 61801-0008. Phone: (217) 328-6666. (Packs)

Granite Gear, Inc., P.O. Box 278, Two Harbors, MN 55616. Phone: (218) 834-6157. (Packs)

Gregory Mountain Products, 100 Calle Cortez, Temecula, CA 92590. Phone: (800) 477-3420, Customer Service Phone: (800) 854-8585. (Internal frame packs, tents)

Gymwell Corportion, 23555 Telo Avenue, Torrance, CA 90505. Phone: (800) 466-7856. (Sleeping pads)

Hartford Easter Seals, Headlite Products, Resource Enterprises, 80 Coventry Street, Hartford, CT 06112. Phone: (203) 243-9741. (Headlamps)

High Sierra, 880 Corporate Woods Parkway, Vernon Hills, IL 60061. Phone: (800) 323-9590. (Packs)

Hitachi, 401 West Artesia Boulevard, Compton, CA 90220. Phone: (310) 537-8383. (Headlamps)

Hi-Tec, 4801 Stoddard Road, Modesto, CA 95356. Phone: (800) 521-1698. (Lightweight boots)

Integral Designs, 5516 Third Street S.E., Calgary, Alberta, Canada, T2H 1J9. Phone: (403) 640-1444. (Sleeping bags)

Jansport, 10411 Airport Road, Everett, WA 98204. Phone: (800) 552-6776, Customer Service Phone (800) 426-9227. (Packs)

Koflach/Atomic For Sport, 9 Columbia Drive, Amherst, NH 03031. Phone: (603) 880-6143. (Heavyweight boots)

Kelty, Inc., 1224 Fern Ridge Parkway, Creve Coeur, MO 63141. Phone: (800) 423-2320. (Packs, child carrier, sleeping bags, tents)

Lafuma USA, P.O. Box 812, Farmington, GA 30638. Phone: (706) 769-6627. (Packs, tents, sleeping bags)

LaSportiva, USA, 3235 Prairie Avenue, Boulder, CO 80301. Phone: (303) 443-8710. (Boots)

Legends Footwear, P.O. Box 505, La Puente, CA 91746. Phone: (800) 533-9653. (boots)

Liberty Mountain Sports, 9325 SW Barber Street, Wilsonville, OR 97070. Phone: (800) 366-2666. (Butane stoves, sleeping bags)

L.L. Bean, Casco Street, Freeport, ME 04033-0001. Phone: (800) 221-4221. Customer Service Phone: (800) 341-4341. (Distributor of a wide variety of hiking equipment, including L.L. Bean brand products.)

Lowa USA/Omni International, RR 3, Box 1521, 31 Falls Road, Hudson, NY 12534-9803. Phone: (800) 289-5354. (Heavyweight boots)

Lowe Alpine Systems, P.O. Box 1449, Broomfield, CO 80038. Phone: (303) 465-0522, Customer Service Phone: (303) 465-3707. (Packs)

Madden USA, 2400 Central Avenue, Boulder, CO 80301. Phone: (303) 442-5828. (Packs)

Markill/Bergsport International, P.O. Box 1519, Nederland, CO 80466. Phone: (303) 258-3796. (Stoves)

Mark Pack Works, 230 Madison Street, Oakland, CA 94607. Phone: (510) 452-0243. (Packs)

Marmot Mountain International, 2321 Circadian Way, Santa Rosa, CA 95407. Phone: (707) 544-4590. (Sleeping bags)

McHale & Company, 29 Dravus Street, Seattle, WA 98109. Phone: (206) 281-7861. (Internal-frame packs)

Merrell, P.O. Box 4249, South Burlington, VT 05402. Phone: (800) 869-3348, Customer Service Phone: (802) 496-4584. (Boots)

MontBell America, 940 41st Avenue, Santa Cruz, CA 95062. Phone: (800) 541-2015. Phone: (408) 476-2400. (Packs, sleeping bags)

Moonstone Mountaineering, 5350 Ericson Way, Arcata, CA 95521. Phone: (707) 822-2985. (Sleeping bags)

Moss Inc., P.O. Box 309, Camden, ME 04843. Phone: (207) 236-8368. (Tents)

Mountain Equipment, Inc., 4776 East Jensen, Fresno, CA 93752. Phone: (209) 486-8211. (Packs)

Mountain Safety Research (MSR), P.O. Box 24547, Seattle, WA 98124. Phone: (800) 877-9677. (Stoves with both the MSR name and Trangia brand; water purifiers)

Mountainsmith, Inc., 18301 West Colfax Avenue, Heritage Square, Building P, Golden, CO 80401. Phone: (800) 551-5889. (Packs, tents)

Mountain Tools, 140 Calle Del Oaks, Monterey, CA 93940. Phone: (408) 393-1000. (Internal-frame packs)

Natural Balance Design, P.O. Box 1573, Fairfield, IA 52556. Phone: (515) 472-7918. (Internal-frame packs)

New Balance Athletic Shoes, Inc., 38 Everett Street, Boston, MA 02134. Phone: (800) 253-7463, Customer Service Phone: (800) 343-4648. (Lightweight boots)

Nike, Inc., 1 Bowerman Drive, Beaverton, OR 97005. Phone: (503) 571-5453, Customer Service Phone: (800) 344-6453. (Lightweight boots, rain gear, outdoor wear)

The North Face, 999 Harrison Street, Berkeley, CA 94710. Phone: (510) 527-9700. (Packs, tents, sleeping bags, outdoor wear)

One Sport, 1003 Sixth Avenue South, Seattle, WA 98134. Phone: (206) 621-9303. (Boots)

Optimus/Suunto USA, 2151 Las Palmas Drive, Carlsbad, CA 92009. Phone: (800) 543-9124. (White gas and kerosene stoves)

Osprey Packs, P.O. Box 539, Dolores, CO 81323. Phone: (303) 882-2221. (Internal-frame packs)

Outbound, 1580 Zephyr, Hayward, CA 94544. Phone: (800) 866-9880. (Packs, sleeping bags, tents, water filters)

Overland Equipment, 2145 Park Avenue, Suite 4, Chico, CA 95928. Phone: (916) 894-5605. (Packs)

Panasonic, 6550 Katella Avenue, Cypress, CA 90630. Phone: (714) 373-7281. (Headlamps)

Patagonia, Box 8900, Bozeman, MT 59715. Phone: (800) 638-6464. (Outdoor wear)

Peak 1/The Coleman Company, Inc., P.O. Box 2931, Wichita, KS 67201. Phone: (800) 835-3278. (Packs, sleeping bags, white gas and multi-fuel stoves)

Peter Limmer & Sons, Inc., Intervale, NH 03845. Phone: (603) 356-5378. (Stock and custom-made boots)

Petzl, Pigeon Mountain Industries, P.O. Box 803, Lafayette, GA 30728. Phone: (706) 764-1437. (Headlamps)

Pop-Tent, Inc., 8800 N.W. 23rd Street, Miami, FL 33172. Phone: (305) 592-5600. (Tents)

PUR, 2229 Edgewood Avenue South, Minneapolis, MN 55426. Phone: (800) 845-7873. (Water Filters)

Pyromid, 3292 South Highway 97, Redmond, OR 97756. Phone: (503) 548-1041. (Stoves)

Quest, 569 Charcot Avenue, San Jose, CA 95131. Phone: (800) 875-6901. (Packs, tents)

Raichle Molitar USA, Inc., Geneva Road, Brewster, NY 10509. Phone: (800) 431-2204. (Boots)

Reebok International, Ltd., 100 Technology Center Drive, Stoughton, MA 02072. Phone: (800) 843-4444. (Boots)

REI (Recreational Equipment, Inc.), P.O. Box 1938, Sumner, WA 98390-0800. Phone: (800) 426-4840. Customer service phone: (800) 828-5533. (Distributor of a wide variety of hiking equipment, including REI brand products.)

Remington/Nelson Weather-Rite, 14760 Santa Fe Trail Drive, Lenexa, KS 66215. Phone: (913) 492-3200. (Packs, tents, sleeping bags)

The Rockport Company, P.O. Box 30, Marlboro, MA 01752. Phone: (800) 343-9255. (Boots)

Rocky Shoes & Boots, Inc., 44 East Canal Street, Nelsonville OH 45764. Phone: (800) 421-5151. (Boots)

Salomon North America, Inc., 400 East Main Street, Georgetown, MA 01833. Phone: (508) 352-7600. (Boots)

Saucony/Hyde Athletic Industries, Inc., P.O. Box 6046, Peabody, MA 01961. Phone: (800) 365-7282. (Boots)

Sebago, Inc., P.O. Box 3000, Westbrook, ME 04098-3000. Phone: (207) 854-8474. (Lighweight boots)

Sierra Designs, 2039 Fourth Street, Berkeley, CA 94710. Phone: (800) 743-7722. (Tents, rain gear, sleeping bags)

Slumberjack, P.O. Box 7048A, St. Louis, MO 63177. Phone: (800) 233-6283. (Sleeping bags)

Streamlight, 1030 W. Germantown Pike, Norristown, PA 19403. Phone: (800) 523-7488. (Headlamps)

SweetWater, Inc., 4725 Nautilus Court South, Boulder, CO 80302. Phone: (303) 530-2715. (Water filters)

Tecnica, USA, P.O. Box 551, West Lebanon, NH 03784. Phone: (800) 258-3897. (Lightweight and mediumweight boots)

Therm-a-Rest by Cascade Designs, Inc., Department B, 4000 First Avenue South, Seattle, WA 98134. Phone: (800) 531-9531. (Sleeping bags and pads)

The Timberland Company, 11 Merrill Industrial Drive, Hampton, NH 03842. Phone: (603) 926-1600, Customer

Service Phone: (800) 258-0855. (Lightweight and medium-weight boots)

Tough Traveler, 1012 State Street, Schenectady, NY 12307. Phone: (800) 468-6844. (Child carriers, sleeping bags)

Ultimate Direction, 1448 North Salem Road, Rexburg, ID 83440. Phone: (800) 426-7229. (Packs)

Vasque, Division of Red Wing Shoe Company, Riverfront Center, Red Wing, MN 55066. Phone: (612) 388-8211, Customer Service Phone: (800) 842-1301. (Lightweight and mediumweight boots)

VauDe/Northern Lights, Inc., P.O. Box 3413 Mammoth Lakes, CA 93546. Phone: (619) 924-3833. (Packs, sleeping bags, tents, outdoor wear)

Walrus Inc., P.O. Box 3875, Seattle, WA 98124. Phone: (800) 550-8368. (Tents)

Western Mountaineering, 1025 South 5th Street, San Jose, CA 95112. Phone: (408) 287-8944. (Sleeping bags)

Wiggy's, Inc., P.O. Box 2124, Grand Junction, CO 81506. Phone: (303) 241-6465. (Sleeping bags)

Wild Country/Journeyman, 624 Main Street, Conway, NH 03813. Phone: (603) 447-1961. (Packs, tents)

Wilderness Experience, 20727 Dearborn Street, Chatsworth, CA 91311. Phone: (818) 341-5774. (Packs)

Wild Things, Inc., P.O. Box 400, North Conway, NH 03860. Phone: (603) 356-6907. (Packs, sleeping bags, tents)

Jack Wolfskin, 920 Mendocino Avenue, Santa Rosa, CA 95401. Phone: (607) 779-2755. (Packs, sleeping bags)

Wolverine, 9341 Courtland Drive, Rockford, MI 49546. Phone: (616) 866-5500. (Mediumweight boots)

Zip Ztoves, 10806 Kaylor Street, Los Alamitos, CA 90720. Phone: (310) 598-3220. (Battery-powered, wood-burning backpacking stoves)

· Appendix 3 ·
Trail Clubs

Adirondack Mountain Club, Inc., RR 3, Box 3055, Lake George, NY 12845

American Discovery Trail, see American Hiking Society

The American Hiking Society, 1015 31st Street, N.W., Washington, D.C. 20007

Appalachian Long Distance Hikers Association, 30 Donovan Court, Merrimack, NH 03054

Appalachian Mountain Club, 5 Joy Street, Boston, MA 02108.

Appalachian Trail Conference, P.O. Box 807, Harpers Ferry, WV 25425

Benton MacKaye Trail Association, P.O. Box 53271, Atlanta, GA 30305

Buckeye Trail Association, 138 Bonita Drive, Dayton, OH 45415

C&O Canal Association, P.O. Box 166, Glen Echo, MD 20812

Chinook Trail Association, P.O. Box 997, Vancouver, WA 98666

Colorado Trail Foundation, 548 Pine Song Trail, Golden, CO 80401

Continental Divide Trail Association, P.O. Box 30002, Bethesda, MD 20814

Desert Trail Association, P.O. Box 537, Burns, OR 97720

Finger Lake Trail Association, P.O. Box 18048, Rochester, NY 14618

Florida Trail Association, P.O. Box 13708, Gainesville, FL 32604

Foothills Trail Conference, P.O. Box 3041, Greenville, SC 29602

Green Mountain Club, P.O. Box 889, Montpelier, VT 05602.

Ice Age Park and Trail Foundation, 630 Riverfront, P.O. Box 422, Sheboygan, WI 53082

Iditarod Trail Committee, Pouch X, Wasilla, AK 99645

Iowa Trails Council, 1201 Central, Center Point, IA 52213

Keystone Trails Association, P.O. Box 251, Cogan Station, PA 17728.

La Canada Flintridge Trails Council, P.O. Box 852, La Canada Flintridge, CA 91011

Lewis and Clark Trail Heritage Foundation, Inc., P.O. Box 3434, Great Falls, MT 59403

Mason Dixon Trail System, P.O. Box 116, Kennett Square, PA 19348

Mormon Trail Foundation, 5300 South 360 West, Salt Lake City, UT 84123

The Mountaineers, 300 Third Avenue, West, Seattle, WA 98119

Natchez Trace Trail Conference, P.O. Box 6579, Jackson, MS 39282

North Carolina Trails Association, Box 1033, Greensboro, NC 27402

North Country Trail Association, P.O. Box 311, White Cloud, MI 49349

Oregon-California Trail Association, P.O. Box 1019, Independence, MO 64051-0519

Ozark Highlands Trail Association, P.O. Box 1074, Fayetteville, AR 72703

Pacific Northwest Trail Association, P.O. Box 1048, Seattle, WA 98111

Pacific Crest Trail Conference, 365 West 29th Avenue, Eugene, OR 97405

Pinhoti Trail, Lower Appalachian Mountain Club, 1404 Stone Hill Road, Sylacauga, AL 35150

Potomac Appalachian Trail Club, 118 Park Street SE, Vienna, VA 22180

Potomac Heritage Trail Association, see Potomac Appalachian Trail Club

Rails-to-Trails Conservancy, 1400 16th Street N.W., Washington, D.C. 20036

Santa Fe Trail Association, Santa Fe Trail Center, Route 3, Larned, KS 67550

Superior Hiking Trail Association, Box 2157, Tofte, MN 55615

The Vulcan Trail Association, P.O. 31104, Birmingham, AL 35222

Washington Trails Association, 1305 Fourth Avenue, #512, Seattle, WA 98101

· Appendix 4 ·
Suggested Reading

The Appalachian Trail Backpacker, by Victoria and Frank Logue. Menasha Ridge Press, Second Edition, 1994.

This guide answers the questions most asked about the nation's longest continuous footpath and provides vital information for a trip of any length on the A.T. The book was formerly titled, *The Appalachian Trail Backpacker's Planning Guide*.

Backpacking With Babies and Small Children, by Goldie Silverman. Wilderness Press, Second Edition, 1986.

Tips for taking your youngsters out on the trail and not only surviving, but learning to enjoy it.

The Basic Essentials of Cooking in the Outdoors, by Cliff Jacobson. ICS Books, 1989.

Ideas and solutions for making food taste better and stay edible longer.

The Basic Essentials of Edible Wild Plants and Useful Herbs, by Jim Meuninck. ICS Books, 1988.

Learn to identify, collect and eat nutritious vegetation found wild.

The Basic Essentials of Women in the Outdoors, by Judith Niemi. ICS Books, 1990.

A guide for for comfortable backcountry travel written just for women.

Be an Expert with Map and Compass, by Bjorn Kjellstrom. MacMillan, 1983.

The standard text on an important backpacking skill.

Cross-Country Skiing, by Ned Gillette and John Dostal. The Mountaineers, Third Edition, 1993.

A guide to cross-country ski equipment and technique.

Emergency Medical Procedures for the Outdoors, by Patient Medical Associates. Menasha Ridge Press, revised 1992.

Unique step-by-step guide to almost all outdoor emergencies.

The Green Consumer, by John Elkington, Julia Hailes, and Joel Makower. Penguin Books, 1990.

Useful information for anyone wanting to do the right thing environmentally.

Gorp, Glop and Glew Stew, by Yvonne Prater and Ruth Dyar Mendenhall. The Mountaineers, 1981.

Recipes for camping and backpacking trips.

Harsh Weather Camping in the '90s, by Sam Curtis. Menasha Ridge Press, revised 1993.

Learn to survive and thrive in adverse weather. Tips on staying dry when it's wet, warm when it's cool and cool when it's hot.

How to Shit in the Woods, *An Environmentally Sound Approach to a Lost Art*, by Kathleen Meyer. Ten Speed Press, 1989.

A guide to disposing of your wastes without disturbing the areas you hike in.

Knots for Hikers and Backpackers, by Frank Logue. Menasha Ridge Press, 1994.

A 32-page booklet with all of the knots essential to backpacking and their uses.

Medicine for the Backcountry, by Buck Tilton and Frank Hubbell. ICS Books, 1990.

A guide to providing emergency medical treatment in the backcountry.

Modern Outdoor Survival, by Dwight R. Shuh. Menasha Ridge Press, 1983.

Learn to use modern gear and knowledge to prevent outdoor emergencies and to cope with the ones that do occur.

The Peterson Field Guide Series. Houghton Mifflin Company.

This valuable series of more than twenty books includes guides to birds, mammals, animal tracks, wildflowers, edible plants, stars and planets, and more.

Shopping for a Better World. Council on Economic Priorities, updated annually.

A product by product guide to shape your buying habits. It is based on a company's record of the environment, employment practices, and more.

Simple Foods for the Pack, The Sierra Club Guide to Natural Foods for the Trail, by Claudia Axcell, Diana Cooke, and Vikki Kinmont. Sierra Club Books, 1986.

Recipes for camping and backpacking trips.

Snowshoeing, by Gene Prater. The Mountaineers, Third Edition, 1993.

The definitive book about this winter off-shoot. It covers equipment and technique.

Wilderness Ranger Cookbook, A Collection of Backcountry Recipes, by Forest Service Wilderness Rangers. Falcon Press, 1990.

Recipes from seasoned veterans of wilderness travel and cooking.

• Index •

· About the author ·

Victoria Logue began her writing career as a newspaper reporter for two small daily newspapers, for whom she garnered several writing awards.

In 1988, with her husband, Frank, Victoria hiked the entire Appalachian Trail. After returning, they wrote *The Appalachian Trail Backpacker's Planning Guide* to help others prepare for a hike of any length on that trail. Since then, they have written and illustrated the *Appalachian Trail Fun Book*, a coloring and activity book for 4-9 year olds.

Victoria and Frank collaborated on *The Best of the Appalachian Trail: Dayhikes* and *The Best of the Appalachian Trail: Overnight Hikes*. Victoria's most recent book is *Camping in the 90s*.

The Logues live in north Georgia where they are restoring a 120-year old house and sharing their love of the outdoors with their daughter, Griffin.

· About the illustrator ·

Leigh Ellis is a professional artist, who specializes in illustrating the natural world. She was formally educated as a zoologist and ecologist before pursuing a career in fine arts. In addition to her science training, she has studied art at the University of Hawaii and Montana State University.

Her work has been exhibited in juried and private shows in several states and is sold in galleries. Leigh teaches watercolor and illustration classes for both children and adult audiences focusing on avian and floral illustration. She lives north Georgia with her daughter, Jessie.